Race, Ethnicity, and the State in Malaysia and Singapore

Social Sciences in Asia

Edited by

Vineeta Sinha
Syed Farid Alatas
Chan Kwok Bun

VOLUME 7

Race, Ethnicity, and the State in Malaysia and Singapore

Edited by

Lian Kwen Fee

BRILL
LEIDEN • BOSTON
2006

This book is printed on acid-free paper.

Library of Congress Cataloging-in-Publication Data

A C.I.P. record for this book is available from the Library of Congress.

ISSN 1567–2794
ISBN 90 04 15096 X

PRINTED IN THE NETHERLANDS

CONTENTS

LIST OF CONTRIBUTORS

Alexius A. Pereira, Department of Sociology, National University of Singapore

Alice M. Nah, Department of Sociology, National University of Singapore

Joseph Stimpfl, Department of Religious Studies, Webster University

Tong Chee Kiong, Department of Sociology, National University of Singapore

Lian Kwen Fee, Department of Sociology, National University of Singapore

Vineeta Sinha, Department of Sociology, National University of Singapore

Lee Kiat Jin, Department of Sociology, New School for Social Research

Sai Siew Yee, Department of Sociology, National University of Singapore

INTRODUCTION

More than 60 years ago when John Furnivall introduced the term "plural society" to describe the lack of social organization in the colonial societies of Netherlands India and Burma, he wrote (1944):

> In a plural society, then, the community tends to be organized for production rather than social life; social demand is sectionalized, and within each section of the community the social demand becomes disorganized and ineffective, so that in each section the members are debarred from leading the full life of a citizen in a homogeneous community; finally, the reaction against these abnormal conditions, taking in each section the form of Nationalism, sets one community against the other so as to emphasize the plural character of the society and aggravate its instability, thereby enhancing the need for it to be held together by some force exerted from outside.

While many scholars have since readily accepted the applicability of the concept, Charles Coppel (1997) argues that the plural character of colonial society has been overdrawn in the urban centres of colonial Java at the turn of the twentieth century, and warned that its further use should be subject to closer scrutiny. It is not the purpose of this volume to assess the accuracy of the description with regard to colonial Malaya. The contributions refer to contemporary Malaysia and Singapore. They support the view, however that even in current conditions, it makes sense to regard each "section" within the "community"—Eurasians, Orang Asli, Malays, Chinese, and Tamils/Indians—in its own right; and for the state to continue to work with these groups as *realpolitik*, whether through coercion or persuasion, in order to hold society together.

There is no doubt that race and ethnicity have and will continue to be of fundamental influence on how societies are structured in this region, so uniquely characterized by Furnivall. The sociological excavation of this, which began in the 1970s, has been intermittent and largely confined to empirical output; the conceptual and theoretical developments have lagged behind.

Until recently, the prevailing understanding in sociology is that race is a category imposed, usually from a position of power, on groups for the purpose of exclusion on the basis of phenotypical features. Ethnicity, on the other hand, is the consequence of self-identification and refers to what contributes to cultural identity. "Racialization" and "ethnicization" denote the social process in which either occurs. Racialization and ethnicization, however, are no longer regarded as mutually exclusive, for the racialization of a group may lead to its ethnicization and vice-versa. So, groups identified in the past as races may be referred to in ethnic terms (Sollors cited in Goldberg, 1992: 554). Indeed, it is not inconceivable that some groups may be referred to as both races and ethnic groups simultaneously; hence, the paradoxical description "ethnorace" (Goldberg, 1992: 555). It is not always self-evident that racialization and ethnicization are mediated through the state as it imposes its will on a modern and plural society.

Racialization and ethnicization are social processes: hence, they require us to examine race and ethnicity as such. Goldberg (1992: 545) recommends a methodological prescription:

> . . . . we proceed not by defining 'race' conceptually—in terms, that is, of necessary and sufficient conditions. We should focus, rather, on a different set of concerns: how has the term been used at different times, what has it signified, and how has it served to articulate a conception for its users of self- and group-identity, of self and other.

He suggests that we should shift our attention to race and ethnicity from a definitional and conceptual issue to addressing them as a problematic of discourse. For example, public, official and political pronouncements and policies about race and ethnicity are usually circumscribed within a state-defined discourse. Of course, political opposition will contribute to this. The overall effect is to racialize and, sometimes, unintentionally ethnicize the population. In private and everyday lives, however, groups and individuals may feel less maligned about such differences. The contributions in this volume have ramifications for the issues I have raised here, some of which I highlight in the last chapter.

The *Southeast Asian Journal of Social Science* devoted two special issues to ethnicity—"Ethnicity in Southeast Asia" in 1982, and "Transformations of Ethnic Identity in Malaysia and Singapore" in 1997. The idea for this volume was mooted when Brill, together with the Department of Sociology at the National University of Singapore, introduced the series *Social Sciences in Asia* as a means of disseminating scholarship on the region to a wider readership. The contributions of Joseph Stimpfl and Sai Siew Yee were published in the 1997 special issue of the *Southeast Asian Journal of Social Science*, while Lian

Kwen Fee's work on the Tamils in Malaysia appeared in *Asian Studies Review* in 2002. I am grateful to the publishers of the two journals for giving me permission to reprint these three articles. I would also like to acknowledge the support of Brill and the encouragement of the editors of this series in putting together these contributions in what I hope is a modest advancement of our understanding of race and ethnicity in Malaysia and Singapore.

REFERENCES

Coppel, Charles A. (1997) "Revisiting Furnivall's Plural Society: Colonial Java as a Mestizo Society?", *Ethnic and Racial Studies* 20(3): 562–79.

Furnivall, John S. (1944) *Netherlands India: A Study of Plural Economy*. Cambridge: Cambridge University Press.

Goldberg, David (1992) "The Semantics of Race", *Ethnic and Racial Studies* 15(4): 543–69.

NO LONGER "OTHER": THE EMERGENCE OF THE EURASIAN COMMUNITY IN SINGAPORE

Alexius A. Pereira

This study examines the "emergence" of the Eurasian community in Singapore from the 1990s within the context of Singapore's multiracialism. I argue in this chapter that the emergence of this very small community could be attributed to two simultaneous processes. First, the Singapore government, after many years of neglect, began to formally recognize Eurasians as one of Singapore's charter communities. Second, the Eurasian community itself has been active in raising its profile. My research, however, finds that the emergence has brought advantages as well as disadvantages for the community. On the one hand, recognition has "empowered" the Eurasian community, as the state has offered economic, political and social support. On the other hand, inclusion into the state's multiracial model will probably lead to essentialization and ascription. I conclude this paper with some observations of the social costs and benefits of the emergence, and its implications for ethnic politics in Singapore.

Introduction

On 5 July 2003, the Eurasian Community House was officially opened by the President of Singapore, Mr. S. R. Nathan. To many Eurasians, this event was significant because it meant that they were no longer "an invisible community" in Singapore. More specifically, many Eurasians felt that they were no longer regarded as the Other in Singapore's CMIO (Chinese, Malay, Indian and Other) racial categorization, but had finally become accepted as one of Singapore's charter communities, even if the community itself constituted less than 0.5 percent of Singapore's resident population. I argue in this paper that the Eurasian community's emergence is a result of both the Singapore government's official support as well as the community's own initiatives. I find that official state recognition has brought about both advantages and disadvantages for the Eurasian community.

I conclude with some reflections on the debates on (ethnic) minority politics in Singapore.

Multiracialism and Minority Groups in Singapore

The Singapore government has, since national independence in 1965, pursued a system of multiracialism (see Benjamin, 1976; Hill and Lian, 1995). This system can be understood as a variant of "multiculturalism". Multiculturalism, as defined in the *Harper Collins Dictionary of Sociology* (1991), is:

> . . . the acknowledgement and promotion of cultural pluralism as a feature of many societies. Multiculturalism celebrates and seeks to protect cultural variety, for example, minority languages. At the same time, it focuses on the often unequal relationship of minority to mainstream cultures (quoted in Wieviorka, 1998: 881)

In the social science literature on ethnic politics, multiculturalism is one of several possible "systems of national integration"; other systems include "assimilation" and "melting pot" (Kivisto, 2002). These debates centre mainly on the state's management of ethnic (and racial) minority groups in society, often regarded as obstacles to national integration. Most systems of national integration involve utilizing a "national culture"—encompassing values, practices and lifestyles—that people in society can identify with. For the system of assimilation, the national culture is usually drawn from the culture of the majority ethnic group. For example, ethnic minorities living in French or Japanese societies are expected to conform to the dominant national culture in order to "fit in". Although the national culture might be a blend of several different ethnic cultures in the melting pot option, the final product is still one distinct national culture that serves as the source for identification. For instance, in Brazil, the national culture is drawn from European, African and indigenous South American cultures but, ultimately, it is distinctively Brazilian. Hence, the assimilation and melting pot systems operate on the assumption that there is a single national culture, which everyone in that society should identify with in order for national integration to take place. Multiculturalism, on the other hand, is a system that "celebrates" diversity. A common assumption is that a multicultural society is not constituted by a single national culture, but accepts several different ethnic cultures, particularly those of ethnic (and racial) minorities. Multiculturalism involves state sanctioned maintenance or promotion of different cultures, including the offering language or religious rights. A classic example would be that of Switzerland, where different groups or regions could be culturally German, Italian or French; in Canada, the province of Quebec is allowed to be culturally French, whereas the rest of the country is culturally English or "Anglo-Saxon" (see Kivisto, 2002). A "multicultural state" will, therefore, have concrete policies—"multiculturalist policies" (Wieviorka, 1998)—to preserve and protect the cultural rights of different groups in that society, including minority groups. In theory, minority ethnic groups ought to view the state's overtures not just as a concession but a basic cultural right and, therefore, reinforce their allegiance towards a system that accepts "cultural" pluralism (Kivisto, 2002). As a model for national integration, multiculturalism attempts to enhance national identity through accepting, maintaining and promoting different ethnic identities.

Societies that adopt multiculturalism as a national cultural system will preserve and even celebrate ethnic differences through various state policies; however, a consequence of policies that promote cultural differentiation is that essentialization might take place. Essentialization refers to a process through which social reality is ignored in favour of the over-simplification of characteristics.[1] In addition, these characteristics will become treated as an "unchanging given" (Kivisto, 2002: 14). For example, ethnic heritage, racial features and [other features] are elevated into exclusive master statuses that totally fix an individual's identity and interest (Joppke, 1996: 449). Essentialization obscures social reality, since there may be considerable variations even within officially recognized ethnic communities. It appears, however, to be an inevitable side effect in multicultural societies.

Also, multiculturalism, as a system of national integration, exacts "social costs"—not just from the various ethnic groups, but also from the state. From the point of view of the majority group, multiculturalism may mean disproportionate concessions to satisfy the cultural, political and/or economic aspirations of minority groups,

[1] The concept of "essentialization" is the direct opposite of "hybridity". These concepts were first developed in post-colonial literary theory, but have more recently been applied to identity studies and post-modern analyses (see Young, 1995).

sometimes referred to as ethnic "affirmative action". For minority groups, it might seem advantageous that the community receives disproportionately higher benefits; this, in turn, might lead to resentment from the majority community. The costs of multiculturalism to the state could be that it ". . . can lead to reified group distinctions that become fault lines for conflict and separatism" (Verkuyten, 2004: 53). Further, critics of multiculturalism argue that the system could easily lead to calls, usually from minority groups, for "structural pluralism". Structural pluralism refers to a society that has parallel institutions for different groups; for example, a structurally plural society might have different systems of education for each ethnic group. This is different from cultural pluralism, which recognizes diversity but within one common educational and economic system.

Finally, multiculturalism neutralizes the individual in favour of the group or community. Since the system is supported by ethnic categorization, individuals will be "induced" to belong to one of the given categories, almost involuntarily. This process is known as "ascription", through which identities are conferred onto individuals simply because of their perceived membership of the group. Individual expression and options, therefore, could be severely limited in a multicultural society.

Singapore's "multiracialism", promoted by the state, is a variant of multiculturalism, both empirically and theoretically. The key difference lies in the Singapore government's utilization of the terms "race" and "ethnicity". The Singapore government does not distinguish between race and ethnicity, often using them interchangeably.

In Singapore, multiracialism is more than just the official name of the government's ethnic policy; at the same time, it is also "a fact, and an ideology" (Hill and Lian, 1995: 93; Benjamin, 1976: 115–6). As a fact, it recognizes that Singapore is racially (and ethnically) heterogeneous, where over 75 percent of the resident population is Chinese, 15 percent Malay, about 8 percent Indian, and 2 percent consisting of members of other races, as officially reported by the Singapore government (Singapore Department of Statistics, 2001). As an ideology, multiracialism is committed to the equal treatment of all races in Singapore.[2] This would mean that in the

[2] Although "race" is a highly charged and contested concept in social sciences, this chapter uses it only because it is treated as an "active" category in Singapore

Constitution of the Republic of Singapore, Article 152, the state guarantees that the economic, political and cultural rights of the minority racial or ethnic groups will be protected (Government of Singapore, 1999). It is interesting to note that as a fact and an ideology, the state assumes that Singapore is constituted by different "races" (Benjamin, 1976: 115). Racial classification can be attributed to the British colonial government, which operated an overt racial division of labour between 1819 and 1940. The independent Singapore government then adopted and perpetuated this classification system (see Turnbull, 1977: 16). More importantly, however, the ideology of multiracialism is regarded as Singapore's "founding myth" (Benjamin, 1976: 116). Put in another way, it was the ideology of multiracialism, which opposed both ethnic discrimination and ethnic affirmative action, that made political merger with Malaysia untenable;[3] as the ruling People's Action Party refused to compromise on this issue, Singapore was excluded from the Federation of Malaysia on 9 August 1965 (see Hill and Lian, 1995).

As a national policy, multiracialism was designed to reduce or eliminate two processes that were believed to lead to ethnic conflict: ethnic assertion and ethnic competition (Lai, 1995). Ethnic assertion was identified as a potential source of ethnic conflict, especially if minority ethnic groups perceive that the majority ethnic group is attempting some form of cultural assimilation. For example, in Singapore, it could be argued that the state could potentially promote Mandarin and Chinese culture—commonly known as the process of Sinicization—simply because over 70 percent of the population is of Chinese racial origin. Such a move, however, might result in anxiety and suspicion among the minority ethnic groups, as the imposition of a dominant Chinese culture would immediately marginalize the minority ethnic cultures (Lai, 1995: 148). In this regard, the Singapore government's multiracialism has been clear in stating that the "traditional" and "ethnic" cultures of the main races (including

by the government. As the rest of the chapter will show, the Singapore government frequently confuses and conflates the concepts of "race" and "ethnicity", often treating them as interchangeable.

[3] Malaysia, on the other hand, stood firm on its policy of affirmative action to not only protect, but also to strategically improve, the status of the indigenous Malay community, known as the *bumiputeras* (see Hill and Lian, 1995).

the minority ethnic communities) are all equally important and ought to be preserved (see Vasil, 2000). Therefore, in the national education system, for example, the cultures of the Malays and Indians have been "preserved" through the offering of their respective "mother tongues"—Malay and Tamil, respectively—along with Mandarin for the Chinese community, as core academic subjects (see Hill and Lian, 1995). Although there have been many discrepancies and inconsistencies in the promotion and practice of multiracialism, the objective of cultural preservation has been to overtly demonstrate to the minority ethnic communities that the system of national integration in Singapore will not require them to abandon their lifestyle and identity. With cultural preservation further reinforced by other policy measures—for example, the maintenance of separate official newspapers, television and radio channels, and the equal distribution of public holidays for each racial community, among others—minority ethnic groups technically cannot blame the state for creating institutions and structures that marginalize their respective cultures.[4] In this sense, Singapore's multiracialism operates on the same principles as other multicultural societies, where the state will formally protect minority rights.

With regard to reducing or eliminating ethnic competition, the Singapore government has overtly pursued a meritocratic ideology in decoupling economic performance from ethnicity. In other words, unlike systems practised in other countries (for example, Malaysia's *bumiputera* policy is a variant of affirmative action as it economically favours the indigenous Malay community), no ethnic or racial group in Singapore is given any special economic or political privileges[5]

[4] On the other hand, many critics feel that these measures still continue to marginalize minority ethnic cultures (see Rahim, 1998).

[5] Although the Malays (and their culture) in Singapore are constitutionally protected, it would not be accurate to equate it with affording the community special privileges or benefits. In Article 152, "Minorities and Special Position of Malays", of the Constitution of the Republic of Singapore, it reads: "(1) It shall be the responsibility of the Government constantly to care for the interests of the racial and religious minorities in Singapore; (2) The Government shall exercise its functions in such manner as to recognize the special position of the Malays, who are the indigenous people of Singapore, and accordingly it shall be the responsibility of the Government to protect, safeguard, support, foster and promote their political, educational, religious, economic, social and cultural interests and the Malay language."

(see Vasil, 2000). Empirically, some studies have shown that income distribution among various ethnic groups have been narrowing, mainly as a result of rapid industrialization and equitable state redistribution (see Pang, 1993). Despite this, other studies have found that the Malay community appeared to be more susceptible to economic marginalization (see Li, 1989; Rahim, 1998). As a result, the state has intervened to alleviate potential economic disparity by improving educational attainments of disadvantaged groups in Singapore society. According to Quinn-Moore, the Singapore government's commitment to "fair opportunity" is manifested in three ways:

> First, the government allows each racial group to create a community-based self-help group to address its cultural, educational and social deficiencies. Second, massive government subsidized housing projects provide people of all income levels relatively similar living conditions to ensure that the rich do not have large environmental advantages over the poor, Finally, after entry into the 'playing field' has been equalized by self-help and housing policy, the procedural equality of the meritocracy is supposed to be guaranteed by the educational system, in which success is determined 'objectively' by standardized testing. The hierarchy established by this system is deemed fair as all enter the social game at similar level, and all determinations of ability are uniform, and therefore, considered unbiased (2000: 345).

With meritocracy and multiracialism, inter-ethnic group competition for economic resources has "officially" been eliminated from social life in Singapore. This implies that if economic disparities emerge, it would not be due to official state policy, but to particularistic and inherent issues within the community, which can only be addressed by "self-help" groups (see Vasil, 2000).

There are several ramifications of the Singapore government's commitment to promoting multiracialism. One consequence is the overall pervasiveness of the so-called CMIO (Chinese, Malay, Indian and Others) model. The CMIO model is an exemplary case of essentialization, where each racial community's ethnicity is not only assumed to be unique and particularistic, but also serves an ascriptive function in Singapore society (see Benjamin, 1976; Hill and Lian, 1995) (see Table 1).

The "problems" or unintended consequences of the CMIO model have been addressed in other studies; some argue that the model is detrimental to national integration (see, for example, Benjamin, 1976; Siddique, 1990; Purushotam, 1998). In direct relevance to this paper,

Table 1. CMIO Model

"Race"	Mother Tongue	Religion	Traditional Dress
Chinese	Mandarin	Buddhism	*Cheongsam*
Malay	Malay	Islam	*Sarong Kebaya*
Indian	Tamil	Hinduism	*Sari*
Others	English	Christianity	"Western" gown

the CMIO model has also been criticized for "essentializing" ethnicity in Singapore (see Benjamin, 1976; Hill and Lian, 1995; Chua, 1998; Tong and Chan, 2001). For example, all Chinese in Singapore are assumed to speak Mandarin, adhere to Buddhism, and practise traditional Chinese customs. The reality is that a Chinese may speak Mandarin as well as other Chinese dialects such as Hokkien or Cantonese, or might even adhere to Christianity or Islam. The consequence of essentialization is not only in the process of over-simplification, but also that people accept the "essential" over the "actual" as the social reality.

Another consequence is the "social costs of multiracialism" (Chua, 2003: 103). For example, the state's promotion of multiracialism as a national cultural system effectively denied the Chinese community the option of living within a culturally Chinese national system, or a primarily "Chinese society" in Singapore. Chua argues that for the community, the Chinese language was reduced to merely a "mother tongue" or "second language". With English as the main operational language of the economy, and with Singapore's national cultural system being mainly "non-ethnic" in character, those that felt more comfortable living and doing business in a culturally Chinese environment were marginalized (ibid.). In addition, those that attempted to highlight this problem publicly were labelled "Chinese chauvinists", and in a few cases, were subjected to political detention and self-imposed exile (ibid.). Chua further claims that multiracialism has exacted costs from the Malay community as well (Chua, 2003: 103–4). Chua then concludes that multiracialism can also be viewed as a process of "neutralization . . . thus [enabling] the government to reduce everyone and every group to cultural equality, contributing to the development and maintenance of Singapore as a country where only merit counts" (Chua, 2003: 104)

The practice of multiracialism and multiculturalism has facilitated both racial and ethnic ascription and essentialization in Singapore. It is within this context that the emergence of the Eurasians was accepted by the state as one of the founding "races" of Singapore in the early 1990s. The rest of this paper will document their emergence and consideration as an ethnic community in Singapore.

Eurasian Marginalization

Before I discuss the marginalization of Eurasians in Singapore, it would be useful to briefly outline the history of the Eurasian community. The Eurasian community in Singapore has always been a very heterogeneous group, both racially and ethnically (or culturally) (see Braga-Blake, 1992). Although the term "Eurasian" is itself heavily contested and has different meanings, in Asia, it usually refers to descendants of marriages between Europeans and Asians.[6] A "community" emerges when individuals become aware that they belong to a particular social group. In this sense, there were many Eurasian communities that were formed in Asia, particularly in cities and towns that had extensive contact with Europeans. This includes Goa, Ceylon, Malacca, Macau, Batavia and Timor, among others. In Malacca during the sixteenth and seventeenth centuries, to which many Singapore Eurasians trace their origins, the Eurasian community tried to pass themselves off as belonging to the "Portuguese" rather than to a distinct Eurasian community. These Portuguese Eurasians occupied a privileged niche in the colonial system, as many of them worked for the Portuguese government and in trading companies (see Boxer, 1969). This community was racially heterogeneous, as early reports indicated that Eurasians usually had Portuguese fathers while the mothers could be Malay, Indian or Chinese (ibid.). Despite the racial heterogeneity, however, the community was ethnically homogeneous, as all the Portuguese Eurasians adhered closely to the Roman Catholic religion and extensively used the Portuguese language (Sta-Maria, 1982). While the Portuguese were in power,

[6] The term "Eurasian" has also been used to describe the people who live in Eurasia, or Central Asia (the former Soviet republics).

these Eurasians enjoyed a high socio-economic status relative to the other Asian communities.

In 1641, the Dutch conquered Malacca in their pursuit to dominate Southeast Asia. The Dutch colonials discriminated against the defeated Portuguese men and Portuguese Eurasians, as the two nations were in a state of war in Southeast Asia. The Dutch made distinctions along religious and cultural lines. For example, the Dutch were Protestants and spoke Dutch while the Portuguese were Catholics and spoke mostly Portuguese. Consequently, the Dutch authorities relegated the Portuguese–Eurasians to a position benerath that of the natives and other Asians in the social hierarchy (Turnbull, 1977: 15–16, 30). Furthermore, the Dutch encouraged intermarriage with Portuguese Eurasians, as a strategy to assimilate the Portuguese Eurasians and entice them away from Catholic–Portuguese culture towards Dutch–Protestant culture (see Boxer, 1965). This policy could be explained by the Dutch experience of Ceylon and the Dutch East Indies (Indonesia), where Dutch–Asian Eurasians proved not only to be a politically loyal group, but also a "useful" class of civil servants. Thus, the first Governor General of the Dutch East Indies, Pietier Both, advocated ". . . inter-marriages with indigenous women, after Roman or Portuguese precedents, or with Christian converts" (Boxer, [1948] 1973: 242–3). In Dutch controlled Malacca, there were some Dutch and Asian marriages that not only increased the size of the Eurasian community, but also added to its racial heterogeneity.

In the eighteenth century, the British became the dominant colonial power in Southeast Asia. They had experience with their own Eurasians (or Anglo–Indians, as they were known) in India (see Gist and Wright, 1973; Hawes, 1999). Just like the Dutch Eurasians, the Anglo–Indians were a valuable economic resource to the colonial power as they were more cost effective as civil servants than the alternative of stationing Britons in Southeast Asia (Sta-Maria, 1982: 84). Some Portuguese–Eurasians left Malacca in 1789 for Penang when the British colonized the island, in search of better opportunities. As many Eurasians—some of whom were posted from India while others came from Malacca—were fluent in European languages, it was easier for them to learn English and join the British civil service (Daus, 1989). By the beginning of the nineteenth century, the Eurasians became even more racially and ethnically heterogeneous. First, there were reports of Eurasian women marrying British officers and businessmen. At the same time, other Eurasians began to adopt British middle-class culture, with the English language becoming their primary language. As Munshi Abdullah wrote in the *Hikayat Abdullah* ([1950] 1970: 38):

> For the first time in Malacca the majority of people knew how to speak English, and those of Dutch extraction who lived in Malacca changed their customs and language, their clothing and habits of their race, men and women alike copying English ways of life.

Due to the structure and politics of European colonial society in Asia, Eurasians were usually a privileged class situated above the Asian communities. In the early colonial period of the Straits Settlements of Penang, Malacca and Singapore, the Eurasians were even identified as being "on par" with the so-called "pure Europeans". This allowed some of them to join prestigious social clubs, such as the Singapore Cricket Club and the British Club, which were at the time open only to "white" people. More importantly, this meant that Eurasians could gain access to certain posts within the British civil service. With the opening of the Suez Canal in 1869, which saw a large influx of Europeans, particularly European women, to Southeast Asia, the White community began to discriminate against the Eurasians. This led to a hardening of the boundary between the Europeans and the Eurasians in the Straits Settlements, and social exchange became more limited. There were indications that the Europeans were concerned about the potential competition for resources and power from the Eurasians. Yet, the Eurasian community, which was earmarked by the Europeans to fill the civil service, was still given more social and economic privileges than any of the Asian communities. With the hardening of the boundaries between Europeans and Eurasians, both communities became much more inward looking. It was argued that the years between 1869 and 1940 were the "golden years" for Singapore Eurasians. The community was tightknit and strong, albeit because it was marginalized by the Europeans (Braga-Blake, 1992). This community, however, was not culturally or ethnically homogeneous, as Eurasians appeared to embrace various aspects of Portuguese, Dutch, British, Chinese, Malay and Indian cultures. It was no surprise that later studies were unable to identify a distinctive and stable Eurasian culture during this period (Willis, 1983; Barth, 1994; Pereira, 1996).

In Singapore, the social status of the Eurasian community changed between 1940 and 1965. During the Japanese Occupation (1942–1945), being racially Eurasian was a reason for being interned as a prisoner of war (Pereira, 1996). After the war, although Eurasians generally returned to their positions within the British civil service, there was an acknowledgement that the colonial power would in the near future withdraw from Malaya. This caused great anxiety for the Eurasian community, as many feared for their personal safety in the light of communal unrest and communist insurgency in Malaya (Braga-Blake, 1992). From 1945 onwards, many Eurasians, especially those who held British passports, emigrated to other Commonwealth countries. It appears that the outflow intensified with Singapore's failed merger with Malaysia in 1965, as many Eurasians were left uncertain about Singapore's future.

After independence in 1965, the Eurasians who chose to remain in Singapore were described as being "socially marginalized", mainly because of Singapore's multiracialism (Willis, 1983). The most overt symbol of Eurasian marginalization was having their "race" classified as "Other" in official documents such as the National Registration Identity Cards (NRIC), as well as in most official documents and reports. This had a deep socio-psychological impact on Eurasian individuals, as they were very ambivalent about their ethnic identity unlike the Chinese, Malay and Indian communities (Willis, 1983; Braga-Blake, 1992; Pereira, 1996). The only formal association that was related to the Eurasian community, the Eurasian Association, was established in 1919 and saw its membership fall to an all time low of 13 members, even though there were about 10,000 Eurasians in Singapore at the time (Barth, 1992: 100). The Eurasian community in Singapore had become the "Invisible Community" (Bachtiar, 1990).

This "othering" process might appear to be a contradiction in terms as Singapore's multiracialism was supposed to retain ethnic identity, promote ethnic pride and encourage cultural preservation (see Benjamin, 1976; Hill and Lian, 1995). In reality, however, the Eurasian community was unable to fit into Singapore's multiracial model as easily as the Chinese, Malay or Indian communities. This was because the Singapore government did not actively promote Eurasian "culture" and identity. The Eurasian community was numerically small; from 1965 until 1990, Eurasians formed no more than 0.5 percent of Singapore's resident population (Braga-Blake, 1992). It could, however, also be argued that the state simply did not know what constituted Eurasian culture; therefore, it was in no position to intervene. Furthermore, it could be argued that the Singapore government treated the Eurasians like the other demographically smaller racial communities in Singapore, such as the Jews, Armenians and the Sikhs, where the state recognized their autonomy in maintaining their traditional heritages. In schools, Eurasian children were allowed the option to select any "second language" on offer, since the community did not have its own "mother tongue". Thus, most Eurasian children grew up learning Malay or Mandarin in Singapore. It was, therefore, not surprising that by the 1980s, studies had found that the Eurasians felt that they "did not know what their culture was", or "did not feel that the country respected their culture". It was argued that Eurasians were clearly marginalized in Singapore (Willis, 1983; Braga-Blake, 1992). This marginalization was further compounded when Eurasians compared themselves with the other communities in Singapore, which appeared to be knowledgeable and proud of their ethnic heritage, as a result of the state's promotion of multiracialism.

By the beginning of the 1990s, the Eurasian community appeared to be significantly more interested in its identity and in improving its social status in Singapore (Pereira, 1997). Based on research conducted in 1996 to 1997, and between 2001 and 2003, I argue in this paper that the reasons for this revitalization can be summarized in two main processes: the "bottom-up" and the "top-down" process. The former process explains that the source and the motivation for revitalization came from within the Eurasian community itself, while the latter process was initiated by the Singapore government. As this discussion will show, these processes were not mutually exclusive; instead, both processes were closely related and mutually reinforcing.

Bottom Up

The "bottom-up" process came from several sources. Some sources were gradual in nature, such as the impact of multiracialism, but others were triggered by specific incidents. For example, in the late 1980s, many Eurasians were "stirred into action" as a result of the "Catherine Lim affair" (Braga-Blake, 1992; Pereira, 1996, 1997). This so-called "affair" arose because a short story written by Lim was selected as a secondary school English literature text in 1988. In this story, the central character was a young Eurasian male adult with a dubious reputation. Many Eurasians were outraged that Lim had chosen to "stereotype" Eurasians as being irresponsible "womanizers" or "party-animals". Not only were many protest letters written to *The Straits Times* and to the Ministry of Education, there was a sudden surge of Eurasians formally joining the Eurasian Association (henceforth known as the EA) to address the "affair". As mentioned earlier, in 1982, the EA had 13 paid-up members; in 1988, the number increased to 126. In 1989, 119 out of a total of 240 members attended the EA's Annual General Meeting, which had tabled a motion to discuss the community's response to Lim's short story (Braga-Blake, 1992: 20). Membership of the EA continued to grow to 660 in 1989 and to 1132 in 1990 (da Silva, 2001: 4).

At the same time, there was a new generation of Eurasians who had grown up within Singapore's multiracial environment. Many younger Eurasians perceived that all Singaporeans belonged to their own particular racial community, each of which had its own distinctive "traditional historic culture". In addition, members of the community were also expected to be proud and fully aware of his/her history and heritage. Younger Eurasians growing up in this socio-cultural environment felt marginalized, as they were unable to "experience" their ethnicity in a similar manner (Pereira, 1996). There was no "traditional historic" Eurasian culture that existed in Singapore, and the state never attempted to promote Eurasian ethnic awareness and pride in the way it did for the other races. Many younger Eurasians were disappointed at only being known as "Other" in Singapore society (Pereira, 1996). In response, several individuals worked towards improving the position of Eurasians. There were three measures adopted by active members of the community in the 1990s.

First, some Eurasians attempted to persuade the government to adopt the racial category of "Eurasian" rather than the generic "Other" category (da Silva, 2001). In other words, some Eurasians wanted the "fifth box"—in addition to the existing CMIO boxes—in official state application forms. Also, there was a plea to the government to consistently use "Eurasian" in the racial specification of the National Registration Identity Card (NRIC). Until that time, many Eurasians were simply identified as "Other". Second, some active Eurasians began chronicling and (re)presenting Eurasian "culture". Although this was ostensibly to raise the awareness of Eurasian culture to the other communities, the aim was to simultaneously help younger Eurasians identify with the culture as well. These activists tended to rely heavily on the cultural artefacts that the Portuguese Settlement in Malacca had created, including cuisine, music, traditional costumes and language.[7] Although the majority of Singapore Eurasians are of Portuguese–Malaccan descent, the adoption of Portuguese–Malaccan cultural artefacts was found to be highly alien to them, as very little of it was practised in Singapore (Pereira, 1996). Yet, the so-called Eurasian culture became essentialized, very much in line with the practice of multiracialism in Singapore. Representatives of the Eurasian community appeared on national television for the very first time during the 1994 National Day Parade, where a troupe of dancers contributed with a so-called traditional Eurasian dance (see Pereira, 1996, 1997).

The third aspect was the high-profile publication of Eurasian literature. In the 1990s, there were two Eurasian authors who published fiction that either dealt with Eurasian affairs or involved Eurasians as central characters. The first author was Rex Shelley, whose first three novels could be described as being archetypal Eurasian literature. The novel titles all had strong Eurasian allusions. The first, *The Shrimp People* (1991), was a reference to the Portuguese–Malay word *geragok*, a term that not only describes the shrimp that Portuguese–Malaccans fished but was also a derogatory term for Eurasians. Similarly, the novels *People of the Pear Tree* (1993) and the *River of Roses* (1998), were English translations of "Pereira" and "Rosario", respectively—both common Eurasian family names. *The Shrimp People* not only turned out to be an award-winning book for its literary merits,[8] but also thrust the Eurasian community into the spotlight for a short while. The other author was Wilfred Hamilton-Shimmen, whose novel, *A Season of Darkness* (1993), was also centred on Eurasians and their plight in (colonial) Malaya and in Singapore. Thus, from a situation where the only literary output on Eurasians was a problematic short story written by Catherine Lim, the decade of the 1990s saw the publication of four full-length novels by Eurasians about Eurasians.

---

[7] For an excellent and critical study of the Portuguese Settlement in Malacca, see Sarkissian (2000).

[8] *The Shrimp People* won first prize in the 1992 National Book Development Council of Singapore awards.

The consequence of these developments was to facilitate the integration of the Eurasian community into a multiracial society. Eurasians wanted to overtly display that they did, in fact, have a historic traditional culture, a "mother tongue", distinctive traditional costumes and food ways. This paved the way for younger Eurasians to become more aware of their cultural heritage, in turn promoting Eurasian ethnic consciousness in Singapore. As the following section will show, this process of ethnic consciousness was welcomed by the Singapore government, as it fitted nicely into its notion of multiracialism. In this paper, I do not, however, suggest that the emergence of Eurasian ethnic consciousness was entirely "bottom-up", in that it was initiated and sustained from within the community alone. Instead, there was a "top-down" process that was taking place at the same time. Also, it is impossible to argue that the two processes were distinct; rather, it could be argued that the two processes fed into each other.

Top Down

As suggested earlier, the Singapore government's active implementation of multiracialism has been central to nation-building in Singapore (see Hill and Lian, 1995; Chua, 1998). Before 1990, it was quite evident that the Singapore government did not directly promote Eurasian ethnicity and culture. After 1990, however, the state had noticed that the Eurasian community was taking an active interest in its ethnic origins. The Singapore government began to encourage and support the Eurasian community, especially since ethnic revitalization was in line with its policy of multiracialism. The most significant measures adopted by the Singapore government were the institutional co-optation of the Eurasian Association and the formal acknowledgement of Eurasian ethnicity and culture.

As mentioned in the previous section, in the later half of the 1980s, the Eurasian Association (EA) was the focus of Eurasian activity and interest. In the 1990s, the EA initiated a series of events that led to its formal recognition. In 1992, the EA approached a minister in the Singapore government, George Yeo, to act as an unofficial Cabinet representative of the Eurasian community. Yeo was selected by the EA because he was "familiar" with Eurasians—on the basis that he was a Roman Catholic and had gone to a Catholic school (St. Patrick's School, which had many Eurasian students). Facing no objection from the Singapore government or from within the ruling People's Action Party, Yeo accepted the appointment (see Hill and Lian, 1995: 104). The "necessity" of having a Eurasian representative in parliament or within the one-party government is a very interesting aspect of Singapore's multiracialism. Although race and ethnicity in Singapore was "de-politicized", the state has always been concerned about the welfare and interests of the various "racial communities" and acknowledged the importance of community representation. This can be seen in the constitutional amendment that saw the Group Representative Constituency introduced in 1988. Under this system, several (electoral) constituencies were grouped into larger constituencies, within which three (or more) candidates were fielded as a team (Hill and Lian, 1995: 110). The logic of the GRC system was to ensure "minority" (racial) representation in parliament, as all teams competing in GRC elections had to necessarily include one candidate who was of a "minority" race (Chan, 1989). In this case, the term "minority" race referred to the Malay, Indian and "Other" communities. At the formal level, there was a Minister of Malay–Muslim Affairs in the Singapore government Cabinet. Furthermore, since the 1980s, the government has been conscious about having the other communities "represented", albeit less formally. For example, several members of the cabinet acted as spokespersons and representatives for the Chinese and Indian communities without a formal portfolio being created; however, by the mid-1980s, this representation was subsumed under the ethnic self-help system, which will be discussed later. In this light, the Eurasian community had not had a representative in parliament since the retirement of E. Barker, a Eurasian and the former Minister of Law, in 1988. It needs to be pointed out that Barker had rarely addressed Eurasian issues in parliament; this was mainly because during his term in government, the Eurasian community was generally "dormant", while interest in Eurasian affairs and issues only began after his retirement. Yeo's appointment, however, has served to complete the multiracial model, at least as far as the Eurasian community was concerned, as it felt that it was finally part of multiracial Singapore.

The overt willingness by the EA to be directly involved in public life in Singapore was clearly welcomed by the Singapore government. Soon after the minister in charge of Eurasian affairs was confirmed, the government began co-opting Eurasian Association as an official "ethnic self-help group". Singapore's ethnic self-help group system emerged in the 1980s when the Malay community tried to understand and alleviate its economic underperformance vis-à-vis the other racial communities (see Lai, 1995; Hill and Lian, 1995; Hirman, 1999). As a result, MENDAKI was formed in 1981 with the objective of improving the educational performance of Malay children; indeed, its original name was an acronym for *Majlis Pendidikan Anak-Anak Islam* (translated as The Council of Education of Muslim Children). In 1989, its name was changed to Yayasan MENDAKI (The Council on Development of Muslims in Singapore) to encompass all spheres in which the Malay community was "lagging behind" (MENDAKI, 1992). This amendment marked the beginning of overt state involvement and direct support for the organization, as MENDAKI became the state's pilot project, which was eventually extended to the other communities. Soon after, the state established self-help groups for the Chinese and Indian communities in Singapore, with the Chinese Development Assistance Council (CDAC), and Singapore Indian Development Agency (SINDA), respectively. The ethnic self-help group initiative became a key strategy for the state to simultaneously address the issue of the "underclass" in Singapore, and to immediately devolve direct responsibility for this problem (Quinn Moore, 2000). These ethnic self-help groups are mainly funded through mandatory contributions from members of the respective communities; again, entirely based on ascription. Each ethnic self-help group does, however, garner significant government assistance through the provision of state funds and other financial resources, including dollar-for-dollar grants for all monies contributed by members. In addition, the government also provides administrative support in terms of granting office space and other logisticresources. As such, the term "self-help" has been described as a misnomer because of the overwhelming amount of government assistance (Hirman, 1999).

Although it began as a social club, the EA metamorphosized into a "self-help" group at the beginning of the 1990s. It put forth a suggestion for a similar contribution scheme for all Eurasians, which would be administered by the EA for the alleviation of poverty and educational underachievement within the community. This led to the formation of the Eurasian Community Fund (ECF), which was set up in 1994. This Fund complemented the EA's own Endowment Fund, which was initiated in 1992, when the EA was granted the Institution of Public Charter Status. Both funds are exempt from tax, with the government pledging to match dollar-for-dollar up to a maximum of S$200,000 per fund. The EA was not allowed to utilize the principal sums from both funds; instead, it was only allowed to use the interest earned from the two funds for its programmes and operational costs. By 2003, the EA had earned almost S$2 million in donations; the ECF had grown to over S$700,000 while the Endowment Fund stood at over S$1.2 million (Eurasian Association, 2002: 4). As with all the other ethnic self-help groups, the Singapore government was very supportive of the EA's initiatives, providing logistic and financial support for all the EA's welfare activities. Before 1988, the EA did not have a clubhouse or office. Meetings were usually held at members' residences or at rented premises. By 1992, however, the EA was given an office on the premises of the People's Association. This was deemed necessary as the EA needed an office to deal with the administration of Eurasian Community Funds. In 1996, the Singapore government allowed the EA to operate out of a small state-owned building along Mountbatten Road rent-free. With further financial support from the government (and other donors), the Eurasian Community House was opened in July 2003. The EA's offices are located in this house, along with classrooms, a restaurant and a proposed museum to chronicle the history of the Eurasian community and display "Eurasian culture".

Directly related to the last point, the third important top-down initiative has been the state's recognition of Eurasian "culture and heritage". This began with the adoption and promotion of the *branyo*, the so-called Eurasian dance that was featured in the 1992 National Day Parade. Since then, the EA has also propagated Eurasian culture through the offering of *Kristang* (the Portuguese–Malay patois once spoken in Malacca and among some older Eurasians in Singapore) classes at the EA's premises, and the promotion of uniquely Eurasian cuisine (see Braga-Blake, 1992). As a result, in typical multiracial fashion, Eurasian culture has been included in the official displays of Singaporean culture. For example, the Eurasian dance troupe has been invited to perform in the Singapore Tourist Promotion Board's cultural shows, which also include Chinese, Malay and Indian dances, both in Singapore and in other countries. Also, Eurasian cuisine has become a mainstay in the annual Singapore Food Festival.

The most significant aspect of the formalization of Eurasian culture has been its presence within the official school curriculum, as part of the social studies programme for primary school children. In the social science textbook for primary two students, *Discovering Our*

World: Our Neighbourhood (published by the Curriculum Planning and Development Division, Ministry of Education, Singapore), the Eurasian community is introduced after the Malay, Chinese and Indian communities. Thus, in the chapter entitled "A Family Gathering at Jack's House", the community is introduced by a Eurasian character named Jack, who says:

> Eurasians are children of European father and Asian mothers, or of Eurasian parents. My grandfather, who is European, married my grandmother who is Chinese. That's why I'm Eurasian (CPDD-MOE, 2001: 13).

Also highlighted in the same chapter are photographs of the *branyo* dance and the *sugee* cake, which are supposedly characteristic of Eurasian cuisine. The chapter ends with Jack teaching his friends a song, "Jinkli Nona". The original lyrics, which are in the *Kristang* language, are accompanied by an English translation. I found that social studies teachers had a recording of this song, which is taught to all students in the cohort. In addition, Christianity has been highlighted as being the "main religion" of the Eurasians.

The Consequences of Official Recognition

Becoming a recognized community in Singapore has brought about several advantages for the Eurasian community. To many Eurasians, the most important advantages are "social" rather than "political" and "economic". Most Eurasians do not feel socially marginalized any longer. Some pointed out that the classification "Eurasian" rather than "Other" in their NRIC and other official documents was "most satisfying and comforting". Others felt that with greater press and media coverage, the community no longer felt so "invisible". A few respondents said that they were heartened by the fact that other Singaporeans seemed to demonstrate a greater awareness and understanding of the Eurasian community; thus, they no longer had to regularly answer questions such as: "Are you a Singaporean?" or "What is a Eurasian?"

While most Eurasians feel less marginalized within Singapore society, several community leaders indicated that official state recognition has direct economic benefits as well. As mentioned earlier, the government matches dollar for dollar all contributions to the Eurasian Community Fund and Endowment Fund up to a maximum of

S$200,000 per year, and it has donated half the S$2 million dollars as of 2003 of both funds. According to a senior member of the Eurasian Association's management committee, the establishment of the two EA administered funds has been directly responsible for improving the lives of around 50 Eurasians. In 2002, S$160,000 was spent on welfare programmes. Although the majority of these Eurasians were elderly or retired persons with very little income and almost no familial support, there were several who were single parents as well. Before the establishment of the funds, many had to turn to the Council of Social Services, a national body. Now, with the Eurasian Community Fund, the Eurasian Association has two full-time social workers and a working fund to support these individuals. Thus, the economic benefits appear to be even more significant when the overall size of the Eurasian community is factored in.

The Eurasian community has also economically benefited in education. A large proportion of the interest earned from the Eurasian Community Fund and the Endowment Fund is annually utilized for educational programmes designed to improve the standing of Eurasians. In 2002, just under S$200,000 was spent on a variety of educational programmes (Eurasian Association, 2002: 5). Examples of such programmes include remedial tuition classes for Eurasian children in subjects such as mathematics and second language (Malay and Mandarin), as well as information technology (IT) courses to introduce computer literacy to less skilled working adults. At the same time, the EA annually sets aside S$20,000 from the Eurasian Community Fund for bursaries, study grants and excellence awards for Eurasian schoolchildren.

Outside of the ECF, the state also financially supports the community in other areas. The Eurasian Community House is perhaps the clearest example of this, as the government underwrote 80 percent of the House's building cost (S$5 million) of S$6.2 million dollars (Eurasian Association, 2002: 4) (the day-to-day operations costs, however, are entirely borne by the EA). Even though donations from the state seem low, they are very high given the relatively small size of the Eurasian community itself (estimated at around 20,000 by the EA).[9] Also, in January 2002, the EA initiated a Worker Assistance

[9] Interestingly, Singapore Population Census 2000 Advance Data Release still

Programme in response to the economic downturn in Singapore; it established CareerLink with the support of the Ministry of Manpower and state funds. CareerLink is located in Toa Payoh, a large public residential estate, and caters to Singaporeans of all races. Although it is a non-profit para-state organization, the EA has been economically benefiting from CareerLink. The Ministry of Manpower "rewards" every successful employment placement with a small grant, not just for EA CareerLink, but for all employment agencies in Singapore. At the end of 2002, it was reported that CareerLink had one of the highest placement rates among all employment agencies in Singapore (with over 50 percent success rate). This has enabled CareerLink to not only become self-funding but, with the grants earned from the government, it has been able to expand its operations. For example, it has increased the number of full-time employment counsellors from four to seven, and has been able to run its own re-training programmes (Eurasian Association, 2002: 8).

Politically, the Eurasian community has benefitted from not only being recognized but also from participating in civic life in Singapore, as witnessed by the EA's welfare, education and worker assistance programmes. Senior leaders of the EA Management Committee have been invited to sit on a variety of national boards and committees. For example, there is at least one EA Management Committee member on each of the Community Development Councils (CDCs) on the island. In addition, the government holds regular feedback sessions specifically for the Eurasian community. These sessions are chaired by a member of parliament and have policy implications. Although the discussions at these sessions are confidential, members of the EA who have attended some of these sessions have indicated that issues raised range from economic uncertainty (national concern) to the problem that many older Eurasians face in seeking re-employment, particularly as many are unable to understand Mandarin (a community-specific issue). Finally, having a minister to represent the Eurasians has brought about a few benefits as well. Several senior leaders of the EA have said that the minister has assisted the EA in a variety of issues, including fund raising for the building of the

enumerates the population using the CMIO categories; as such, it is impossible to ascertain the size of the Singapore Eurasian community.

Eurasian Community House. He was also credited for initiating the replacement of the race label "Other" with "Eurasian" in official documents.

In addition, social life for the Eurasian community has improved. As mentioned earlier, the Eurasian community has become more "visible" in society, particularly at official state-organized events such as the National Day Parade, Cultural Heritage Festivals, and even at tourism promotion events. Viewed from a broader perspective, the Eurasian community has become the fourth "charter" community in Singapore, after the Chinese, Malay and Indian communities. As such, it would even be possible to argue that Singapore's multiracial model ought to be modified to read CMIEO, with the addition of the Eurasian community. The Eurasian community appears to be placed on equal status with the other communities within the multiracial model, despite the fact that it constitutes less than 0.5 percent of the resident population.

As I discussed earlier, although Eurasians now enjoy some economic, political and social advantages, formal state recognition may have intended or unintended consequences. The most serious ones are the essentialization of Eurasian culture, the homogenization of the hybrid Eurasian community, and the potential isolation of the community. Eurasian culture, which might be defined as the ethnic and cultural practices of the Singapore Eurasians, has been elusive and difficult to pin down, mainly because it has been described as "hybrid" (Braga-Blake, 1992; Pereira, 1997) and "undistinctive" (Willis, 1983). It does not even share much in common with the Malaccan Eurasian community, which claims to be heavily "Portuguese" in culture (see Sta-Maria, 1982; Sarkissian, 2000). Furthermore, even though Eurasians of so-called Portuguese descent appear to be the numerical majority within the community, Singapore Eurasians tend to embrace a wide variety of different cultures and ethnic practices (Pereira, 1996). Singapore Eurasians are comfortable with aspects of several European cultures (British, Dutch, Portuguese and even Italian) as well as Asian cultures (Chinese, Malay, Indian and even Peranakan). This hybridity and lack-of-distinctiveness only becomes a socio-psychological "problem" when the CMIO model is actively promoted and maintained. In such a situation, the expectation is that one "race" will practise a corresponding "ethnic culture". In this sense, all cultures in Singapore undergo the process of "essentialization" in order to neatly fit into the CMIO model. As it turns out, Eurasian culture has itself undergone a similar process of essentialization. The clearest evidence of this is in the teaching of "Eurasian culture" in primary school textbooks. Conforming to the CMIO matrix, Eurasians are ascribed to speak English as their mother tongue,[10] adhere to Christianity for their religion, wear Portuguese-styled traditional clothes, and enjoy so-called traditional dishes such as *sugee cake* and *devil's curry*. Therefore, essentialization becomes a very artificial process in which the social reality—where Eurasians actually have a very wide range of ethnic and cultural practices—is replaced by simplified and convenient artefacts, which may or may not be actually practised by Eurasians. It would, therefore, not be surprising if in future, Singapore Eurasians are expected to adhere to the prescribed "Eurasian" ethnic practices.

As a related process, homogenization is very likely to take place. Given that the Eurasian community can now be clearly defined and identified, not just by their "race" (as stated on their NRIC and other official documents) but also by their "culture". Individuals might find that, in future, a once ethnically heterogeneous community may become a distinctive and "delimited" community. An example of this is when a person who has a Caucasian father and a Chinese mother might not be accepted as a Eurasian, because the "official" view defines a Eurasian as one who not only has Eurasian parents but also must necessarily practise the "essentialist" notion of Eurasian culture. Rather than having a relatively fluid boundary, the Eurasian community may unintentionally create boundaries between themselves and others.

Finally, if the boundaries for the Eurasian community are being even more clearly defined, particularly, as a result of formal state recognition and essentialization, there is the possibility that they may be pressured into choosing "Eurasian" as their primary identity. As other studies have shown, Eurasians have tended to primarily identify themselves as "Singaporeans" rather than as members of an ethnic (or "racial") community (Benjamin, 1976; Braga-Blake, 1992;

---

[10] This might appear to be ironic, as English is seen, for the other communities, officially as the language of business and administration, but for the Eurasians could be adopted as a "mother tongue". It could also be argued that *Kristang* could be equally ascribed as the "mother tongue" for Eurasians; however, this only goes to show how confusing a rigid application of the CMIO matrix might turn out to be.

Pereira, 1996). The consequence of this would be that the Eurasian community would exist as a distinctive but very small minority community, rather than as members of a much larger community of "Singaporeans". This would be an irony as the whole exercise of gaining formal state recognition was an escape from marginalization.

It could be argued that these aspects are "unintended consequences" rather than costs or disadvantages to the Eurasian community. In other words, compared to the benefits that Eurasians currently enjoy, these "costs" appear to be minor. Yet, I would argue that essentialization—and by extension, ascription—will become "problematic" for Eurasians, as it leads once again to social marginalization, albeit of a different nature. Eurasians used to be socially marginalized in Singapore because they were not culturally distinctive enough. By becoming "essentially" distinctive, however, they are now socially marginalized because it is highly likely that only a few Eurasians can actually identify with the essentialized version of Eurasian culture, as many do not practise it in their everyday lives. As such, the marginalization will once again be socio-psychological, where once this community ". . . had no culture" but currently, this community has a culture that many ". . . cannot identify with" and ". . . do not practice".

Conclusion

This case of the emergence of the Eurasian community gives an indication of ethnic politics in Singapore. On the surface, it appears to be a "win-win" situation. Indeed, the "costs" of including the Eurasians clearly outweigh the benefits, both to the community and by the state. The Singapore government will be satisfied that the Eurasians are now fully "included" in the CMIO model; in other words, the community can no longer claim to be disgruntled that the state is marginalizing them. The Eurasians, too, seem satisfied with the current situation as they are enjoying the economic, political and social benefits of inclusion.

The Singapore government has been careful to maintain cultural pluralism; it even introduced several features that might seem to resemble "structural pluralism" without actually creating separate institutions and structures. For example, it could be argued that the ethnic self-help groups in Singapore could be a form of structural pluralism since they represent parallel institutions aimed at dealing with poverty in Singapore. The state would argue that this form of structural pluralism is a pragmatic response and a more effective solution to the problem of poverty in Singapore. Further, parallel structures in the sphere of social welfare do not appear to directly threaten the main social institutions in Singapore, which remain culturally plural within a larger national system.

It is interesting to note that although race and/or ethnicity are salient in Singapore because of the pervasiveness of multicultralism (that is, Singapore is officially culturally plural), Singapore remains an ethnically (or racially) neutral society (the state does not favour any particular ethnic group). As mentioned earlier, Singapore's national identity is not premised on any one (or more) ethnic cultures but is, instead, premised on "values" such as meritocracy, pragmatism and multiracialism. With the inclusion of the Eurasian community into the CMIO model, the state has shown once again how it has reinforced two main elements of multiracialism: cultural "equality" (as opposed to generating cultural assertion) and "fair opportunity" (as opposed to creating political and economic competition among ethnic groups). Multiracialism, therefore, appears to be an efficient and pragmatic policy in managing (ethnic) minority groups, mostly benefitting the minority groups concerned without causing the state to incur significant costs.

REFERENCES

Abdullah, A. K. (Munshi) (1970) [1950] *The Hikayat Abdullah*. Trans. A. H. Hill. Kuala Lumpur: Oxford University Press.

Barth, V. (1992) "Belonging: Eurasian Clubs and Associations", in M. Braga-Blake and A. Oehlers, eds., *Singapore Eurasians: Memories and Hopes*. Singapore: Times Editions, pp. 97–108.

Bachtiar, Ida "The Eurasian Awakening", *The Straits Times*, 8 February 1990.

Benjamin, Geoffrey (1976) "The Cultural Logic of Singapore's Multiracialism", in R. Hassan, ed., *Singapore in Transition*. Singapore: Oxford University Press, pp. 115–133.

Braga-Blake, M. (1992) "Eurasians: An Overview", in M. Braga-Blake and A. Oehlers, eds., *Singapore Eurasians: Memories and Hopes*. Singapore: Times Editions, pp. 11–24.

Boxer, C. R. (1965) *The Dutch Seaborne Empire: 1600–1800*. New York: Knopf.

———. (1969) *The Portuguese Seaborne Empire: 1415–1825*. London: Hutchinson.

———. (1973) [1948] *Hildagos in the Far East: 1550–1770*. The Hague: Martinus Nijhoff.

Chan, H. C. (1989) "The PAP and the Structuring of the Political System", in K. S. Sandhu and P. Wheatley, eds., *Management of Success: The Moulding of Modern Singapore.*, Singapore: ISEAS, pp. 70–89.

Chua, B. H. (1998) "Racial Singaporeans: Absence after the Hyphen", in J. S. Kahn, ed., *Southeast Asian Identities: Culture and the Politics of Representation in Indonesia, Malaysia, Singapore and Thailand.* Singapore: ISEAS, pp. 28–50.

———. (2003) "Singapore: Multiracial Harmony as a Public Good", in C. Mackerras, ed., *Ethnicity in Asia.* London: Routledge, pp. 101–7.

CPDD-MOE (Curriculum Planning Division, Ministry of Education) (2001) *Discovering Our World: Our Neighbourhood.* Singapore: Federal Publications/Times Media.

Da Silva, A. (2001) *The Eurasian Association Singapore: From Social Club to Self-Help Group.* Unpublished B. A. (Hons) Thesis. Department of History, Melbourne, University of Melbourne.

Daus, R. (1989) *Portuguese Eurasian Communities in Southeast Asia.* Singapore: ISEAS.

Gist, N. and R. D. Wright (1973) *Marginality and Identity.* Leiden: Brill.

Glazer, N. (1997) *We Are All Multiculturalists Now.* Cambridge: Harvard University Press.

Government of Singapore (1999) *Constitution of the Republic of Singapore.* Reprint. Singapore: (Singapore) Government Printers.

Hawes, C. J. (1996) *Poor Relations: The Making of a Eurasian Community in British India, 1773–1833.* Richmond: Curzon.

Hirman, A. (1999) "Ethnic-Based Self-Help and its Impact on the Ideology of Multiracialism". Unpublished B. Soc. Sci (Hons) Thesis. Department of Political Science, Singapore, National University of Singapore.

Hamilton-Shimmen, W. (1993) *Seasons of Darkness.* Klang, Malaysia: Wilfred Hamilton-Shimmen.

Hill, M. and K. F. Lian (1996) *The Politics of Nation Building and Citizenship in Singapore.* London: Routledge.

Joppke, C. (1996) "Multiculturalism and Immigration", *Theory and Society* 25(4): 449–500.

Kivisto, P. (2002) *Multiculturalism in a Global Society.* Oxford: Blackwell.

Lai, A. E. (1995) *Meanings of Multiethnicity: A Case Study of Ethnicity and Ethnic Relations.* Kuala Lumpur: Oxford University Press,

Li, T. (1989) *Malays in Singapore: Culture, Economy and Ideology.* New York: Oxford University Press.

MENDAKI (1992) *Making the Difference: Ten Years of MENDAKI.* Singapore: Yayasan Mendaki.

Pang, Eng Fong (1993) "Singapore", in C. Y. Ng and E. F. Pang, eds., *The State and Economic Development in the Asia Pacific.* Singapore: ISEAS, pp. 27–40.

Pereira, A. A. (1995) *Singapore Eurasians: Their Management of Ethnic Identity.* Unpublished M. Soc. Sci Thesis. Department of Sociology, Singapore, National University of Singapore.

———. (1997) "The Revitalization of Eurasian Identity in Singapore", *Southeast Asian Journal of Social Science* 25 (2): 7–24.

Purushotam, N. (1998) "Disciplining Difference: 'Race' in Singapore", in J. S. Kahn, ed., *Southeast Asian Identities: Culture and the Politics of Representation in Indonesia, Malaysia, Singapore and Thailand.* Singapore: ISEAS, pp. 51–94.

Quinn-Moore, R. (2000) "Multiracialism and Meritocracy: Singapore's Approach to Race and Inequality", *Review of Social Economy* 58(3): 339–360.

Rahim, L. Z. (1998) *The Singapore Dilemma: The Political and Educational Marginality of the Malay Community.* Kuala Lumpur: Oxford University Press.

Sarkissian, M. (2000) *D'Albuquerque's Children: Performing Tradition in Malaysia's Portuguese Settlement.* Chicago: University of Chicago Press.

Shelley, R. (1991) *Shrimp People.* Singapore: Times Books.

———. (1993) *People of the Pear Tree.* Singapore: Times Books.

———. (1998) *A River of Roses.* Singapore: Times Books.

Siddique, S. (1990) "The Phenomenology of Ethnicity: A Singapore Case Study", *Sojourn* 5 (1): 35–62.

Singapore Department of Statistics (2001) *Singapore Population*. Singapore: Singapore Department of Statistics.
Sta Maria, B. (1982) *My People My Country*. Malacca: Malacca Portuguese Development Centre.
Tong, Chee Kiong and Chan Kwok Bun (2001) "One Face Many Masks: The Singularity and Plurality of Chinese Identity in Singapore", *Diaspora* 10(3): 258–285.
Turnbull, C. M .(1977) *A History of Singapore*, 1819–1975. Kuala Lumpur: Oxford University Press.
Vasil, R. K (2000) *Governing Singapore: Democracy and National Development*. Singapore: Allen & Unwin.
Verkuyten, M. (2004) "Everyday Ways of Thinking About Multiculturalism", *Ethnicities* 4(1): 53–74.
Willis, J. (1983) *The Serani and the Upper Ten: Eurasian Ethnicity in Singapore*. Unpublished B. A. (Hons) Thesis. School of Sociology, Sydney, University of New South Wales.
Young, R. J. C. (1995) *Colonial Desire: Hybridity in Theory, Culture and Race*. New York: Routledge.

NAMES AS SITES OF IDENTITY CONSTRUCTION, NEGOTIATION, AND RESISTANCE: SIGNIFYING ORANG ASLI IN POSTCOLONIAL MALAYSIA*

Alice M. Nah

The purpose of this paper is to examine the complex and multi-faceted interplay between naming practices, identity construction and exercises of power, with particular focus on the Orang Asli, otherwise known as the aborigines of Peninsular Malaysia. Numbering around 130,000 people (Department of Statistics, 2000), the Orang Asli—literally "original people" in the Malay language—comprise at least 19 linguistically and culturally different groups spread across the Peninsula.

Presently, every Orang Asli individual is governed within a matrix of State-provided names (see Figure 1), which indicate their official social location within Malaysian society. According to State definitions, the Orang Asli population can be divided into three "races" (or "main groups")—Negrito, Senoi and Proto-Malay. Each of these "main groups" is further broken down into six "aboriginal ethnic groups" (or "sub-groups"), thus resulting in 18 fixed and mutually exclusive categories that an Orang Asli can be classified into. This is the standard matrix that is reproduced in almost all introductions to the Orang Asli, and can be found in official literature, museums, government web sites, and in research reports.[1] In addition to this, each Orang Asli individual is known by an official personal name, one that is recorded on birth certificates and identity cards.

---

* An earlier version of this paper was presented at the Asian Research Institute (ARI) at the National University of Singapore, on 1 April 2003. I conducted fieldwork in 2002 and 2003 as a postgraduate student of the Sociology Department at the National University of Singapore (NUS). I am thankful to the Department of Orang Asli Affairs (JHEOA) and the Economic Planning Unit (EPU) for official permission to conduct this research, as well as for the assistance provided by the National Archives and the Centre of Orang Asli Concerns (COAC). I am grateful to Peter Pels, Lian Kwen Fee and two anonymous reviewers for comments on an earlier version of this paper.

[1] Having said this, these names of ethnic groups have been problematized repeatedly by anthropologists and administrators, among them Williams-Hunt (1952), Benjamin (1974), and Carey (1976). See Lye (2001) for a detailed discussion.

Figure 1. Orang Asli Aboriginal Ethnic Groups

Race	Negrito	Senoi	Proto-Malay
Aboriginal Ethnic Groups	Kensiu	Temiar	Temuan
	Kintak	Semai	Selemai
	Lanoh	Semoq Beri	Jakun
	Jahai	Che Wong	Orang Kanak
	Mendriq	Jahut	Orang Kuala
	Bateq	Mah Meri	Orang Seletar

Source: Plaque on display at the Orang Asli Museum, Gombak. Viewed in December 2002

Naming practices, I hope to demonstrate in this paper, are not neutral ways in which groups and communities are understood but are always, and inextricably, linked to exercises of power. This is a matter that is sometimes forgotten by the people involved in the recording of names, who may disavow that these are creative acts, and who sometimes presume that the subject peoples exist in precisely the ways they are being recorded.[2] As we will see in the case of the Orang Asli, we will be able to trace the ways in which the State came to know about them, through ethnography, science and statistics. In identifying, counting and documenting the presence of the Orang Asli for the purposes of national security and modern administration, State authorities contributed to the creation of the Orang Asli in ways that did not previously exist. Some of these categories of identification have been internalized, consumed and appropriated by the peoples themselves, who now understand (and were made to understand) their socio-political location in society through these categories.

The act of recording, enumerating and documenting demonstrates State recognition of the existence of the Orang Asli as citizens, which has become a way through which rights and privileges of these peoples can be negotiated. Gaining aggregates, averages, and spatial fixes on the population under its management has been important for security reasons and continues to be necessary for planning pur-

[2] See Hirschman (1986) for an introduction and construction of a racial paradigm by British administrators in colonial Malaya. Hirschman (1987) elaborates on the link between racial ideology, the aims of colonial administration, and the changing ethnic categories in censuses.

poses. State actors use such data to determine allocation of resources—schools, medical services, pipes, roads, and electricity—services and facilities that serve the Orang Asli.

The influence of the State on the Orang Asli, particularly in the form of the *Jabatan Hal-Ehwal Orang Asli* (JHEOA, Department of Aboriginal Affairs), however, goes beyond the scope of "just" providing amenities and supplies to the peoples under their administration. Through counting, enumerating and documenting, as well as through policy-making and everyday interaction with Orang Asli communities, JHEOA officers have been involved in the psychological and social transformation of the Orang Asli, influencing how they think about themselves, how they think about others, and how an "ideal" self should be imagined. In short, the practices of the State contribute to identity (re)construction both at a collective and individual level.

Although the Orang Asli, in part, are constructed by the linguistic functions of their names, there are slippages and negotiations within these modes of subjectification (Foucault, 1994). First, despite the authoritative and homogenizing ways in which these ethnic categories are presented, the subject peoples find ways of slipping in and out of these categories, demonstrating the limitations of such categorization. Second, these naming processes signal the State's perception of the peoples identified, and become ways in which the State (both directly and indirectly) communicates its views about the communities concerned. These become grounds for the named peoples to claim rights and benefits that state authorities are subsequently required or expected to provide. Knowing that they are constituted within such categories, the Orang Asli have turned the very ways they are fixed into sites of resistance and collective protest. Last, it is important to note that the matrix of State-provided names (related to ethnicity/race) I will discuss is but one of many ways in which people are "ordered" and "known". There are alternative ways in which Orang Asli are placed, constituted and related to others from different socio-political locations. These have consequences in altering the ways in which power operates through the establishment of difference.

In the first section of this paper, I review some of the socio-political processes behind the ordering of peoples into the matrix of State-provided names. This required sustained attempts by the colonial authorities to identify, categorize, label, and count aboriginal groups through ethnography, "scientific" theories, and statistics. The ordering of these groups was neither an easy nor a straightforward task, as very little was known about these scattered populations. Nevertheless, it was a necessary project, driven by the political motive of governing aboriginal groups with greater effectiveness and efficiency during the war against Communism (1948–1960). I then proceed to review the different responses to these acts of naming and placing, which have included varying degrees of acceptance, accommodation and negotiation. I also discuss how State-provided names have been used to argue for political positioning and rights within the nation-state.

In the second section of this paper, I examine *personal names*, elaborating first on the ways in which names function as a marker of identity with multiple socio-political meanings. The colonial authorities in the 1950s asserted that an official name be identified, fixed and utilized for each aboriginal person. As different aboriginal groups used alternative ways of recording their names (some using a number of interchangeable names to refer to specific individuals),[3] the process of registration was difficult to implement. The colonial administrators decided to set a particular standardized method for registering personal names, and chose the format used by other ethnic and religious groups. As their naming system parallels those of other majority groups, and as identity and difference—ethnic/racial, gender, religious—are encoded in personal names in Malaysia, this creates specific complications and tensions concerning identity for the Orang Asli.

Names to Create: Race-ing the Subject

I have previously argued that colonial conceptions of difference between the "Malays" and "Orang Asli" (then "aborigines") were related to how the British administrators exerted colonial rule over Malaya (Nah, 2003, 2004). Broadly speaking, the "Malays" were of political importance to British administrators and entrepreneurs from the late nineteenth to the middle of the twentieth century, as it was

[3] See Benjamin (1968), for example, on Temiar names.

through Malay–Muslim rulers and chiefs that the British established an economic foothold in the Peninsula. Early descriptions of the "other" indigenous people in the Peninsula tended to be made vis-à-vis understandings of "the Malay". Significantly, the "Malay" was always recognized by his "Mohammedan religion", and the "indigenous other" was often described as "pagan" (for example, Skeat and Blagden, 1906). As the people who comprised the "Indigenous Other" were few, scattered, and insignificant to political developments, they were summarily lumped together under the catch-all term, "the aborigines" or the "*sakai*" (as the Orang Asli were popularly known to the British).[4]

Although the idea of "the aborigine" existed, it was unclear precisely who they were, despite the fact that there were early attempts to enumerate them.[5] Most of the Malay Peninsula was covered in dense jungle, and it was difficult to find the aboriginal groups, much less identify or enumerate them. Nevertheless, attempts were made to pin down these groups and various approaches were used in order to "map" the communities that were found, whether through philology, anthropometric measurements, or other "scientific" methods concerning origins. These tended to be the work of ethnographers, missionaries and anthropologists curious about the customs, practices and beliefs of the different aboriginal groups.

There were many earlier theories proposed on the ways in which "the aborigines" in the Peninsula should be classified, some of which, as R. O. D. Noone (who became Adviser to the Aborigines) points out, was "based at times on the flimsiest evidence" (Noone and Holman, 1972: 6). Theories focused on "breeding", "stocks" and "strains", and scholars keen on establishing the origins of the "aborigines" took out their calipers to measure, mark, and examine the

[4] Aboriginal groups that British anthropologists and administrators had dealings with also saw themselves as being distinctly different from Malay–Muslim communities (Skeat and Blagden, 1906; Noone, 1936). By the time the British arrived, these "aborigines" had already suffered at the hands of "Malays"; some had been captured, enslaved, raped and murdered (Carey, 1976a; 1976b; Couillard, 1984; Endicott, 1983; Favre, 1848; Newbold [1839] 1971; McNair, 1878) and would not have identified themselves as "Malays".

[5] "Aborigines" in Penang, Malacca and Singapore were first enumerated in the 1881 Straits Settlements Census (Hirschman, 1987). Aborigines in the Federated Malay States (comprising Perak, Selangor, Negri Sembilan and Pahang) were first enumerated in 1901.

physical evidence before them. There was also debate on whether "way of life" or "physical characteristics" should constitute the basis for divisions on race (Williams-Hunt, 1952). Attempting to specify clearly which "ethnic groups" belongs to which "racial group" was a difficult task, for "race", as Carey (1976a) notes, did not just refer to genetic typology, but included "culture" and "language". Some ethnic groups were seen to possess the "culture" and "race" of one group but the "language" of another.

Eventually, it was reconciled and accepted as conventional wisdom that "the aborigines" comprised three different *racial* groups that migrated into the Peninsula in "waves", the first being the "Negritos", followed by the "Senoi" and then the "Proto-Malays". This is the dominant view held today by the State.[6] Geoffrey Benjamin (2002), who rejects this approach, refers to this as the "*kuih lapis* (layered cake) ethnology", and points out that this not only refers to "race" (in the biological and genetic sense), but presents the communities "as if they occupied different steps on a culture-evolutionary staircase" (2002: 19), with "Negritos" assumed to be more primitive than the "Senoi" who were, in turn, less civilized than the "Proto-Malays".

Categorizing Difference: The Politics of Ordering the "Other"

It is critical to consider the political circumstances surrounding the drive for identifying, naming and placing "the aborigines". After the World War II, Malayan Communists campaigned against British colonialism and were forced to flee into the jungles to survive. Some of the Communists had already befriended "the aborigines" during the war against Japanese forces, and relied on them to sustain them with rations, information, and to act as guides. The aborigines were valorized by the Communists as *orang asal* ("original people"), and they set up a network of cells called the Asal Organisation, in which the aborigines were recruited as participating members (Carey, 1976a; Leary, 1989).

The choice of the term "*asal*" was not accidental. It signalled a recognition of them as the "original people" of the Peninsula, at a

[6] See description on http://www.jheoa.gov.my/e-orangasli.htm, accessed 25 January 2004.

time when they were referred to as "aborigines" and "*sakai*" by the British government—terms that had derogatory connotations (Jimin et al., 1983).[7] The Communists promised that in a "liberated" Communist Malaya, they would be given special recognition and privileges because of their "status" (Holman, 1958). The Asal Organisation was an effective one, and the British began to realize that the Communists could not be defeated if the latter continued gaining the support of the aborigines. The British government then began a campaign to "win the hearts and minds" of the aborigines, whom they could no longer ignore.[8] This included the provision of basic supplies—medicine, rations, food—as well as a quest to understand more about the aborigines, so that they could woo them.[9] This prompted an unprecedented collection of statistics and generation of knowledge about the aborigines.

Efforts were made from quite early on by the Federal Department of the Advisor on Aborigines to compile data on the aboriginal communities. As described in a Memorandum released in September 1950, the Department was "charged with the task of instituting research into aboriginal life and custom, collating information on a federal basis and advising measures that might be taken".[10] The resettlement of some aboriginal communities (to "protect" the population against the Communist insurgency of the 1950s), was an opportunity for more concrete data to be collected. Major P. D. R. Williams-Hunt, who was appointed in 1949 as the Adviser of the Aborigines,

---

[7] Having said this, it is necessary to point out that "*sakai*" does not necessarily have the same sort of pejorative connotations everywhere. Anne Hamilton (2002) and Nathan Porath (2002) for example, point out that in Thailand, the term is used in a fairly neutral way. Some Malaysians, too, (particularly members of the older generation in my experience), use the term merely to refer to Orang Asli without the intention of deriding them. In the course of my fieldwork, however, I met several Orang Asli who have expressed an intense dislike of this word. One individual was so against the very mention of the word that he refused to articulate it, spelling it out instead for my benefit.

[8] As General Templer remarked quite frankly, "the only reason why I directed that something must be done about the aborigines of Malaya was that they had become a vital factor in the Emergency" (Holman, 1958:ix).

[9] To this end, P. D. R. Williams-Hunt wrote a book entitled *An Introduction to the Malayan Aborigines*, published in 1952, as a simple introduction for troops fighting against the Communists.

[10] Circular Memorandum No. 15, "Some Notes on a Suggested Policy for Aboriginal Advancement", dated September 1950, 1963/0000926, BA Selangor 70/1950: Aboriginal Matters.

drew up a census form and provided specific instructions on how "accurate" data was to be gained. As recorded in a Memorandum dated 25 June 1950[11] under "A Note on Aboriginal Nomenclature", enumerators were instructed,

> If a specific ethnic group is mentioned an attempt should be made to give the group name—i.e. what the aborigines call themselves—*if* this can be ascertained but it is emphasized that many groups will not give their group name. Vague general terms such as "orang bukit" or "orang paya" should be avoided (emphasis mine).[12]

Major Williams-Hunt had quite an intimate knowledge of some of the aboriginal groups, and knew that attempts to make aborigines fall into neat schemes was going to be a difficult task. He provided each enumerator with a list of provisional names— a list of "aboriginal ethnic group names believed to be correct"—for their reference. He further stated,

> It is suggested that local authorities do not attempt to describe groups on a racial basis unless the advice of a trained anthropologist is available.
>
> It is not suggested that existing documents such as identity cards should be amended on the lines given above but it is suggested that all future documents should conform to the proposed nomenclature.[13]

In his later book, Williams-Hunt discussed the complications inherent in trying to establish distinctive names for each aboriginal ethnic group:

> A group may have three names, one used by itself, one by which it is called by the Malays and one or more by which it is known to adjacent Aboriginal groups. Furthermore many tribes will conceal their group name to outsiders' (1952: 19).

Nevertheless, after much deliberation, the present set of 18 categories, set out into three "racial groups" as shown in Figure 1, were decided upon, and are now taken to be normative knowledge of who the Orang Asli comprise.[14]

---

[11] "Letter from the Adviser on Aborigines", F. M. dated 25 June 1950, 1963/0000926, BA Selangor 70/1950: Aboriginal Matters.

[12] "Orang bukit" translates into "man of the hill", while "orang paya" denotes "man from the mangroves".

[13] In the same memorandum, he notes that "Aboriginal groups who have embraced Islam do not normally come within the scope of this Department but have been included here for the sake of completeness".

[14] Geoffrey Benjamin (1974) problematized the very idea that distinct '"ethnic

Slippages in Racial and Ethnic Categories

There have been, and continue to be, different contemporary responses to the matrix of names employed by State officials. First, some do not use State-chosen names to refer to themselves and, in fact, consider themselves outside of the so-named group.[15] Second, while some Orang Asli are aware of the name of the specific "sub group" in which they are officially categorized, some do not have emotive connections to these names, seeing them as names given by others.[16] Third, Orang Asli may consider themselves members of the "sub group" as named by the State, but deny that others similarly categorized are legitimate members of the group.[17] Furthermore, those

groups" essentially exist, suggesting that it could well be produced *because* of the necessity of one group to administer another, that is, a by-product of the State.

[15] Williams-Hunt (1952: 15) remarked, "one group whose name was *Yakin*—which sounds remarkably like a corruption of *Jakun* to my ear—were most indignant when it was suggested that they were *Jakun*. *Jakun*, they said, were wild hairy men with blue tongues and tails and were the ancestors of the Malays! The *Yakin* were nice friendly people and had nothing to do with such monsters." Another example is an amusing newspaper article published in 1956, entitled "Surprise! These 'Jakuns' find that they are really 'Semoq-Beris'". In this article, the writer notes how officials from the Aborigines Department "re-discovered" the identity of the community they visited, thus "rescuing" them from extinction (Nicholas et al., 1989: 162). Later, Iskandar Carey (1976a: 21) noted that, "Many of the Orang Asli that have been questioned on [the use of the word Jakun] were of the opinion that the Jakun are a kind of wild people, and may be compared with the monkeys but whom they, themselves, had never met. The people who are usually called Jakun in the literature of the Orang Asli, call themselves 'Orang Dusun', 'Orang Dalam', 'Orang Hulu', or 'Orang Darat'. In English these terms mean 'people of isolated villages', 'inland people', 'up-stream people', and 'people of the interior' respectively".

[16] The work of Juli Edo—the first Orang Asli anthropologist to write a Phd thesis about his own people—attests to the constructed nature of ethnic labels. He chose not to use the official term "Semai" in his PhD thesis, saying that, "(f)rom the people's point of view . . . the term 'Semai' is not their word and has no meaning, either good or bad. They refer to themselves as *Seng-oi*, which means people. Since the term 'Semai' has been introduced by the state without any specific meaning, this study will employ the term *Seng-oi* to refer to this people" (Juli, 1998: 17). Howell (1984) also explains that the Che Wong obtained their name through a misunderstanding between a British forester and a worker for the Forest Department. When the latter was asked what the name of the aboriginal group was, he gave his own name, Siwang, which was recorded officially as the name of that aboriginal group.

[17] Nicholas (2002: 125) describes his experience with Jahais as follows, "when meeting with the Jahais in Perak and Kelantan in 1993, the Jahais of Banun (Perak) emphatically denied that those in Jeli (Kelantan) were also Jahais. Similarly, the Jeli Jahais strongly insist that they were the *real* Jahais. This is despite both groups having similar physical features and linguistic affiliations".

classified within the same "sub group" may see divisions and sub-groupings among themselves, and use alternative signifiers to demarcate "intra-category" difference (see Dentan, 1975).

Another common phenomenon is for Orang Asli to have complex understandings of the internal dynamics and tensions within their "own" group, and to have little personal experience with other groups such that they assume a homogeneity that does not exist among these other groups.[18] In addition, with frequent intermarriages among members of different aboriginal ethnic groups, the children of such unions are uncertain about how they should identify themselves. This is not obvious in the government population tables, which list the exact numbers of the Orang Asli right down to the last individual.

Finally, there are examples of how these identity slots may be incomplete in number.[19] Williams-Hunt (1952) and Carey (1976a) refer to the *Dossin Dolak*, a group of Orang Laut converted to Islam. Williams-Hunt, in 1950, notes the existence of the Ple/Pleh, which he records as being "mixed Negrito–Sakai",[20] as well as the "Semaq Palong", whom "security forces stumbled upon".[21] Not too long ago, the newspapers published an article with the headlines, "New Orang Asli tribe identified!" (*Sunday Star*, 2 June 2002). It was explained that the "Temok" had only just been found, as they were not registered on the JHEOA lists. Colin Nicholas of the Center for Orang Asli Concerns (COAC) refuted this "discovery", pointing out that the Temoq/Temok had been identified and researched by individuals as early as 1949 (see Collings, 1949). Benjamin (1974) had already highlighted that some distinct groups were not clearly identified in admin-

---

[18] When I was on fieldwork, the Orang Asli individuals that I met seemed more comfortable using the State-designated names to refer to individuals from other groups than they were in using them on themselves.

[19] There may be different reasons for this lack of completion. Their absence from the State's list of categories may be a matter of how different groups were separated out into various ethnicities. These "dividing practices" (Foucault, 1994), Benjamin (1974) suggests, may be drawn from everyday perceptions of difference—sometimes based on locality, sometimes based on lifestyle—not necessarily based on genetic "stocks". It becomes a matter of judgment which specific markers constitute sufficient difference, so that they may be called into being as a separate ethnic category.

[20] Letter from the Adviser on Aborigines, F.M. dated 25 June 1950, 1963/0000926, BA Selangor 70/1950: Aboriginal Matters.

[21] Letter from the Adviser on Aborigines, F.M dated 18th July 1950, 1963/0000926, BA Selangor 70/1950: Aboriginal Matters.

istrative data.[22] Lye (2001) furthermore, suggests that there are between 17 to 25 indigenous ethnic minorities that may be considered Orang Asli. Benjamin (2002) notes that some smaller groups are subsumed under other ethnic categories. Nevertheless, while popular perceptions of ethnic groupings did not (and still do not) conform perfectly to the categories used and promoted by the State, the ubiquitous use of these categories have been consequential. These are now comprehensible ways of referring to Orang Asli individuals, both for Orang Asli and non-Orang Asli (Gomes, 1988, 1994).

From "Aborigines" to "Orang Asli"

In 1966, a decision was made by the government to rename the aborigines "Orang Asli" (Jimin et al., 1983). Iskander Carey explains the reasons for this:

> The Malaysian Government, some years ago, felt that the word 'aborigines' had certain pejorative connotations; it was associated with concepts such as backwardness, under-development and primitiveness. The Malay words 'Orang Asli', however, do not have these connotations. The word '*orang*' merely means 'people' and the term '*asli*' comes from the Arabic word '*asali*', meaning '*original*', '*well-born*' or '*aristocratic*'. It was decided accordingly that the Malay term, 'Orang Asli', should be used even in English correspondence (1976a: 3).

This renaming signalled the post-colonial government's intent towards the people under its care. Yet over the past few decades, there have been further attempts to change this name, perhaps indicative of the struggles authorities have in "placing" the Orang Asli within the nation-state. Nicholas (1997) notes, for example, that

> In 1974, the state introduced 'Saudara Lama' (which literally means, old relatives) to replace Orang Asli. This was probably to complement another term, 'Saudara Baru' (meaning new brothers/sisters), a term which particularly refers to non-Malays who converted to Islam.
>
> In 1984, the Sultan of Johor . . . declared that the Orang Asli should be referred to as 'Bumiputra Asli' (original indigenes), arguing that the only reason that they are not Malays is that they are not Muslims . . . (np)[23]

---

[22] However, his comments were summarily dismissed as being a case of "academic hair-splitting" in Jimin et al. (1983: 4).

[23] The comment by the Sultan of Johor was reported in Tan, C. K. (1984) "We

The choice of these names indicate an existing and ever-present question on the minds of State authorities: How do the Orang Asli fit in a nation-state whose political legitimacy is based on claims to indigeneity, as waged by the politically dominant group, the "Malays"?[24] How do their religious beliefs matter, in a nation-state in which Islam is the "religion of the Federation" (Federal Constitution, Article 3(1)), and the Malay language is given primacy (Federal Constitution, Article 152(1)), being the nationalist "emblems of nation-ness" (Anderson, 1991: 133)? This remains to be resolved, but creates tensions with regard to the administration of the undeniably indigenous Orang Asli.

One of the attempts to re-name the Orang Asli prompted a collective response by the community. In 1973, the Minister of Rural Development, Ghaffar Baba, announced that the name Orang Asli would be changed to *Putrasli*, a suggestion that sparked great concern among various aboriginal groups. Fourty-one Orang Asli individuals met together to deliberate this change. A memorandum[25] was subsequently presented to the Director of Orang Asli Affairs, in which they affirmed that they wanted to retain the name "Orang Asli", and that they saw it as being appropriate to them. In addition, these individuals expressed dislike of being seen as "objects", always acted upon, and instead desired greater inclusion and participation in deciding the affairs of their own community. As we can see in this response, the re-naming practice proposed by the Minister signaled an exercise of power that was perceived to be coercive when conducted without the consultation of the communities involved. This core group eventually formed an association that has evolved into the Peninsula Malaysia Orang Asli Association (*Persatuan Orang Asli Semenanjung Malaysia, POASM*), presently a broad-based, community organization whose membership has grown to over 19,000 people.

Should Lead By Example", *The Star*, 26 April, pp. 1, 8; and commented upon by Nicholas, C. (1984) "Another Semantic Debate Over the Orang Asli", *The Star*, 9 May, p. 21.

[24] For further discussion about the tensions between the Malay "Self" and Orang Asli as a "new-Other" in postcolonial Malaysia, see Nah (2003).

[25] POASM document entitled "Minit Perjumpaan Mengkaji Usul Putrasli" dated 12.10.73.

"Orang Asli" has become a term that is embraced and used in everyday discourse, both by Orang Asli and non-Orang Asli (Juli, 1998; Nicholas, 2002).[26] It is the way in which, if the topic of ethnic identity surfaces, Orang Asli introduce themselves to other members of the Malaysian population. It has become the way they distinguish themselves as being different from others—sometimes with pride, and sometimes with shame (Nah, 2004). This sense of identification has become the banner under which groups of people, geographically distant from one another and speaking different languages, band together to lobby for social change, despite the difficulties of representing plural interests.[27]

The signifier "Orang Asli", as I have reviewed, holds within it State recognition of the peoples as "indigenous" to the land. This takes on particular meaning in Malaysia, for all the rights and privileges assigned to the "Malays" on account of them being "indigeneous" should logically, then, always extend to the Orang Asli, who are undeniably indigenous, as evidenced by their name. This may be the reason why some Orang Asli are accorded *bumiputra* privileges on an everyday basis—for example, in terms of university quotas and scholarships—although their "special position" is not inscribed formally in the Federal Constitution, the way it is for "Malays" and "natives of Sabah and Sarawak" in Article 153.[28]

[26] Although the term "aborigine" is still used in legislation dating before this official change. Juli Edo provides three reasons why people have ascribed to the term "Orang Asli". Firstly, he says, this has become a platform on which political consciousness and unity is built. Second, it is a name that is retained to resist manipulation of their identity by dominant groups, a matter he states is related to pride and desire to resist the appearance of assistance by virtue of a superficial name change. Lastly, it provides them with a convenient umbrella ethnic classification that covers mixed marriages within ethnic sub-groups (Juli, 1998: 13–14).

[27] While aboriginal groups (segmented according to ethnicity, geographical distance, religion or political opinion) may unite under the banner of "Orang Asli", differences, fragmentation and tensions exist among them (see Howell, 2002; Nicholas, 2002; Nah, 2004).

[28] In Malaysia, "indigenous" groups are given special status and privileges; *bumiputra* translates as "sons of the soil" in Malay. The matter of whether the Orang Asli are considered *bumiputra* is a point of some ambiguity among scholars and the Orang Asli themselves. While it seems commonsense that the Orang Asli are undeniable indigenous and, therefore, should (obviously) count as *bumiputra*. The source of legal authority for this "special position", however, is Article 153 of the Federal Constitution, which explicitly does *not* refer to the Orang Asli. Nevertheless, in a lived sense, everyday bureaucrats, officers and corporate employees who mete out *bumiputra* benefits also do so for the Orang Asli. Furthermore, the JHEOA explicitly recognizes

"Traces of Aboriginal Origin": Slippery Boundaries between "Self" and "Other"

> The *natural evolution* of the 100,000 or so aborigines in the Federation of Malaya is to graduate from pure wandering hunting communities to shifting agriculture then to a more and more settled way of life until they become closely similar to the Malays, eventually embrace Islam and disappear into the Malay population . . . Such evolution must take its course and is a matter of many years or even centuries.
>
> Some Notes on a Suggested Policy for Aboriginal Advancement, September 1950[29]

> . . . any community of Aboriginal descent which is converted but which retains any elements of Aboriginal social organisation should be regarded as Aboriginal until all traces of its Aboriginal origin has disappeared.
>
> Williams-Hunt (1952: 10)

> They are an indigenous community whose social, economic and cultural development prevents them from sharing fully in the rights and advantages enjoyed by other sections of the population. It is right therefore that the Government should adopt suitable measures designed for their protection and advancement with a view to their ultimate integration with the Malay section of the community.
>
> *Statement of Policy Regarding the Administration of the Aborigine Peoples of the Federation of Malaya*, Ministry of the Interior (1961: 3)

> Most Malays and indeed many other Malaysians as well have been inclined to interpret "integration with the Malay section of the community" as meaning *masuk Melayu* or 'becoming Malay', in short embracing Islam.
>
> Baharon Azhar (1972: 7)
> Director General of the JHEOA from 1969–1986

them as a *bumiputra* community in its public literature. For further discussion concerning *bumiputra status* and *bumiputra privileges*, see Nah (2004).

[29] Circular Memorandum No. 15 by the Department of the Adviser on Aborigines (1963/0000926, BA Selangor 70/1950: Aboriginal Matters).

For most Orang Asli, embracing Islam is synonymous with *masuk Melayu*, that is, to "become Malay". The desired "integration" of the Orang Asli with the Malays, to have them indistinguishable and completely assimilated into the latter, is a fear among many Orang Asli individuals (Dentan and Endicott, forthcoming; Dentan, 1997, 2002; Dentan et al., 1997; Nah, 2004; Nicholas, 1996; Wazir, 1995).[30]

In 1983, the JHEOA officially noted its intentions for "the Islamisation of the whole Orang Asli community and the integration/assimilation of the Orang Asli with the Malays" (JHEOA, 1983: 2), a policy that sparked concern among the Orang Asli. Over the years, there have been many initiatives to "encourage" the Orang Asli to become Muslims (Dentan et al., 1997; Mohd Sabri, 1999/2000; Nicholas, 1996; Wazir, 1995; Zakuan Sawai, 1996/97). Many see this as a way of dominating the community, of "erasing" their existence, and facilitating the extinction of the Orang Asli. Some are suspicious of why the JHEOA supports/facilitates proselytization and are wary, at the same time, of the State-invested "power" that the JHEOA holds. For some Orang Asli, the JHEOA has become the "policing" authority that tells them what is "legal" in Malaysia, which makes it unclear what type and level of authority they hold when it comes to proselytization. As a young Semelai man said to me, expressing his reservations,

> The *Jabatan*'s mandate is for economic development and education, not for Islamicizing Orang Asli. But, they promote this. Now, many Orang Asli have become Muslims (*masuk Islam*). In my own view, there is a hidden agenda, a hidden motive, [that is] to co-opt the Orang Asli, especially the ones that are smart. This strengthens their [Malay Muslim] position. When the Orang Asli become Muslims, they change their thoughts, mindset, behaviours. When there are marriages, deaths, and so on, all our cultural practices become Islamic. Orang Asli are afraid to break the law, so they follow along. They are afraid of going

[30] There are different ways in which Orang Asli "ward" off Islamicization. While on fieldwork, I was told that some Orang Asli embrace the Baha'I and Christian faiths in order to avoid becoming Muslim. Some also joked that they hung the meat of wild pigs out to dry when Muslim proselytizers came to their villages. I sensed a mix of emotions concerning Islamicization among non-Muslim Orang Asli—a combination, of fear, reluctant acceptance, anger, frustration, and helplessness. The link Orang Asli made between the JHEOA and Islamicization was ubiquitous, as was their perception that becoming a Muslim meant becoming Malay, thus leading to the extinction of their Orang Asli identity.

> against the authorities. If the authorities tell them to bury [the dead] in a certain way, they will do it. They go along rather than resist (Interview, 15 September 2002).

For many people at an everyday level, to become Malay (*masuk Melayu*) after conversion is a particularly "easy" transition for Orang Asli because in a variety of ways, they are already indistinguishable from "Malays". Physically, it is often difficult to tell the difference between an "Orang Asli" and a "Malay" person. Many Orang Asli are also able to converse fluently in the Malay language, which is the official language of Malaysia. With the changes in social practice required by Islam, the behaviour and appearance of Muslim Orang Asli are more similar to "Malays" than to other non-Muslim Orang Asli.

Muslim Orang Asli occupy a contested space, a restricted sociopolitical location that is open, in small ways, to reinterpretation. Some Muslim Orang Asli proudly retain their Orang Asli identity, arguing that religion does not, and should not, erode their ethnic identity. Yet others embrace the Malay way of life altogether, and for all intents and purposes pass as Malays, and "are" Malays. The choice to "retain" Orang Asli identity is a personal one, but is something that takes extra "work" in order to accomplish socially; one has to "prove" to the outside world, particularly to other Orang Asli, that he/she remains loyal to the Orang Asli identity after he/she embraces Islam. Even so, to most Orang Asli, this person is considered "Malay".

Some Muslim Orang Asli take refuge in the definition of "aborigine" in The Aboriginal People's Act (1954, revised 1974), which expressly states that an "aborigine" remains an "aborigine" no matter what religion he or she ascribes to. This becomes the way in which they argue for a separation between their ethnic identity, as Orang Asli, and their religious identity, as Muslims. Some Orang Asli, however, are still concerned about what Islamicization means in terms of the ethnic/racial identity of their children.[31] As we will see later, the ambiguity that exists around the issue of whether an Orang Asli can still be Muslim without being Malay, as well as the

[31] As an Orang Asli individual said to me, "The government doesn't care about us—it's the next generation they want".

anxiety that surrounds the desire to remain Orang Asli despite pressures to become Muslim/Malay, gets played out in relation to the meanings ascribed to *personal* names.

Personal Names

In this section, I will reflect on the ways in which power is exercised through the mobilization of *personal names* in postcolonial Malaysia. The first is directly linked to State control over individuals. By fixing each individual with a name, and requiring this signifier to be proven on personal identity documents for basic activities, State authorities were (and are) able to regulate, track and place every individual in a multitude of ways. For the Orang Asli, who did not find it necessary for each individual to be fixed with one particular personal name, and did not have a "standard" system for naming, the State prescribed the method by which their names were to be recorded, based on their observations of other cultural practices in the Peninsula.

The second way in which power works relates to the capacity of names to function as markers of difference, indicating socio-political positioning on a number of dimensions. This is made possible because everyday naming practices systematically inscribe ethnicity, religion, gender, and "indigeneity" into personal names. The naming system imposed on the Orang Asli parallels the systems other ethnic and religious groups used to name themselves. As these naming practices are "common sense" among Malaysians, Orang Asli are sometimes mistakenly affiliated to these other ethnic and religious groups. It gets more complicated when particular naming system take on different meanings, for example, when the Muslim connective terms *bin* (son of) and *binti* (daughter of) usually used by Malays become shorthand notations for *bumiputra* identity, and certain Orang Asli find themselves caught in a nexus, as (the relatively rare) non-Muslim *bumiputra.*

Names for State Control: Fixing, Tracking, Placing Individuals

Attempts at fixing an official personal name for each and every aborigine of the Peninsula took place at about the same time as they became strategically important in the fight against the Communist insurrection in the 1950s. Part of the strategy employed against the Communists was to systematically "starve them out". In order for this to be done, it was necessary to keep close track of the movements and activities of individuals, in order to prevent the smuggling of food and supplies to the Communists. Procedures were taken to register each and every person in Malaya and to assign identity cards to them, a system of individual documentation that prevails until today. Failure to produce identity cards resulted in imprisonment or fines.

Many aborigines did not comply with registration, and in Perak, a particularly "Communist-infested" state, special procedures were drawn up by the Perak State Executive Council in May 1950 to register the aborigines.[32] Known as the Registration of Aborigines (Perak) Rules, 1950, the Protector of Aborigines was to maintain a register of each aboriginal tribe, which had recorded in it the personal details of each member of the tribe. This included his/her name, father's name, (estimated) age, sex, and any other details deemed important by the Protector. Each individual was to be given a metal identity disc on which his or her name would be stamped, along with a registration number. The disc was to be returned to the Protector upon his/her death.

Major Williams-Hunt recognized the complications inherent in implementing this system. Not only was it difficult to contact (and maintain contact with) some aboriginal groups, many aboriginal groups remained unknown. Furthermore, he explained:

> Many aborigines will not give their personal names, some groups have a change in name at different ages, some groups take on the name of their first child and drop their own name, some groups name their children in order of birth irrespective of sex so that out of a group of, say, thirty aborigines ten may have the same name and some groups claim to have no personal names at all [*sic*].
>
> Many groups will not name children usually up to the time the child will walk but sometimes for longer or shorter periods.
>
> Some groups have male and female prefixes—e.g. with some of the Senoi Semai, Bah for males and Wa for females. These will have to be distinguished from groups that take their childrens' names—e.g. Temoq, Pak Tandur, father of Tandur.[33]

[32] Letter from the Adviser on Aborigines, F.M. dated 18 July 1950, 1963/0000926, BA Selangor 70/1950: Aboriginal Matters.

[33] Letter from the Adviser on Aborigines, F.M. dated 18 July 1950, 1963/0000926,

Obtaining a "father's name" for each individual, was also difficult for enumerators. As Williams-Hunt, in his 1950 memorandum continued to advise,

> Nearly all the wilder aborigines have a tabu on mentioning the name of anyone who is dead and may refuse to give their deceased fathers name. The recorder in these cases need to have some knowledge of aboriginal language or he may go astray. There are many identity cards issued at the moment which such entries as . . . s/o Bah Kebus the recorder being under the impression that this was the father's name. Actually Bah Kebus means— father dead.[34]

Nevertheless, since the 1950s, continuous efforts have been made to register each and every individual with an official personal name. With regard to children, birth certificates are necessary for enrollment at schools, thus, most Orang Asli are careful to register their children in time. Adults possess identity cards, which are necessary for admission into hospitals, registering as members of organizations, securing contracts, voting in elections, obtaining loans, and for other purposes.[35] In relation to practices of the State, personal names are used to account for the population ascribed and enumerated in statistics. Personal names are also an essential means in which property, marriage, children, social networks, professional qualifications, and entitlements, are marked on registers as belonging to individuals.

Personal Names as Markers of Difference

Personal names are salient markers of identity. They act as signs that suggest social location along various dimensions of difference—

BA Selangor 70/1950: Aboriginal Matters. Geoffrey Benjamin was later to note the same sorts of issues in his detailed analysis of the complexities of Temiar naming systems (Benjamin, 1968). He observed that individuals could be referred to by variety of names—including autonyms, birth-order names, teknonyms, necronyms, burial names, and designations—which seemed to "change almost daily" (1968: 99). Furthermore, he writes that "it is only with the greatest difficulty that a Temiar can be persuaded to divulge either his own [autonym] or someone elses . . . to address a person of higher generation by name is regarded as a heinous act, and a foolish one insofar as it tempts fate in some undefined way" (p. 103).

[34] In relation to "age", he notes, "most aborigines have no idea of their age", and that "even mothers who have recently given birth can not say how many days old their child is". He proposes instead a way in which enumerators may guess the age of each individual, by examining the teeth and physical characteristics of each person.

in particular, ethnicity, religion, gender, "culture" and "indigeneity". As systems of naming are relatively stable in Malaysia, personal names denote ethnic and religious identity, and in contentious situations are a source of "proof" of affiliation or membership. As these meanings are socially established, however, there is sometimes a conflation in meaning; a particular signifier may have multiple meanings depending on the level of sophistication of the reader of the name, thus causing confusion.

The naming practices for the Orang Asli, as we have seen above, are State defined, and based on existing systems for other ethnic and religious groups. For most Orang Asli, their personal names are a combination of three elements, the person's first name, a connective term, and then his/her father's first name. There have been struggles and resistances mounted through (official) personal names in the past few years, which illustrate how important names are for proof of "ethnic/racial" affiliation. In a recent case concerning land rights for the Orang Asli, *Sagong bin Tasi & Ors v Kerajaan Negeri Selangor & Ors [2002] 2 MLJ 591*, the plaintiffs were required to demonstrate that they "still continue to practice their Temuan culture", in order to qualify for recognition as "aborigines" under the legal definition as outlined in the Aboriginal People's Act. One way in which they proved this was by showing that their naming practices still followed "aboriginal customs". In this case, the ruling Judge accepted that "[personal] names are derived from incidences or events that occurred during the respective infancy, for example, Dabak . . . got his name because he had bruises (debam) all over his body and Sagong . . . because he cried noisily (*macam gong*)". This was part of legal evidence to prove that they were "following an aboriginal way of life, [and] practising customs and beliefs".

While on fieldwork, I encountered other examples of how personal names have become ways of demonstrating identity on an everyday basis. For example, a young Orang Asli woman I met had a name that was recorded in the "Chinese" way (because her grandfather was Chinese) but could pass as Malay by physical appearance. When she was asked why she did not wear a scarf (*tudung*), as a "good Muslim" would, and questioned when she was found eating during the fasting month of *Ramadan*, she informed them that she was Orang Asli, proving this by showing them her "Chinese" name on her identity card. Since all Muslims, including Chinese converts, have "Muslim" names, she was able to demonstrate her non-Muslim identity through her "non-Muslim" "Chinese" name.

The Ambiguity of Connective Terms

An issue concerning personal names that has had greater impact on the Orang Asli and their demonstration of identity is the use of connective terms. For the Orang Asli, in place of the term "son of" or "daughter of", some have the sign "A/L" (to denote *anak lelaki* or "son of") or "A/P" (to denote *anak perempuan* or "daughter of"). Others have the sign "*bin*" (a Muslim signifier for "son of") or "*binti*" (a Muslim signifier for "daughter of"), while yet others use the non-gendered term "*anak*" (translated as "child of").

In Malaysia, the use of "A/L" and "A/P" are reminiscent of Indian communities,[36] for this is one way in which their ethnicity and gender is inscribed into their name. Some Orang Asli do not like the use of these signifiers for their own names for this reason. The terms *bin* and *binti* also pose a problem for the Orang Asli because they are markers of Muslim identity. This is a salient issue for many Orang Asli individuals, who, as stated earlier, are similar to Malays in physical appearance. This gives rise to cases of mistaken identity, which are particularly thorny during the Muslim fasting month, *Ramadan*, as the earlier example illustrates. As this religious practice is policed by the various *Jabatan Agama Islam* (Islamic Religious Departments) some Orang Asli have been hauled up by the authorities for eating regular meals during this period, as they have been presumed to be Muslim on account of their physical appearance.[37]

---

[35] While on fieldwork, I spent some time with a community development organization that was helping several villages participate in a co-operative development scheme. Most, if not all, of the members had difficulty filling out the forms, despite their desire to participate in the scheme. They produced their identity cards and birth certificates, however, and all necessary personal details were thus available.

[36] This is also used for Siamese communities.

[37] Islamic identity, however, is marked clearly the new technologically sophisticated chip-based MyKad identity cards introduced in September 2001, which help officials in determining which citizens are subject to Islamic law and practices. At the moment, not all Malaysian citizens have migrated to the new system, and some still possess the paper-based identity card.

Some Orang Asli are able to "prove" their non-Muslim Orang Asli identity by virtue of their name having "A/L", "A/P" or "anak", thus signifying their *difference* from Malay Muslims.This becomes difficult, however, for those who have *bin* and *binti* in their names.[38]

Complications arise with the terms *bin* and *binti*, as they have also been taken as short-hand notations of *bumiputra* identity. This is not surprising as most *bumiputra* in Peninsula Malaysia are Malay Muslims, and for the most part, this rule works. This, however, makes it problematic for people who fall outside the norm, such as non-Malay *bumiputra* or non-Muslim *bumiputra*, for their names do not contain *bin* or *binti*. In such cases, their claims for *bumiputra* benefits are cast in doubt because they do not have the appropriate, expected, short-hand markers of *bin* and *binti*.[39]

This matter of having *bin* or *binti* in one's name is, thus, a source of discontentment for some Orang Asli. This discontentment is likely linked to feelings that there is pressure on them to be Muslim, and to be Malay. Having *bin* or *binti* makes it "easier" for Orang Asli to be Muslims, or so it is popularly thought. Orang Asli read this as a way in which the State exercises control over their identity, and resist this by being very careful in the way they register their children's names. I have come across frustrated Orang Asli individuals who deliberately avoided using *bin* and *binti* when registering the names of their children, in order to prevent problems of mistaken identity in the future and in order to assert their Orang Asli identity. They were told, however, that as Orang Asli, it was necessary for them to use either *bin* or A/L for males, and *binti* or A/L for females. This was summarily carried out despite their personal reservations and protests. Some Orang Asli who are keen to re-establish their non-Muslim Orang Asli identity have even changed their names officially in order to avoid ambiguity.

---

[38] Similarly, Orang Asli are able to "pass" as Malays if their names have *bin* or *binti* in them. One young man informed me that he would sometimes attend Muslim talk sessions (*ceramah*) to "find out their thought patterns" (*cara pemikiran mereka*) despite the fact he is a Christian. His official personal name, which included a *bin*, became a way he could "disguise" (*menyamar*) himself as a Malay–Muslim.

[39] Examples of these would be some Indian Muslims with Malay blood, who by physical appearance seem to fall under the category of "Indian" and, thus, have their names inscribed with A/L and/or A/P by registration officers, despite their equally plausible claims of being *bumiputra*. Some such individuals have deliberately changed their names to include *bin* or *binti* in order for their claim for *bumiputra* status to be more assured.

The issue of connective terms has been raised repeatedly at POASM General Meetings. At the 8th POASM General Meeting in 1997, recommendations were mooted to, ". . . agree to fix [naming practices] so that the word 'ANAK' or 'a/k' is used to replace the word 'BIN', 'BINTI', 'A/L' and 'A/P' for the Orang Asli effective today" (POASM, 1997).[40] This matter was discussed yet again at the 14th General Meeting in April 2003. A young Orang Asli man, a Semelai, exclaimed during the meeting:

> We have no title [name], no image; the government doesn't give us an image. This is our identity. If we are Muslims, [using] *bin* and *binti* is fine. But we are Orang Asli. During the fasting month I need proof from the JOA [JHEOA] that I am Orang Asli! We are free to choose our names, yes, but we should have a way of reflecting our identity [in our names].

This was followed by a comment by another Orang Asli individual, a Temuan, who advocated strongly for the use of the term *anak*

> . . . *anak* is a term that all religions can use. But *anak* should only be used for those who are really asli (*betul-betul asli*) . . . But your name is secondary, what is important is your [religious] belief. You can have the name A/L but still be Muslim . . . *Anak* can be used for both men and women. It can be used by anyone who is Orang Asli and who wants the Orang Asli identity.

A third person, a Temuan woman, spoke up, stating:

> Using *anak* is easier for those who are non-Muslims. Perhaps we can use *anak* by default, and then adopt *bin* and *binti* if you become Muslim. [In this way] it is allowed to be your choice. We should do this not just for today, but for a long time . . . At the moment, during fasting month it is really difficult . . . We need a term that is usable across all the different groups (*suku*), so that we can perpetuate (*mengekalkan*) Orang Asli identity.

These comments highlight the salient link between the choice of connective term and Orang Asli identity.

---

[40] This was noted after a recommendation "to pressure the Director-General of the JHEOA to withdraw and nullify the circular JHEOA Bil. A1. 072–(66) dated 27th September 1996 which instructs that 'BIN', 'BINTI', 'A/l' [sic] and 'A/P' be used for the Orang Asli." (POASM, 1997).

The Cultural Politics of Removing Connective Terms

In the past few years, there have been deliberations about whether the use of connective terms should be dispensed with altogether. The National Registration Department, in April 2002, announced that it would consider introducing surnames for all Malaysian citizens, "regardless of race"[41] and, thus, remove the use of connective terms for all communities. It was reported that: "The proposal would change the traditional use of *bin* and *binti* by the Malay/Islam communities in Malaysia, the words a/l and a/p by the Indian and Siamese communities as well as the word ak by the Orang Asli in the peninsula and bumiputra communities in Sabah and Sarawak."[42]

This prompted a flurry of contrasting responses from various ethnic/racial communities. Members of the Dayak community in Sarawak, for example, wanted to retain the option of using the term "anak",[43] while someone from the Bisaya community, also an indigenous group in Sarawak, suggested that the institution of surnames would help them "preserve native identity" through the continued usage of 'indigenous' names.[44] Some Malays were opposed to the removal of *bin* and *binti*, stating that these terms signified legal birth, while the absence of it would connote illegitimacy.[45]

In August 2003, a public announcement was made that the use of connective terms would be left optional, for parents to decide.[46] In the article, Tan Sri Bernard Dompok, a Minister in the Prime Minister's Department, was cited as being supportive of this decision. In relation to *bin* and *binti*, he said, "(w)hile it is up to the Muslims to use them, I will strongly oppose any attempt to make it compulsory for others to use *bin* and *binti* or other terms. The preference not to use them should be respected." While on fieldwork in 2003, I came across some birth certificates of Orang Asli children, issued in December 2000 that recorded the names of babies. While a personal name was given, as well the name of their father, the

[41] "NRD proposal to omit *bin, binti*, a/l, a/p and ak", *The Star*, 18 April 2002.
[42] "Home Ministry Studying Proposal To Drop '*Bin*' From Documents", *Bernama*, 15 November 2002.
[43] "Group wants option to retain 'anak'", *The Star*, 26 April 2002.
[44] "Surnames will help preserve native identity", *The Star*, 1 May, 2002.
[45] "Malays register mixed reactions over surnames", *The Star*, 27 April 2002.
[46] "Use of connective terms optional", *The Star*, 12 August 2003.

connective term was not included. This, I presume, leaves the decision open to parents about which connective term to use.

Conclusion

In this paper, I have sought to examine the ways in which naming practices contribute to an understanding of the Orang Asli in Malaysian society. Naming practices are ways in which power is exercised in a variety of ways. For State authorities, it is a pragmatic way of recognizing their own citizens, keeping track of them, and administering them as "appropriately" as they can. They have done this through the construction of social categories and systems for recording names, so that each and every Orang Asli can be triangulated within a coherent framework. The names of these social categories have become reified ways of knowing the Orang Asli, "creating" them such that different groups of people, across disparate territories and of different languages, are viewed homogenously both politically and legally. The naming of these groups as "Orang Asli", despite differences in genealogical origins, had the unintended consequence of political mobilization to protect Orang Asli identity.

On an individual level, systems for recording personal names are ways in which socio-political differences are identified. The State's practices of recording Orang Asli names draw on parallel systems used by other ethnic and religious groups, but have resulted in cases of mistaken identity. Orang Asli are wary of whether their naming systems are methods of State control over their ethnic and religious identities. Reactions against such naming systems—for example, in avoiding the recording of names in particular ways, or re-registering their names—are ways in which perceived pressures by the State are resisted. I have attempted to show in this paper that names act as sites through which identity can be displayed, and as texts upon which social meaning is inscribed, negotiated, and resisted.

REFERENCES

Anderson, B. R. O'G. (1991) *Imagined Communities: Reflections on the Origin and Spread of Nationalism*. London: Verso.

Baharon, A. (1972) *Some Aspects of the Relationship of the Orang Asli and other Malaysians*. Mimeographed report, JHEOA.

Benjamin, G. (2002) "On Being Tribal in the Malay World", in G. Benjamin and

C. Chou, eds., *Tribal Communities in the Malay World: Historical, Social and Cultural Perspectives*. Leiden: IIAS *and* Singapore: ISEAS, pp. 7–76.
———. (1974) *Working Paper 25: Prehistory and Ethnology in Southeast Asia: Some new Ideas*. Department of Sociology, Singapore: University of Singapore.
———. (1968) "Temiar Personal Names". *Bijdragen Tot de Taal- Land- end Volkenkunde* 124:99–134.
Carey, I. (1976a) *Orang Asli: The Aboriginal Tribes of Peninsula Malaysia*. Kuala Lumpur, Oxford University Press.
———. (1976b) "The Administration of the Aboriginal Tribes of Western Malaysia", in D. Banks, ed., *Changing Identities in Modern Southeast Asia*. The Hague: Mouton, pp. 43–69.
Collings, H. D. (1949) *Aboriginal Notes*. Bulletin of the Raffles Museum, Colony of Singapore, series B, #4:86–103.
Couillard, M. A. (1984) "The Malays and the 'Sakai': Some Comments on their Social Relations in the Malay Peninsula", *Kajian Malaysia*, 11(1):81–108.
Dentan, R. K. (2002) "Ideas Redeemed but Political Memories Do Run Short: Islamicization in Malaysia", *Social Justice: Anthropology, Peace and Human Rights* 3(3–4): 153–189.
———. (1997) "The Persistence of Received Truth: How the Malaysian Ruling Class Constructs Orang Asli", in Robert Winzeler, ed., *Indigenous Peoples and the State: Politics, Land, and Ethnicity in the Malaysan Peninsula and Borneo*. Monograph 46/Yale University Southeast Asia Studies. New Haven: Yale University Southeast Asia Studies, pp. 98–134.
———. (1975) "If There Were No Malays, Who Would the Semai Be?", in Judith A. Nagata, ed., *Pluralism in Malaysia: Myth and Reality*, Contributions to Asian Studies 7: 50–64.
———. and Endicott, K. M. (forthcoming) "Ethnocide Malaysian Style: Turning Aborigines into Malays", in C. Duncan, ed., *Legislating Modernity*. Ithaca, NY: Cornell University Press.
———. K. Endicott, A. G. Gomes and M. B. Hooker (1997) *Malaysia and the Original People: A Case Study of the Impact of Development on Indigenous Peoples,* in eds. The Cultural Survival Studies in Ethnicity and Change. Boston: Allyn & Bacon.
Department of Statistics (2000) *Population Distribution and Basic Demographic Characteristics*. Kuala Lumpur.
Endicott, K. (1983) "The Effects of Slave Raiding on the Aborigines of the Malay Peninsula, in A. Reid and J. Brewster, eds., *Slavery, Bondage, and Dependency in Southeast Asia*. Brisbane, Australia: University of Queensland Press, pp. 216–245.
Favre, P. (1848) "An Account of the Wild Tribes Inhabiting the Malayan Peninsula, Sumatra and a Few Neighbouring Islands", *The Journal of the Indian Archipelago and Eastern Asia* 2 (1): 237–282.
Foucault, M. (1994) "The Subject and Power", in J. D. Faubion, ed., *Essential Works of Foucault 1954–1984, Volume 3: Power*. London: Penguin, pp. 326–348.
Gomes, A. (1994) "Modernity and Semai Ethnogenesis", in ed. *Modernity and Identity: Asian Illustrations*. Bundoora: LaTrober University Press, pp. 176–191.
———. (1988) "The Semai: The Making of an Ethnic Group in Malaysia," in A. Terry Rambo, Kathleen Gillogly and Karl L. Hutterer, eds., *Ethnic Diversity and the Control of Natural Resources in Southeast Asia*. Ann Arbor: Center for South and Southeast Asian Studies, University of Michigan, pp. 99–118.
Hamilton, A. (2002) "Tribal People on the Southern Thai Border: Internal Colonialism, Minorities, and the State", in G. Benjamin and C. Chou, eds., *Tribal Communities in the Malay World: Historical, Social and Cultural Perspectives*. Leiden: IIAS *and* Singapore: ISEAS, pp. 77–96.
Holman, D. (1958) *Noone of the Ulu*. London: Heinemann.

Howell, S. (2002) "We People Belong in the Forest": Chewong Re-creations of Uniqueness and Separateness, in G. Benjamin and C. Chou, eds., *Tribal Communities in the Malay World: Historical, Social and Cultural Perspectives*. Leiden: IIAS and Singapore: ISEAS, pp. 154–172.

JHEOA (1983) *Strategi Perkembangan Ugama Islam Di Kalangan Masyarakat Orang Asli*. Kuala Lumpur: Jabatan Hal-Ehwal Orang Asli.

Jimin, I., Mohd Tap Salleh, Jailani M. Dom, Abd. Halim Haji Jawi and Md. Razim Shafie (1983) *Planning and Administration of Development Programmes for Tribal Peoples (The Malaysian Setting)*. CIRDAP.

Juli, E. (1998) *Claiming Our Ancestors' Land: An Ethnohistorical Study of Seng-oi Land Rights in Perak Malaysia*. Unpublished thesis. Australian National University.

Leary, J. (1989) "The Importance of the Orang Asli in the Malayan Emergency 1948–1960. Working Paper No. 56. Melbourne: Centre of Southeast Asian Studies, Monash University.

Lye, T-P., ed. (2001) *Orang Asli of Peninsula Malaysia: A Comprehensive and Annotated Bibliography*. CSEAS Research Report Series No. 88. Kyoto: Center for Southeast Asian Studies.

McNair, J. F. A. (1878) *Perak and the Malays: 'Sarong' and 'Kris'*. London: Tinsley.

Ministry of the Interior (1961) *Statement of Policy Regarding the Administration of the Aborigine Peoples of the Federation of Malaya*. Federation of Malaya.

Mohd Sabri bin Ismail (1999/2000) "Perkembangan Islam di Kalangan Orang Asli dari tahun 1987–1997: Satu Tinjauan dari Sudut Penerimaan Masyarakat Asli di Post Brook Gua Musang" Kelantan, Sarjana Usuluddin Akademi Pengajian Islam, University Malaya.

Nah, A. M. (2004) *Negotiating Orang Asli Identity in Postcolonial Malaysia*. M.Soc.Sci thesis. Sociology Department, National University of Singapore.

Nah, A. M. (2003) "Negotiating Indigenous Identity in Postcolonial Malaysia: Beyond Being 'Not quite/ not Malay' ", *Social Identities* 9(4): 511–534.

Newbold, T. J. (1971) *Political and Statistical Account of the British Settlements in the Straits of Malacca, Volume II*. London: Oxford University Press.

Nicholas, C. (2002) "Organizing Orang Asli Identity", in G. Benjamin and C. Chou, eds., *Tribal Communities in the Malay World: Historical, Social and Cultural Perspectives*. Leiden: IIAS and Singapore: ISEAS.

———. (1997) "Becoming Orang Asli: Survival in the Face of Modernity". Paper presented at the Conference on Tribal Communities in the Malay World, IIAS-Institute fur Ethnologie/ISEAS/Engender. Singapore. 24–27 March.

———. (1996) "The Orang Asli of Peninsula Malaysia", in C. Nicholas and R. Singh, eds., *Indigenous Peoples of Asia: Many People, One Struggle*. Bangkok: Asia Indigenous Peoples Pact, pp. 157–176.

Nicholas, C., A. Williams-Hunt, T. Sabak (1989) *Orang Asli in the News: The Emergency Years: 1950–1958*. Compilation. Kuala Lumpur.

Noone, H. D. (1936) "Report on the Settlements and Welfare of the Ple-Temiar Senoi of the Perak-Kelantan Watershed". *Journal of the Federated Malay States Museums*, 19 (Part 1):1–85.

Noone, R. O. D. and D. Holman (1972) *In Search of the Dream People*. New York: Morrow.

POASM (1997) "Perhimpunan Agung Tahunan Kali ke-8 Tahun 1997 Sessi 1995/1997". 26th April 2003. Kuala Lumpur.

Porath, N. (2002) "Developing Indigenous Communities into *Sakais*: South Thailand and Riau", in G. Benjamin and C. Chou, eds., *Tribal Communities in the Malay World: Historical, Social and Cultural Perspectives*. Leiden: IIAS *and* Singapore: ISEAS, pp. 97–118.

Skeat, W. W. and C. O. Blagden (1906) *Pagan Races of the Malay Peninsula*. London: MacMillan & Co.

Wazir, J. K. (1995) "Malaysia's Indigenous Minorities: Discrepancies between Nation-Building and Ethnic Consciousness", in R. Razha, ed., *Indigenous Minorities of Peninsular Malaysia: Selected Issues and Ethnographies*. Kuala Lumpur: INAS, pp. 18–35.
Williams-Hunt, P. D. R. (1952) *An Introduction to the Malayan Aborigine*. Kuala Lumpur: The Government Press.
Zakuan Sawai (1996/97) *Dakwah Islamiah kepada Orang Asli: Kajian Khusus Mengenai Transformasi Minda Masyarakat Semai Selepas Memeluk Islam*. Bahagian Pengajian Usuluddin Akademi Pengajian Islam, University Malaya.

GROWING UP MALAY IN SINGAPORE*

Joseph Stimpfl

Introduction

Malay school children in Singapore are attempting to cope with the question of Malay identity in the ethnic environment of modern Singapore. They are required to adjust to the ascribed minority status of being Malay, which inevitably results in difficulties in achieving social success in a materialistic society dominated by non-Malays.

In this article I attempt to decipher the concept of Malay identity as articulated in one Singapore school and housing estate. I focus on the tensions and cultural processes in national identity formation as it affects Malay students and examine how state-engineered identity is perceived and experienced in schools by the Malay minority in Singapore. Are these students drawn into a national identity that demands an opportunistic movement away from ethnicity to national "secularism"? Is a dichotomy perceived between education for Muslim moral virtue and education for personal advancement in a national meritocracy? How do children navigate between the demands of being ethnic Malays and national identity? How is the identity of the Malay constructed, maintained, adapted, transformed or surrendered? What are the varying perceptions of educational success for the central figures in schools: for students, parents, teachers in the schools, the school administration and various other interest groups? What are the desired and perceived outcomes for the schooling experience?

Schools in Singapore provide a myriad combination of choices for students that result in interpretations and reinterpretations of identity based on situations that vary by place, participation and purpose. Being Malay in Singapore is a complex process that requires

* This is a revised version previously published in *Southeast Asian Journal of Social Science*, Vol. 25 No. 2 (1997), under the imprint Times Academic Press by Marshall Cavendish International.

a negotiation of identity in the context of competing and, sometimes, conflicting models that change with both physical and social location. The application of these characteristics to day-to-day situations defies the simplistic assumption that that there is one clear identity dominated by Chinese identity characteristics. At the start of my research, I assumed that Malay students who chose to "remain Malay" were excluded from material success in Singapore society. This dichotomy failed to explain the complex interrelations between Malays and non-Malays. In Singapore, Malay identity is constructed, collected, negotiated and renegotiated in an expansive number of situations, thus no one identity model is adequate for expressing the complications of identity choices. Choice is limited only by the number of identity characteristics the individual chooses and the self-imposed limitation or exclusion of participation in the numerous and diverse cultural situations available to the average Singaporean.

Schools and Culture

This article makes two theoretical assumptions in its analysis of schools. The first is that when an ascribed minority group is assigned a status position in the socio-economic system of the dominant group, it will often accommodate the assignment but resist its application. This resistance can be in non-conformity to the mores and principles of status in broader society, or maladaption to institutions of that broader society as applied to the minority. The second is that minority identity, defined ethnically, is ecologically described and articulated by the niche to which it is assigned in the social, economic and political system in which it exists. The idiosyncratic nature of Singapore has created an organic regional identity (Rahim, 1998: 25).

Singapore's schools are national schools, which are dynamic venues for cultural accommodation and conflict. They provide a common institutional system based on a nationally held curriculum, through which all children must pass and from which they are presented a common set of symbols, values and goals. Yet, even in this levelling context, schools may offer cultural groups a method of boundary-maintenance by which children are discouraged from participating in the social system of the dominant cultural group. Schools are institutions that provide structural integration in conjunction with cultural reproduction of a dominant social hierarchy ". . . where cultures and ideologies are produced and dominant ideologies may ultimately be maintained" (Weis, 1983: 257). The school serves as an institution of "differential socialization", allocating students to work roles while socializing them to perform adequately in those roles (Wilcox, 1982: 271). In schools, students learn behaviour and styles of interaction that are appropriate to their positions in the status mobility system. Socialization for children includes the acquisition of a specific cultural identity and the responses to this identity. The process of socialization is a matter of control: a particular moral, cognitive and affective awareness is evoked and given specific form and content. Socialization sensitizes children to orders of society and the roles they are expected to play (Bernstein, 1972).

A significant amount of research in these areas comes from studies of students in American and British schools. Ogbu (1978, 1981, 1985), in studying American minorities, explained disproportionate and persistent school failure among subordinate minorities as a reaction to limited social and economic opportunity. Poor school performance was an adaptive response to the cultural and structural imperatives of the dominant group in a society (Ogbu, 1986: 178). He found that achievement was related to the group's "status mobility system", a socially or culturally approved strategy for getting ahead.

> A status mobility system is the approved method and folk theory of self-betterment in a society or social group. Members of a society or social group share this theory about how their status mobility system works, and the theory includes the range of available status positions (e.g., types of jobs open to people), rules for eligibility for competition for the available position, and how to qualify for successful competition (Ogbu, 1982: 128).

According to Ogbu, "ideal personality types" are inherent in such a system, and these may be in conflict with the normative practices of broader society. He found that the way different cultural groups prepare their children for adulthood, both in and outside of schools, is influenced by the "ideal types" that may be in conflict with the normative practices of broader society. He found that the way different cultural groups prepare their children for adulthood, both in schools and out, is influenced by the ideal types and characteristics of successful members of that group. "These images are incorporated into the value system of parents and others responsible for the upbringing of children" (Ogbu, 1986: 180). The system of status mobility present in a society reflects the social and economic realities of its members.

> In the case of subordinate minorities like black Americans, the schooling offered to them by the dominant groups usually reflects the dominant group members' perceptions of the place of the minorities in the opportunity structure; equally important, however, are the responses of the minorities, which reflect their perceptions of their social and economic realities, their strategies for getting ahead (Ogbu, 1986: 180).

Where group members see no choice but to accommodate a system that works to their disadvantage, they may find ways to resist normative conformity. This resistance, while not a direct challenge to the over-arching authority of the dominant group, provides an alternate form of status for the resisting group. Status may be acquired or lost through group membership. When status is subtractive (membership decreases status), a group will redefine the meaning of success. Lower academic performance may be an adaptive response of minority students to social stratification, which they assume predetermines the status positions they will have as adults. Subordinate minorities may perceive formal schooling as one-way acculturation into the inequitable cultural frame of reference of the dominant group. Instead of aspiring to status positions defined by the dominant group, an out group will create or maintain its own status position. Such positions may be questioned or even rejected by the dominant group.

McDermott (1974), in studying African-Americans in the USA, referred to a group with clearly identifiable characteristics associated with deviance or failure by the dominant group as a "pariah group". In spite of low status, pariah children reproduce pariah cultural forms, apparently in reaction to the condemnation and oppression of the dominant culture (McDermott, 1974: 84). For such a group, identity characteristics become very important.

> If a social organization shows a division into pariah and host groups, then this is a division produced in everyday life; in their daily dealings, pariah and host people must classify each other into different groups and then treat each other in accordance with the dictates of their classification (McDermott, 1974: 88).

This research by McDermott and Ogbu supports the contention that the interactions of everyday life—the group dynamics of a society—

are replayed in the classroom. It becomes important for children to acquire characteristics that they and broader society design and define as inherent in group identity. If school failure is markedly associated with group identity, then failure may be a social achievement.

> School failure and delinquency often represent highly motivated and intelligent attempts to develop the abilities, statuses, and identities that will best equip. the child to maximize his utilities in the politics of everyday life (McDermott, 1974: 113).

Reproduction of lower status in school is often resisted by out groups through struggle for control of the classroom. Everhart (1983), in a study of classroom management in an American junior high school, found that lower status students resisted traditional classroom management and successfully restructured the instructional forms to meet their own needs. The school represents a hierarchy of culturally valued knowledge, with implied superiority for those who have this particular knowledge and inferiority for those who do not have it.

> Opposition often signaled, at least in the student's mind, a recognition of their role as members of an organization wherein they had been relegated to positions of low status where, almost invariably, they were the passive recipients of knowledge or activities planned for them by adults (Everhart, 1983: 183).

Assignment of low status is opposed and resented by those holding status roles judged to be inferior. Everhart found that students in classrooms restructured activities as a means of "resisting the institutional imperatives for teacher-directed knowledge" (Everhart, 1983: 176). The strategies of resistance generated by students were collective, norm-referenced activities that aided in defining student relationships (Everhart, 1983: 187).

> Student opposition is an important activity because it is part of a lived culture that is created and recreated in their everyday life. It must be seen as part of the students' understanding of their own present and historical role in the school. This understanding will be conditioned (but not necessarily determined) by factors such as class, culture, and gender (Everhart 1983: 170).

Alternative forms of doing—the normative behaviour of an out group—may be at odds with conformity in broader society. In the context of resistance, group norms may condemn those who work "too hard" or are "too studious" (Weis, 1983: 253). Resistance in accommodating the system allows a measure of self-esteem and community but, at the same time, it traps the group in a "web of dependency" (Anyon, 1983: 34).

> Day-to-day resistance, because it is by its very nature collective, can also impart a sense of community strength and teach the rudiments of organization. At the same time it can imply accommodation to a regime, in contrast to insurrection (Weis, 1983: 254).

For those excluded from status mobility, status acquisition is only possible through resistance. In resistance, ethnic identity is reaffirmed and class standing is rejected. Ethnic separateness results in different definitions of success and an alternative status mobility system based on occupational outcomes that may contrast markedly with those in the hierarchy of the dominant group. The process ultimately works to undermine group consensus and identity by linking individuals of the out group in a dependent relationship with the dominant group. Resistance becomes a strategy designed to alleviate true struggle and arrive at "productive" accommodation. Ironically, this resistance ultimately aids in the reproduction of unequal social relations (Malmstad et al., 1983: 359).

The problem becomes a matter of negotiating identity in the context of competing/conflicting models. Hanna, in an essay on ethnic boundaries, describes what appear to be two competing models of ethnic identity in the face of modernization: (1) primordial, in which modern economic and political structures cause a decline in ethnic groups; and (2) reactive, where high levels of economic and political modernization may lead to a renewed movement towards ethnic boundaries (Hanna, 1979: 254). He resolved this discontinuity by offering circumstances where both might occur. Culturally-related identities are often hierarchical and multiple, with larger and larger group memberships available as one moves away from an individual or core identity (Hanna, 1979: 255). In the development of the modern nation-state, power usually accrues with larger groups. In this circumstance, smaller group designations are often subsumed in larger over-arching "ethnic identities". "As long as the smallest scale identities remain strong and salient to collective action, the likelihood of effective and sustained action on the basis of widely shared ethnic identities is low" (Hanna, 1979: 255). When the status mobility structure of a society becomes institutionalized and groups are assigned positions in this structure, then "ethnicity", serving as a mechanism for the consolidation of power, supersedes cultural identity and polarizes society.

Singaporean National Identity

Singapore is a nation of immigrants with a history of economic and political cultural group differentiation. The creation and maintenance of Singapore is a result of British political interests and it fell to that colonial government to arbitrate and mediate "ethnic difference". When Britain turned over control of the government to Singaporeans, it turned it over to the elite class of the English-speaking and English-educated, a group dominated by British-educated Chinese. The result is that Singapore has a strong tradition of preservation and replication of colonial forms and traditions. The dominant Chinese social attitude of respect and deference for legitimate authority has helped to institutionalize these forms and traditions. When government and governing were turned over to Singaporeans, they superseded the extensive cultural differentiation of the population into many ethnic groups by ascribing an overarching ethnic designation (Chinese, Malay, Indian, Other) to each citizen. They also decided to adopt and adapt the Western cultural model to co-opt indigenous cultural forms into a new national identity. The strategy was to avoid the creation of many "ethnic groups" from the numerous cultural groups in Singapore, and include all citizens into a collective identity that would avoid sectarianism.

Although this new "national model" was dominated by Chinese culture, it was still strongly influenced by Western mass culture. Introduction of mass culture into Singapore was to help create an over-arching coordinating and controlling institutionalized state culture that would solve the problems of ethnic factionalism due to the realization and establishment of cultural boundaries. The state conceded a form of ethnicity while at the same time attempting to supersede such fragmentation with an integrating and controlling "national culture." National identity was constructed to avoid ethnic communalism. The aim was to make industrial modernity the metanarrative of national identity (Wee, 2003: 147). The result, an emerging culture much dependent upon the resolution of cultural differences at school level, has not acted to perform the social control function that the Singapore government had intended.

Singapore exemplifies a state-instituted plural society. Perhaps the conscious beginning of being "Singaporean" came with the formal creation of Singapore citizenship with the Citizenship Ordinance of 1957. Under the constraints of the system, one must choose an ethnic identity that creates a paradox for personal identity.

> The concept of Singaporean national identity requires that every citizen have two overlapping social identities: his identity (politically defined) as a Singaporean, and his identity (culturally defined) as a member of an ethnic group (Clammer, 1985: 119).

The practice of the Singapore government is the assumed neutral "ideology of pragmatism" (Chan and Evers, 1978: 119). This pragmatism, based on shared wealth through increased productivity, has been enforced by the government's "paternalistic authoritarianism" (Skolnik, 1976: 10). "The revolutionary ideology, democratic socialism, has been elected to a political religion, and the state has become a moral entity" (Bell, 1972: 627).

Many aspects of life in Singapore are mandated or dictated by the central government. These include things such as two years of national service for all males 18 years of age, a penalty for failing to vote, state acquisition of private land, resettlement of people in public housing (HDB), and participation in a national social security scheme (Central Provident Fund or CPF). Government control extends from a tightly policed tax structure to a very serious attitude towards such mundane things as littering, eating on public transport, chewing gum and flushing urinals in public restrooms. The government also has very strict health rules as well as a strongly enforced licensing scheme for small businesses such as food and drink hawkers, that is, generally unregulated small businesses in Southeast Asia.

For many Singaporeans, the challenge of multicultural living has resulted in a chameleon-like ability to adapt to different cultural and locational situations. In order to survive productively in this multicultural setting, many have become "cultural brokers."

> They inhabit more than one system of cultural values and they not only pass continuously from one to another of these systems, but their very role in the society is vital as they represent the channels of communication from one cultural 'zone' to another. Singaporean society is an overlapping network of such zones. No one individual inhabits all the zones, but many act as mediators between two or more zones by being simultaneously members of a plurality of such zones (Clammer, 1981: 28).

Ethnic identification, however, is absolute. "By analogy, the individual's relationship to his defining culture will be regarded as organic: it will be claimed that amputation of one's traditional culture will lead to personal disorganization" (Benjamin, 1976: 119–120). To allow for distinctiveness of cultures, differences must be heightened and similarities underplayed. Constant reiteration of state-defined ethnic categories has forced people to identify themselves with these categories. "Ethnicity in Singapore is accordingly regarded as an unchangeable and irreducible fact of life which individuals and the state must come to grips with" (Benjamin, 1976: 30).

> The egalitarian model of Singapore's 'multiracialism' is administered as a form of social control relying on the codification of selected cultural differences: where each constituent race are defined by the list of stereotypic behavioral traits ascribed to it, followed by the institution of active programmes of social management aimed at adjusting the internal consistency of the content of these categories to achieve outward compatibility with various national interests (Chew, 1982: 187–188).

The government in Singapore has attempted to mitigate the dangers of ethnic boundaries by sponsoring the second or national identity that eschews ethnic culture in favour of "being modern". This hybrid was to incorporate the "desirable" elements of home culture in the context of Western "mass-culture". "The objective of building one nation out of many races calls for an integrated national culture embodying the sentiments and values of the four great cultures that exist in our midst" (speech by the Minister of Social Affairs, *The Mirror*, 27 January 1973).

The political structure of Singapore is predisposed to ". . . the imposition of standards of national relevance based on utility or convenience through the programmes of public policies enforced as limits to viable traditional practices" (Chew, 1982: 185). Government policies and practices directed at establishing a "national identity" inevitably result in activities dominated by the Chinese majority's behavioural norms. Malays in Singapore perceive, whether calculated or not, that the Singapore government designs programmes in an attempt to expurgate Malay behaviour from national culture and replace it with Chinese culture in Malay trappings.

National Development Minister S. Dhanabalan, speaking on the subject of ethnic balance (*The Sunday Times*, 20 August 1989), said that where ethnic groups are of the same size, the potential for tension and conflict is very high. He stated Singapore is better off with one dominant ethnic group and added that since the Chinese in Singapore form a large majority, even though surrounded by countries with Muslim majorities, they do not feel threatened. "Because they do not feel threatened, they would also be prepared to make more effort to meet the sensitivities of the minorities".

The government did not anticipate that Western forms would result in Singapore cultural forms that often reflect Western "mass-culture", even providing the base of "counter-culture". When they realized this, the government decried this process of enculturation. Former Prime Minister, Lee Kuan Yew, and the government have said they fear the acquisition of a national identity based on norms outside Chinese traditional culture (interestingly, many of these Chinese traditionalists are English-educated) and, particularly, norms beyond government control. This fear is articulated in the government criticism of "Westernization". Westernization has been viewed as a form of social pollution. More to the point ". . . Western culture in Singapore is a rapid solvent of ethnic distinctions and poses a corresponding threat to the maintenance of the Multiracial ideology" (Benjamin, 1976: 123). In order to avoid this, strong ethnic boundaries must be encouraged and maintained. In short, members of ethnic groups must embrace the stereotypical view of the "others" and co-operate in public expressions of their cultural stereotypes.

The government willingly adopted an anti-Western cultural stance that ignores the history of Singapore's cultural adaptation. Nearly the entire structure of government has been borrowed from Western models. In spite of this, the government maintains that the current problems of structural developments in social relations are a result of "pseudo-Westernism". One result has been a government-sponsored movement to identify "core values". Lee Kuan Yew has stated that he fears the loss of what he has described as "core Asian values". He has attributed this loss to the influence of "Western culture" which, when transplanted to Singapore, becomes "pseudo-Westernism". Along with others, he has identified the single greatest threat to Singapore to be the rise of individualism, or a preoccupation with self over a responsibility to "community". The government has consistently claimed that freedom of expression and the idea of individual rights adopted from the West has led to unproductive and unhealthy questioning of the relevance and appropriateness of government policy.

The government has addressed this problem by creating the concept of a "rugged society". A rugged society is defined as one that prizes self-discipline and social responsibility in individuals but, at the same time, that ranks individual concerns as being always secondary to an obligation towards the good of society (Busch, 1974: 33). The government describes the attributes of good citizens as "Confucian ethics", especially citing "duty" (to family, to the state, to the elderly, to friends) as a traditional value threatened by "pseudo-Westernism". According to one minister I interviewed, this "really means respect and deference to authority".

Part of the developing identity in Singapore is a result of secularization, a process of "rationalizing" one's world-view. This process is closely associated with the growth of urbanization, the expansion of technology and the spread of bureaucratization (Clammer, 1985: 50). All Singaporeans have been "exposed to insecurities, frustrations and disorientations of a general nature arising form Singapore's development thrust" (Betts, 1975: 294). A hybrid ideology based upon Confucian principles comfortably fills the void.

The result is an isolation of groups inside cultural or ethnic composites that, however arbitrary, institutionalizes difference within the construct of stereotypical perceptions. "Each culture turns in on itself in a cannibalistic manner, struggling to bring forth further manifestations of its distinctiveness" (Benjamin, 1976: 122).

> Individuals make decisions in the light of their cultural knowledge and it is through these culturally informed practices that individuals come to be channeled to higher or lower positions in the national socio-economic hierarchy. In turn, a cumulative and unintended outcome of these culturally informed practices is to sustain and institutionalize the hierarchical conditions within which individuals and groups find themselves constrained (Li, 1989: 122).

A successful Singaporean is one who has "achievement motivation, a money orientation, a competitive spirit and a desire for upward mobility", things that are "fundamentally congruent" with the historical performance of Singapore Chinese (Betts, 1975: 299–300). These are the things that "closely approximate those values, attitudes and motivations which had contributed so substantially to Singapore's growth and development" (Betts, 1975: 300).

Malays and Non-Malays

The Malay minority in Singapore is composed of Muslims indigenous to the area. They have a tradition of kingship and subsistence based on farming and fishing, usually in a village structure known as a *kampung*. Malay villages are usually structured around the practice of Islam, expressed through local custom (*adat*). Each village has a common prayer site (*surau*) and is hierarchical in structure with a village headman (*ketua*). Traditional behaviour offers respect to a political hierarchy but resists outside interference to local affairs.

Malay culture emphasizes social obligation, most dramatically in the form of participation in formal occasions such as marriage sand religious activities, particularly during religious holidays. It is not uncommon for a Malay to explain this obligation with the phrase *balik kampong*, which can be translated as "I need to return to my village". Malay lifestyle, traditionally based on subsistence, expresses a preference for temporary, migratory, seasonal, entrepreneurial or commission work over wage labour. Participation in village and community rituals is seen as an absolute obligation. These include Friday public prayers, prayers during the fasting month (Ramadan), marriages, and the many village activities that are part of Malay culture. In fact, although family ties are important and carry certain expectations of support, community membership and co-operation, particularly at the village level, are absolutely necessary for individuals to maintain their Malay identity.

This proves a contradiction for Singapore Malays. The majority of Malays in Singapore have been dispersed and resettled in public housing estates in which there are government prescribed limits on the percentage of Malays in a given building (HDB block). The government has attempted to replace the former village socio-political structure with a government-sponsored, affiliated and maintained management system. Resettlement to national housing is government controlled, and the location of Malays has been random, with no attempt at maintaining the integrity of former residence groups. Malays are widely dispersed in public housing dominated by Chinese and an ever-present and overwhelming (to Malays) Chinese culture.

Over 90 percent of the population is now living in public housing, in most cases, high-rise apartment blocks controlled by the Housing and Development Board (HDB). Yet, even though Malays have been displaced, in many cases involuntarily, they continue to preserve and adapt their own unique social structure based on former residence patterns. Malay groups have strong cultural bonds, usually in terms of land and village, and their social structure is hierarchical. Aspirations to status positions are directly related to family history and status. When Malays have voluntarily relocated to urban settings, they have reorganized themselves on this rural village model; the class structure transfers from village to city.

Ethnic stereotypes are common and commonly accepted by Singapore Malays. In fact, they are actively "embraced", with members of the state-defined ethnic groups applying stereotypes to prescribe their own behaviour. The basis of these stereotypes is found in colonial history when roles and occupations were often ethnically assigned. Limiting occupational outcomes led to cultural stereotyping and, consequently, a hierarchy of cultural or racial competencies. The Malays and the Chinese hold stereotypical views of each other and of themselves. For instance, Malays will say that a Malay who hoards money is miserly and is obsessed with money like the Chinese. Malays often say that money and work are in the flesh and blood of the Chinese.

This stereotype reflects the immigrant experience of the Chinese in Singapore. During the nineteenth and early twentieth centuries, Chinese lived in self-contained communities that were closely affiliated with old China. Change, when it came, was a result of political change in China (Busch, 1974: 21). The character of the immigrant Chinese community in Singapore was built on the values of enterprise and effort. Small family businesses, established through entrepreneurship, were the backbone of the Singapore economy, but this Chinese entrepreneurial spirit is based on familiar solidarity and exclusivity. Chinese social interaction is family based and is the source of almost every daily activity. Everything is done to protect the family from unwelcome intrusions. Due to a tradition of close-packed urban living, Chinese homes are often constructed like fortresses. With their myriad locks and bars, they create a barrier to the outsider and discourage cultural interaction with neighboors.

Malays have a moral sense of superiority to the Chinese. They regard the Chinese as socially irrelevant (Li, 1989: 134–5). "The perception that Chinese profit through trickery, while Malays are constrained by moral and religious scruples, is a fundamental part of the ethnic self-image of Malay businessmen" (Li, 1989: 140). The difference is a source of pride and an acknowledgement of inability to compete with Chinese.

> It is fundamental to the image Malays hold of themselves as an ethnic group, in the context of Singapore, that Malays are co-operative and caring neighbors in contrast to the Chinese who are said to only look after themselves (Li, 1989: 135).

Among some upwardly mobile Malay parents, the association of their children with Chinese is a matter of pride. "Many Malay parents hope that by living close to the non-Malays, particularly the Chinese, their children will hopefully learn to appreciate the importance of education" (Ong, 1974: 12). A Malay who speaks Chinese is often admired by other Malays while also regarded by them as an object of suspicion. The situation of Chinese and Malay interrelationships is particularly difficult for students. One parent insisted that her daughter who studied Chinese should attend special religious classes at the mosque. She explained: "A Malay must be very careful when associating closely with Chinese. We must not be Chinese, only like the Chinese".

Conversely, there is always some resentment and fear of the intrusion of Chinese culture into Malay society. Malays are quite sensitive to the preference of Chinese language over Malay language (Bahasa Melayu). The Malays interviewed were very conscious of the decreasing use of Malay words in the context of Singapore. An example is the Redhill subway station that is referred to by its English name rather than its Malay name (Bukit Merah); the latter term was used from the earliest days of colonial Singapore. More problematic are such things as the increase of Chinese names given to schools and housing estates, the Chinese lion dance used as a symbolic representation for distinguished visitors, a government sponsored "Speak Mandarin" campaign, the Yin/Yang logo of the Singapore Air Force, a preponderance of public notices and signs written only in English and/or Chinese, and the government's emphasis on Confucian ideas. These and many other examples are often discussed among Malays as "proof" of the Chinese cultural bias of the Singapore government.

Chinese culture and religion are syncretic and ever-present in Singapore. Chinese social, religious and economic rituals are unavoidably intertwined. thus the expression of Chinese cultural forms is ever-present in Singapore. Gambling, eating pork and consuming alcohol are important ways of establishing identity and group membership, and rituals involving these things permeate all aspects of Singapore life. For Malays, these things are taboo. The Islamic prohibition against eating pork represents a key cultural identity marker for Malays. This identity marker is important not only in its religious context but also when juxtaposed to Chinese culture, which incorporates the use of pork into many formal and informal rituals.

To Malays, Chinese are impure and Chinese food is polluting. Many Chinese religious occasions are celebrated by group dinners. Part of the ritual of these occasions is unavoidably enmeshed in drinking alcohol and eating Chinese food, particularly pork. This type of formal dinner is common for business, political and social interactions; it is very unlikely that a group would have a formal Chinese dinner without serving pork and alcohol. It is difficult for Malays to attend such functions. First, a Malay cannot participate in drinking alcohol and eating pork. It is forbidden (*haram*) not only to eat pork but to eat in a place where pork is served. The only compromise possible I saw on several occasions was to have a formal dinner with separate tables for Malays. Malay food would be catered separately and Malays would not participate in the activities taking place at the Chinese or non-Malay tables.

Eating in public places always presents a problem for Malays. According to a strict interpretation of Islam, a Malay should avoid places where pork and alcohol are served. Common "hawker centres" in many shopping areas of Singapore must be physically divided so as not to put the Chinese and Muslim eating stalls together. Muslims hesitate to eat fast food unless it is approved (*halal*). Kentucky Fried Chicken, for example, is *halal* but no official approval (in the form of a *halal* certificate, recognized by all Muslims) is allowed because it also sells beer (is this accurate in the Singapore case???).

The question of ritual impurity is a difficult one for Malays. As a result of pork consumption, Chinese are considered impure. Close proximity to non-Muslims in social situations predicated by public housing is very threatening to many Malays. As a result, they feel ". . . an increasing concern to intensify their practice of Islam and to preserve Malay culture and language, so as to ensure the survival of Malay identity" (Nurliza, 1986: 11). For example, many Malays kept cats as pets in the *kampung* although cats are not allowed in HDB flats. Although the hygienic reasons are very logical, Malays know that many Chinese consider cats "dirty animals". Dogs, common pets in Chinese homes, are considered "unclean" (*kotor*) by most Malays, but are allowed as pets in HDB flats.

Malays are quick to point out the Chinese insensitivity to the practice of Islam. One mosque official told me that the conflict for Malays and Chinese in the community is that the state-mandated and approved community centres in HDB block housing cannot replace mosques. He explained that Chinese social habits are incompatible to Islam, and he believed that the Chinese were unwilling to make the necessary concessions to garner Malay co-operation and participation. He gave the example that many social activities and meetings conflict with Malay evening prayers (Muslims have ritual prayers several times a day). Chinese pragmatism would not allow such an unyielding commitment to a daily event. In fact, many Chinese mentioned to me that Malays use the excuse of the Muslim obligation for daily prayer to avoid work. As one official from the Ministry of Education explained, "I know many Malays and they are not that religious, but they always claim to go to the mosque. I don't believe it".

A majority of the Malays interviewed resent Chinese control and being forced to live in a Chinese environment. They refer to the fact that Chinese funerals often held under in the void decks of housing estate blocks (the ground floor of a flat blocks is usually an open, common space) are very loud and last several days. Malays who have made complaints based on guidelines from HDB authorities about noise point out that little is done to control the level of noise at Chinese funerals and other events, such as the performance of Chinese operas.

Chinese religion is not simply contained in temple precincts. It is common practice for Chinese HDB residents to erect small altars in almost every conceivable place in a housing estate, and for a wide variety of contexts. They also burn paper, very often in the form of paper money, in conjunction with their rituals. Malays claim that the smells, sights and sounds of Chinese ritual practices permeate the air and offend the senses of Malays who live in public housing. The result is that Chinese ritual practices have a distancing effect on Malays. The Chinese religious rituals are at once frightening and threatening to Malays. In fact, Malays fear that even knowing about a ritual or showing interest may validate and encourage Chinese dominance in everyday life.

Malays resent that they must make tremendous adjustments to be active participants in the economic and political structure of Singapore. "The widespread and deeply held belief among Malays in Singapore is that their problems and disadvantages have been imposed on them on a racial basis by the Chinese majority" (Li, 1989: 179). As one prominent Malay businessman said to me: "I am Malay and I do not need to hide it, but sometimes I must disregard my culture so that people don't judge me by what they think of other Malays".

The stereotype of the Malay is accepted and reproduced by Malays and non-Malays alike. One stereotypical observation of Malay culture is that Malays are lazy. As early as the mid-nineteenth century, the negative stereotype of a lazy Malay had established itself. As one colonial writer commented, "The Malay never rises to be more than a hawker; and this is a result no doubt, of that want of ambition to be rich" (quoted in Trocki, 1979: 87). The concept of Malay "backwardness" is a very current topic and has been for nearly 100 years.

> The image of backwardness and its supposed cultural causes have themselves become part of the cultural fabric of Malay and Singapore society, and they have real practical effects as they are incorporated into the daily lives of ordinary Singaporeans and into national political processes" (Li, 1989:1 67).

Malays have never faired well in the urban economic system of the industrial age. In Singapore, the educated elite favour a socio-cultural explanation for this "Malay failure". The explanation was popularized by Malaysian Prime Minister Mahatir Mohamed. He has explained that the structure of Malay society discourages mobility and demands acceptance of a fixed hierarchy. Malay proponents of this theory often cite the misinterpretation of Islam and misrepresentation of the Koran as controlling factors.

> The pre-Islamic values which are preponderate rely heavily on magico-animistic explanations for worldly phenomena which not only retard the growth of a scientific orientation, self-confidence and entrepreneurship but also encourages passive resignation, self-reproach and a lack of achievement orientation (Yang Razali, 1980: 132–133).

"Informed" Malays "embrace" this stereotypical view of other Malays. One Malay commented in a newspaper (*The Straits Times*, 14 April 1985) claims: "They take life so easy. They don't seem to have depth. They don't look to the future". Singapore Malays tend to accept the blame, as a community, for the statistical and demographical picture of Malay failure in relation to other groups. The fault is described at a failure to "inculcate values" that are "conducive to achievement in education and work" (Tham, 1979: 107).

Members of the Malay ruling elite in Singapore consistently told me that Malays are incapable of competing with Chinese. As one person put it, "They suffer from a social malaise: a love of enjoyment".

> There is a happy go lucky style for Malay men. Prospects for employment are not good. And it is common for Malays to live beyond their means: they do not support and take care of parents. They can't even take care of themselves properly (comments by a Malay MP).

Regardless of the source, there is a general perception among both Malays and non-Malays that Malays are incapable of operating successfully and independently in a modern productive society.

> Insufficient interest exists among Malays on the whole concept of seeking new skills and career upgrading. While Singapore society is racing ahead, certain segments of the society including many Malays are remaining stagnant (comments of a Chinese MP).

Most non-Malays have low regard for the Malay capacity for hard and sustained work and for Malay mental ability. In fact, many Chinese remarked to me that Malays are less hard-working and less achievement-oriented than the Chinese, and that this is the result of traditional Malay cultural values (Li, 1989: 119).

> The idea that Malays have cultural impediments to progress has been incorporated into the practices of daily life through the common idea that the pattern of interaction in lower-income Malay neighborhoods is undesirable, and that lower-class Malay society has to be avoided if mobility is to be achieved" (Li, 1989: 178).

The Singapore Malay has been a marginal participant in Singapore's development. Malay employment has historically been on the periphery of urban commerce. In 1957, for example, the government reported that almost 50 percent of all Malays were involved in uniformed groups such as the police and army, or were common labourers. By 1966, about 50 percent of employed Malays were working in the service sector, usually in marginal jobs. In 1957, over 75 percent (10,843) of policemen, firemen and security forces were Malay. By 1970, both the percentage (21.7 percent) and the number (7,563) had decreased.

Number of Malays in the Police, Fire Brigade and Armed Forces

Years	Malays	All	Malay (%)
1957	10,843	14,350	76
1970	7,563	34,891	22
1980	10,534	81,475	13

Malays have traditionally been concentrated in low levels of the service industry as well as the armed forces and police force. One informant explained that sons often expect to inherit or follow their fathers in their occupations. He referred to this as "lateral mobility".

> It is very simple. If your father was a policeman, then you became a policeman. As we used to say, "Don't seek another job, follow your father." Now Malays have been shut out of many of their traditional occupations. We must look to other things, and many of those jobs are uncertain and indefinite. The old security is gone.

Many believe that Malays have not participated in the modern economic structure of Singapore because of this sense of cultural continuity, rather being satisfied with traditional occupations. They also have resisted occupations that require a compromise in cultural values or activities. As Wilson relates, traditional Malay economic activities form a coherent cultural pattern outside of which Malays are confused and uncertain (Wilson, 1967: 108).

> Malays have tended to retain their traditional social forms and many of their occupational patterns despite urbanization, while Chinese have embraced the process much more wholeheartedly, and indeed in Singapore have largely created it (Clammer, 1985: 121).

In the past, many authors cited Malay resistance to change as a reason for the failure of economic growth and development among Malays (Wilkinson, 1957; Swift, 1965; Parkinson, 1967). Clammer relates this to resistance to change traditional cultural patterns.

> Malays tend in Singapore to have a less rigid system of social classification . . . than the other groups, and are thus less influenced by pressures to become assimilated to the urban, industrialized, time conscious and competitive world of many Singaporeans. They are thus more marginal to the mainstream ideology than any other group and this is reflected in the fact that Malays are rarely employed in front line units during military service, or are not called-up at all, but are put in the part-time or paramilitary forces such as the Vigilante Corps, and that, at the margins of the mainstream society, people express their marginality by, amongst other things, the slackening of physical control, made manifest by longer hair and a more unkept appearance than the average citizen (Clammer, 1981: 25–26).

Malays have been historically resistant to wage labour. Many Malays expressed the idea that they would rather be self-employed than become the "slave" of another. When asked why Malay employment patterns are so unstable, young Malays often told me they prefer to remain free (*bebas*). On the other hand, many older Malay men say the young men are lazy. According to an official in the national manpower office, many of the offspring of urban Malays try to avoid what they consider to be dirty work, or work that is physically demanding—perhaps reflecting a new and developing Malay status hierarchy.

There are also barriers to Malays getting jobs. Some of these have to do with technical or educational qualifications. Most often they have to do with the fact that Malays have a poor work reputation. Li found that "discrimination by Chinese against Malays is based on the Chinese opinion that Malays are culturally inferior and incapable of hard work" (Li, 1989: 179). Many Malays possess what one Malay politician called an "exploitative mentality"—they tend to think that they are always being "mistreated" and that as long as their status positions are limited, there is nothing to be done about their inferior position in society.

Malays in School

Much of my research was focused on Malay students in one secondary school in Singapore. The secondary school was located in a public housing estate composed mainly of working-class families. This particular secondary school did not have a good status so applications for admittance to it were not very competitive. The student body was over 24 percent Malay and less than 65 percent Chinese. In relation to the disbursal of Malays throughout the island, this was one of the highest proportions of Malays in any Singapore secondary school.

In Singapore, students who finish primary school and "pass" the exit examination (Primary School Leaving Examination or PSLE) may apply to a secondary school for admittance. The Singapore system allows self-selection of schools by parents. Schools with a very good reputation attract more students than those that lack a tradition of producing students who are high achievers. Since Malay students have a reputation for poor academic performance, a school with a high proportion of Malay students would be considered a "poor academic choice".

A Singapore secondary school is divided into two "streams". These two streams, "Normal" and "Express", reflect performance in the PSLE. "Normal" students are thought to be a little slow and are given five years to complete their secondary school education. The majority of students enter the four-year secondary school "express" programme, which ends in an examination ("O levels") that determines if a student goes on to a pre-university course of study or a technical school, or leaves school to enter the job market. The majority of Express students continue with their education. Most of the normal students become "school leavers". Of the students who move from primary to secondary school, about 60 percent are in the Express stream and 40 percent in the Normal stream. In the secondary school I studied, which was in an average working-class housing estate, the proportion was close to 50–50.

In this school, Malays were concentrated in the Normal stream (about 80 percent), as is common throughout Singapore. While the government pays close attention to Malay performance in school, their attitude is one of benign neglect. They encourage Malays to formulate self-help programmes and offer moral and administrative support; officially, however, they consider the meritocracy system to be fair and Malays to be underachievers for a variety of cultural and biological reasons. Surprisingly, many Malays accept some of these reasons. At any rate, it is up to the Malay community to formulate and implement programmes to increase performance in school.

The government of Singapore has officially designated itself a "meritocracy". All positions in the government service are filled according to ability level, and this ability level is almost exclusively based on educational attainment, which is predicated on examinations. The educational system has tended to institutionalize inequality under the guise of meritocracy, which inevitably assures limited access to the undereducated and their offspring. The result is an organic development of segregation in schools, jobs and social relations (Rahim, 1998). The possibility of upward mobility in education has affected the identity choices available to students in school. Performance and outcomes are closely tied to factors of school stream and gender as well as ethnicity and social class. Male Malay ideology and behaviour in Normal stream contrasted dramatically with Malay behaviour in the Express stream, and Malay female behaviour generally:

1. They felt that true Singaporean identity was based on "Chineseness" or Chinese characteristics, and that being Muslim excluded them from membership.
2. They thought they were unable to achieve entry in the "meritocracy" because of educational exclusion as a result of examination scores based solely on subjects that favoured Chinese students (Mathematics, English language).
3. They portrayed and identified as "successful" occupational and status outcomes that were marginal to broader society as normatively expressed in the hierarchy based on the government-constructed "meritocracy". Examples include musicians, particularly rock stars (Malay "rock" was a complex field that included many sub-areas well known to Malays but few others), athletes, film stars, and sailors (excluding those in the navy). Attitudes and career choices reflected a marked resistance to participation in wage labour activities.
4. While voluntarily attending school, they managed to resist the specific processes of schooling through such strategies as non-cooperation in class, poor attendance in school, tardiness and cutting of classes, failure to follow the uniform code, and disinterest and non-participation in school-sponsored projects.

"Malay secondary students perceive bias. Statistics bear out the argument that there is a differential calculus at work among Singapore teachers concerning the competence and performance of Malay students" (Rahim, 1989: 205–207). Generally, Malay students try to use school to create opportunities for social interaction. Such social interaction reinforces over-arching Malay values and establishes peer group solidarity. The result is a feeling of interdependence among most Malays. As one Malay teacher observed: "It is the character of Malay children to depend on Malay society". Many Malay students say they are in school because they are interested in the potential for "pleasant" social interaction and the opportunity to forego low status employment. "School is like a heaven to students as they come here to study and enjoy with the company of their friends" (comment by a Malay student). The social aspects of school are very important. Peer standing and association provide a source of status. Security and support are absolute for those who conform to standards of behaviour set by Malay students. Conformity to Malay norms, however, usually means non-conformity to school norms.

Malay students are often criticized by non-Malays for demonstrating a preference for social interaction and co-operation with Malays over individual effort in class and achievement in examinations.

Malays are weak and lazy. They prefer to enjoy themselves. They like to listen to television or the radio and sleep. Because of broken homes, working parents or parental indifference, they have no one else to turn to so they go to their friends. That is why peer influence is so strong (a Malay teacher).

For many Malays, school is entertaining and provides a simple answer to the complex questions of future planning. By going to school, occupational decision-making is deferred and students are left with a great deal of time for social interaction. School provides a way to avoid work and marriage at an early age. The longer one stays in school, the longer the decision to work is deferred and leisure time is guaranteed. If a girl is not interested in marriage, she stays in school. If a boy is not in wage labour, he will stay in school. When they lose interest or fail, they may quit. As one female in the Express stream explained, "Once Malays try and fail, they become disappointed and discouraged, and tend to give up".

Malay students, particularly those in the Normal stream, are very clear about the minimum acceptable performance levels necessary to survive examinations or keep teachers happy, especially in difficult or uninteresting classes. They are very conscious of what subjects they need to pass and quick to dismiss those in which they have little real chance. When the primary concern in school is having the opportunity for social interaction rather than using school as a path to status and wealth, achievement is less important.

Malay students are not usually combative or confrontational. They try to adjust and blend with the environment, adopting an attitude of relaxation and ease, but within the construction of "acceptable" Malay behaviour. During the first term, the Malay students in one Normal class seemed to be causing a lot of trouble for a variety of teachers. The most successful teacher did not try to control them but rather tended to interact freely with them. His teaching did not show an improvement in examination performance but students were usually present in class. None of the teachers complained about discipline problems for these students but rather, that they could not get them to be involved in the lesson. If they scolded them too harshly, they would simply stop paying attention to the lesson. Social co-operation may lead Malays to disruptive behaviour. This is particularly obvious in the case of boys. Non-cooperation by girls is also common. Malays sometimes do not co-operate in a lesson, although they do not articulate this non-cooperation into any overt or challenging form of resistance. The result is that teachers often consider them inefficient, uncooperative or lazy.

> Malays aren't stupid; they are lazy. They are concerned with being at ease and relaxed. They like to go home and relax, listen to music. My Malay friends are always interested in distracting me (comment by a Malay Express student).

The general interpretation of life by Malay students is a world orchestrated and controlled by God. Each person has his or her fate (*rezeki*). One has no choice but to accept the personal fate ordained by God. "We must trust in Allah for the right direction and decision" (comment by a Malay student). This idea of control of fate is a sensitive point for many Malay religious authorities in Singapore. They say that the concept of *rezeki* as intractable is a misinterpretation of Islam, commonly found among the improperly educated.

There is an inherent paradox for Malays in school: being in school with friends is good, therefore, school is good. Being in class and being forced to do things is a loss of freedom (*tak bebas*) and is bad. This paradox is born out by the record of Malay absenteeism at the school I studied. Generally, the average rate of absenteeism by Malays was no different from the school average; however, a greater percentage of Malays were absent from school sometime during the year. If absenteeism associated with Malay holidays or special occasions are factored out, Malay school attendance is higher on average than any other group. The solution is to be in school but to avoid attending classes as much as possible, as long as you are able to stay on in school. "Students may have fun 'at school', but not 'in school.' It's not much fun in class; they learn" (comment by Chinese teacher of Normal stream students). Many Malay students said they come to school even if they have no interest in it because they want to see their friends. "I know that I will not do well on my exams, but I like to see my friends. I can always find work if I want it" (comment by a Malay male in the Normal stream). Tardiness and students being out of the class are higher for Malay students than for any other group. According to the teacher in charge of attendance records, it is "uncountable".

Social interaction in the Malay community is very important for all Malays. During Hari Raya, the most important Malay holiday, it is proper to visit other families. Malay students often miss classes during these holidays. For many Malay students and their families, social interaction supersedes the importance of attending school. Forms of Malay interaction do not lend themselves to the classroom lecture method of teaching. For most Malays, conforming to group norms of interaction is more important than conformity to the form of schooling. In Normal classes with a large representation of Malays, Malay students are very hesitant to disregard what are commonly considered the "normal" forms of Malay behaviour.

> Malay students disturb other students, especially other Malay students. It is not proper to ignore a Malay, even when the student is acting improperly. When we work together it is not nice if one does differently than the others (comment by Malay female in the Normal stream).

The most easily observable patterns of interaction in classes are among Malay boys in the Normal stream. Variations appear between Normal and Express streams, and according to the number of Malay boys in class; ultimately, boys either choose to follow the group or select a form of self-imposed ostracism in an attempt to be successful in school. Group conformity is of paramount importance for "Normal boys", as is the need to be perceived as "acting" Malay. Express students or males in a class with low Malay enrolment may act quite differently in and out of class. One Malay boy, who was a good student in an Express class, would join another Malay group when he was done with his school work.

> You see, Malays follow their friends; they want to have a sense of belonging to their own culture, in this case young Malays. Malays take things easy; failure is nothing new to them. It is more important to follow friends than do well in school. Besides the inevitable is always hanging over their heads: factory jobs or national service. They tend to lose interest in studies in the face of this reality. Many Malays who have low aspirations feel that the government has a prejudiced attitude (comments by a Malay teacher).

Malay boys inevitably work and act as a group. Responses in class come easily from groups: if one student is singled out, that student is shy and hesitates to answer. One student explained why he did not answer if called on, but offered answers when not called on. "I Compo! Compo! Compo! (Compositions) I get fed up. I like nice things, you know? Here school work always hangs over your head. My friends, we don't like to have to worry."

Protests seldom occur unless there is a cadre of Malay boys in the class. In fact, Malay boys seem to like the attention a "fussing" teacher gives to them. This "fussing" is similar to the interaction Malay boys have with their mothers, and is similar to the mother–son relationship of cajoling and non-cooperation found in most Malay *kampungs*. One teacher told me, "Unless I am constantly fighting with them, I just don't have their attention."

Resistance to instruction is a common cause. Normal Malay boys clearly have little tolerance for lectures and would rather be out and about. Sitting in school is not something that is part of Malay male self-characterization.

> Malays don't like to ask questions. They don't like to study. They like to avoid any kind of confusion. It is bad for the balance. They don't like to "think too hard" (comment by a Malay male in Normal stream).

The most overt resistance to instruction comes from boys in the Normal stream. First, they tend to be small offenders of the uniform dress code. They wear patches for rock groups and will even draw on their shirts. They often leave their shirt tails hanging out or their shirts unbuttoned, and this is an almost constant irritation to teachers. Malays also grow their hair dangerously close to the unacceptable standard or "collar length". This resistance to school conformity causes instructional problems for many teachers. It has resulted in a general disregard for Malay behaviour and a distaste for teaching most Malay Normal boys. The classes with the most problems are inevitably those with the largest representation of Malay boys.

The Malay Express students were mostly from upper middle-class families, with a surprising number being the progeny of non-village (*kampung*) originated families. Such Malays are clearly differentiated as Malays in name only, and not true (*totok*) Malays in the fashion of *kampung* Malays. Most Malays in the Express stream did not accept the axiom that to be a successful Singaporean meant one had to surrender "Malayness" and become "Chinese". Rather, they defined success, and thus Singaporean identity, as a composite of characteristics that, while admittedly predominantly Chinese, did not constitute "Chineseness". Being a successful Singaporean was seen, metaphorically, as "choosing clothes appropriate for the occasion, thus covering the body in different ways, but not changing the body beneath the clothes". This situational ethnicity was at once negotiable by context and intent (note: the metaphor appeared to mirror reality for females, who commonly dressed in radically different attire depending on the occasion and the place).

Malay behaviour is also differentiated culturally by gender. Whereas males are traditionally expected to be somewhat resistant to conformity and "fixed residence", females are expected to be co-operative, undemanding and yielding in the face of established (usually male) authority. This conformity among females has predicated their success in schools to a much greater extent than for males. The result is that there are many more Malay females in tertiary education than there are males, thus creating a marriage bind for the females.

All students in the Normal stream (whether Malays, Chinese, Indians or other minorities) expressed and exemplified the primary importance of ethnic identity. Since school success was usually presumed to be unattainable for Normal students, inclusion in a peer ethnic group became very important. Behaviour that compromised ethnic identity, especially stereotypical identity characteristics (examples could include dress and music for Malays, or the practice of gambling and language use for the Chinese) were of paramount importance. Behaviour that compromised ethnic identity was discouraged. Ethnic participants effectively "embraced the stereotype" of their group, assuming characteristics superimposed by outsiders and other groups.

This stereotype extended to performance in schools. Malays constantly referred to mathematics as a "Chinese subject" that Malays were prone to do poorly in (a less than 10 percent pass rate). It was an accepted truism that success in mathematics was only possible if a student studied the "Chinese way". Those who passed mathematics were subject to accusations of associating with Chinese and avoiding the company of other Malays. In contrast to performance in mathematics, Malay students in both streams scored very highly in Malay language and Islamic studies (over 95 percent pass rate).

In contrast to the Normal students, Express students tended to de-emphasize ethnicity in lieu of a more interactive composite identity that centred on the use of English and conformity to the schooling process. Whereas a teacher would have to justify work given to Normal students, Express students would co-operate in almost any work assignment if it were billed as "possible exam material".

A Malay student in school is faced with, basically, three choices. First, he or she may remain a pure Malay (*Melayu totok*), in this case with purity defined culturally by *adat* and antithetically by non-Malays, particularly Chinese. Second, a student could disregard and even denigrate *adat*, rather emphasizing "international Islam". Third, a student might attempt to walk a narrow line between Malay and non-Malay culture by associating with non-Malays in daily circumstances while emphasizing "situational Malayness" through careful attendance of Friday prayers at the *masjid* and formal Malay celebrations. A successful Express student could choose between the three, usually making the second or third choice, depending on living circumstances, and socio-economic status. The Normal student is usually limited to the first choice.

Conclusion: Renegotiating Identity

The factors that contribute to the negotiation and construction of Malay identity are numerous and complex. They vary from individual to individual and situation to situation. In this research, I have attempted to describe those aspects of Malay life, history, customs and relationships that affect the formation of cultural identity for Malay students in Singapore. Factors that affect Malay identity lead to a number of choices, and these choices vary and are significantly affected by the situation and the intention of the Malay actors. Foremost among factors that affect Malay identity is the historical tension between Malay political control through centralization of power and the independent, self-sufficient nature of the idiosyncratic structure of the Malay *kampung*. This particular tension has led to others. Purity of Islam and language, balanced against autonomous cultural practices and syncretic Islam; distinction between indigenous insiders and outside intruders; and the new youth-oriented Malay counter-culture contrasted with the traditional Malay practices that are so closely related to Islam.

Another point of contrast, played out in schools and other areas of institutionalized culture in Singapore, is the comparison of state-mandated cultural forms, largely based on Western and Chinese idioms, and the state-sponsored ethnicity that overarches cultural identity and supersedes subgroup distinctions. In this play between ethnicity and national identity, ethnic boundaries are of paramount importance and choices are formed in dichotomies. This may lead to the faulty conclusion that Malay identity in Singapore is a dichotomy. One might conclude that no matter what the outcome, the choice is an absolute or exclusive one. Closer to the truth is the conclusion that identity in Singapore is negotiated and renegotiated, and constructed and reconstructed according to a wide range of factors. This choice will always depend on the place, the people, the people involved and the specific outcome desired. Far from a dichotomy, Malay identity is situationally negotiated, and the option of alternative choices is always available to Malays, even after they surrender it and choose to be viewed as exclusive and excluding.

For children in school, the negotiation of identity is not a matter of choices but is a matter of situations. Within the context of these situations, students must evaluate who they are, who they want to be, and how they want to be perceived by others. Since these factors change with time, place and participants, there is usually a range of choices available to students. Choices may be strongly affected by the socio-historical roots of Singapore's Malay community, but they are viewed much more simply by students and do not depend on extensive knowledge of such influential factors. For most students it becomes a matter of degrees or interpretations of being Malay or being Singaporean. The state, in the form of the PAP, would prefer other distinctions to be made so as to portray an absolute choice in terms of productivity versus non-cooperation, or individuality versus social welfare. For the state, behaviour that is not state-sponsored or state-endorsed must be sequestered to the fringes of social importance.

The government has created a hybrid national personality based on English-educated Chinese, a hazy reflection of the culture of China, and the reinterpretation of Western colonial models. The companion to the state personality, that of the "good citizen", is ethnic classification. This state-mandated ethnicity acts to supersede any real cultural identity and replace it with a stereotype that is both accepted and embraced by all Singaporeans. Incorporation of ethnic groups into a collective national identity institutionalizes a hierarchy based on ethnic stereotyping and demands cultural adaptation in the form of either incorporation or assimilation to the norms of the dominant group. To be truly successful in Singapore's social structure, a citizen must hold and utilize ethnicity only situationally, and then demonstrate it only stereotypically. Malays who wish to be successful must have a closely structured identity that is adaptable to circumstances. A Malay may conspicuously demonstrate ceremonial ethnic identity while actually living on the fringe of acceptable "Malayness". In this case, Malayness becomes a balance between the desirability of social solidarity and the practical benefits of social distance. Membership may provide social and psychological resources to a Malay, but it may also remove opportunities of success in the status mobility system in broader Singapore society; thus, a balance must be struck.

To advance up the status scale in that system, a Malay must understand state-mandated "good citizenship" and know when to "wear it". In Singapore, the main attribute of a "good citizen" is conformity to the system. For students, this means co-operation in the schooling process, trust in the status mobility system, and success in national examinations. In a letter to MOE, Prime Minister Lee Kuan Yew said, "The litmus test of a good education is whether it nurtures citizens who can live, work, contend and cooperate in a civilized way". Conformity also means acquiescence to the paternal power of the state. Characteristics of that which have been mentioned are loyalty, patriotism, filial piety and respect for elders. According to the Prime Minister, "good citizens" are law abiding, humane, responsible, trustworthy, tolerant, clean, neat, punctual and well-mannered. To be successful in Singapore's social structure, being Malay must be in having a closely structured identity that is adaptable to circumstances. The decision to be Malay is based on a balance between the desirability of social solidarity, as opposed to the practical benefits of social distance.

Being a Malay in Singapore is a compromise. The instances of this compromise are articulated on a continuum that runs from the hegemony of an over-arching Malay ethnicity to the dissolution of this Malayness into a hybrid cultural identity. Lower school performance is an adaptive problem for Malays in Singapore. In fact, school failure in particular is most often referred to as "the Malay problem". The real problem may be that co-operation in the system means acknowledgment of inferiority.

Malays, who base their social interactions and cultural values on the ideals and practices of the *kampung*, resist this "normalization". Resistance for Malays in Singapore means maintaining their identity as Malays. Since cultural difference is referred in the governmentally-sponsored system of "multiracialism", resistance may simply be conspicuous Malayness. The principle of "meritocracy" restricts placement into managerial positions to all but only the most adaptive students. Conversely, it requires the production of a workforce that accepts assignment of lower status positions in the status mobility system.

In school, status outcomes are closely tied to school performance and in secondary school, school performance is highly correlated with the streams: Express students are more likely to succeed, and Normal students are more likely to fail. The system, however, is not logical. If Normal classes—with less efficient, adaptive and learning-ready students—cannot compete with Express classes, why is there a parallel curriculum between the two streams? Such a parallel promises the opportunity of success to students in both streams, but the clear difference between behaviour in the two streams indicated that students do not believe this. Despite the best efforts of the government and the schools, students in the Normal stream very often refuse to co-operate in terms of socialization, instead choosing alternative forms of socialization. They resist incorporation into the dominant system by reproducing their own alternative system of normative behaviour.

REFERENCES

Anyon, Jean (1983) "Intersections of Gender and Class: Accommodation and Resistance by Working-Class and Affluent Females to Contradictory Sex-Role Ideologies", in L. Barton and S. Walker, eds., *Gender, Class and Education*. London: Falmer Press, pp. 19–37.

Banks, David J. (1983) *Malay Kinship*. Philadelphia: Institute for the Study of Human Resources.

Bedlington, S. S. (1974) *The Singapore Malay Community: The Politics of State Integration*. Unpublished Ph.D. dissertation. Cornell University.

Bell, David S. (1972) *Unity in Diversity: Education and Political Integration in an Ethnically Pluralistic Society*. Unpublished Ph.D. dissertation. Indiana University.

Benjamin, Geoffrey (1976) "The Cultural Logic of Singapore's 'Multiracialism'", in Riaz Hassan, ed., *Singapore: Society in Transition*. Kuala Lumpur: Oxford University Press, pp. 115–133.

Bernstein, Basil (1972) "Social Class, Language and Socialization", in P. P. Giglioli, ed., *Language and Social Context*. London: Harmondsworth, pp. 157–178.

Betts, Russel H. (1975) *Multiracialism: Meritocracy and the Malays in Singapore*. Unpublished Ph.D. dissertation. Massachusetts Institute of Technology.

Busch, Peter A. (1974) *Legitimacy and Ethnicity: A Case-Study of Singapore*. Lexington: D.C. Heath and Co.

Chan, Heng Chee and Hans-Dieter Evers (1978) "National Identity and Nation-Building in Singapore", in Peter S. J. Chen and Hans-Dieter Evers, eds., *Studies in ASEAN Sociology*. Singapore: Chopmen Enterprises, pp. 117–129.

Chew Sock Foon (1987) *Ethnicity and Nationality in Singapore*. Athens, Ohio: Ohio University Monographs in International Studies, Southeast Asia Series Number 78.

Chew Soo Beng (1982) *Fishermen in Flats*. Monash Papers on Southeast Asia #9. Monash University.

Chiew Seen-Kong (1983) "Ethnicity and National Integration: The Evolution of a Multiethnic Society", in Peter Chen, ed., *Singapore: Development Policies and Trends*. Singapore: Oxford University Press, pp. 29–64.

Clammer, John R. (1981) "Malay Society in Singapore: A Preliminary Analysis", *Southeast Asian Journal of Social Science*, 9 (1–2): 19–32.

———. (1985) *Singapore: Ideology, Society and Culture*. Singapore: Chopmen Publishers.

Everhart, Robert B. (1983) "Classroom Management, Student Opposition, and the Labor Process", in M. Apple and L. Weis, eds., *Ideology and Practice in Schooling*. Philadelphia: Temple University Press, pp. 169–192.

Hanna, Wilard A. (1966) "The Malays' Singapore, Part 1–5", New York: American Universities Field Staff Reports, Southeast Asia Series, XIV: 2–6.

Hannan, Michael T. (1979) "The Dynamics of Ethnic boundaries in Modern States", in John W. Meyer and Michael T. Hannan, *National Development and the World System*. Chicago: The University of Chicago Press, pp. 253–275.

Hussin Mutalib (1990) *Islam and Ethnicity in Malay Politics*. Singapore: Oxford University Press.

Jones, Gavin W. (1994) *Marriage and Divorce in Islamic South-East Asia*. Kuala Lumpur: Oxford University Press.

Lee Kwee Eng, (1982) *The Maintenance of Group Identity: The Case of the Malays in Singapore*. Academic exercise. Department of Sociology, National University of Singapore.

Li, Tanya (1989) *Malays in Singapore: Culture, Economy and Ideology*. Singapore: Oxford University Press.

McAmis, Robert Day (2002) *Malay Muslims*. Grand Rapids: William B. Eerdmans Publishing Company.

Malmstad, Betty J., Mark B. Ginsburg and John C. Croft (1983) "The Social Construction of Reading Lessons: Resistance and Social Reproduction", *Journal of Education* 165:4.

McDermott, R. (1974) "Achieving School Failure: An Anthropological Approach to Illiteracy and Social Stratification", in George Spindler, ed., *Education and Cultural Process*. New York: Holt, pp. 82–118.

Nurliza Yusof (1986) *Being Malay in Singapore: Perceptions and Articulations of Identity*. Unpublished academic exercise. Dept of Sociology, National University of Singapore.

Ogbu, John U. (1974) *The Next Generation: An Ethnography of Education in an Urban Neighborhood*. New York: Academic Press.

———. (1978) *Minority Education and Caste*. New York: Academic Press.

———. (1982) "Societal Forces as a Context of Ghetto Children's School Failure", in Lynne Feagans and Dale Farran, ed., *The Language of Children Reared in Poverty*. New York: Academic Press, pp. 117–138.

———. (1983) "Minority Status and Schooling in Plural Societies," *Comparative Education Review* (27)2: 168–190.

Ogbu, John U. and Signithia Fordham (1986) "Black Students' School Success: Coping with the Burden of 'Acting White'", *The Urban Review* 18(3): 176–206.

Ong Boon Geok (1974) *The Social Structure of the Resettled Malay Community in Geylang Serai, Singapore*. Unpublished academic exercise. Department of Sociology, University of Singapore.

Parkinson, Brien K. (January 1967) "Non-economic Factors in the Retardation of the Rural Malays", *Modern Asian Studies* 1:1.

Provencher, Ronald (1971) *Two Malay Worlds: Interaction in Urban and Rural Settings.* Berkeley: University of California, Center for Southeast Asian Studies.
Peletz, Michael G. (1996) *Reason and Passion, Representations of Gender in a Malay Society.* Berkeley: University of California Press.
Rahim, Lily Zubaidah (1998) *The Singapore Dilemma: The Political and Educational Marginality of the Malay Community.* Kuala Lumpur: Oxford University Press.
Roff, William (1967) *The Origins of Malay Nationalism.* New Haven: Yale University Press.
Sloane, Patricia (1999) *Islam, Modernity and Entrepreneurship among the Malays.* London: Macmillan Press Ltd.
Suriani Suratman (1986) "The Malays of Clementi: An Ethnography of Flat Dwellers in Singapore". Unpublished M.A. thesis, Monash University.
Swift, Michael G. (1965) *Malay Peasant Society in Jelebu.* London: Athlone Press.
Tham Seong Chee (1977) *Malays and Modernization: A Sociological Interpretation.* Singapore: Singapore University Press.
———. (1979) "Social Change and the Malay Family", in Eddie C. Y. Kuo and Aline K. Wong, eds, *The Contemporary Family in Singapore.* Singapore: Singapore University Press, pp. 88–133.
Thomas, Elwyn (1985) "Stress as a Factor in the Education of Adolescents in Singapore," Fifth ASEAN Forum on Child and Adolescent Psychiatry. 17–19 November. Singapore.
Thomas, R. Murray (1987) "Education and Intergroup Relations—An International Perspective: The Cases of Malaysia and Singapore", in Thomas J. La Belle and Peter S. White, *Educational Policy Analysis and Intergroup Relations.* New York: Praeger.
———. (1980) "Singapore", in R. Murray Thomas and T. Neville Postlethwaite, *Schooling in the ASEAN Region.* New York: Pergamon Press, pp. 181–221.
Trocki, Carl (1979) *Prince of Pirates: The Temenggongs and the Development of Johore and Singapore. 1784–1885.* Singapore: Singapore University Press.
Wee, C. J. W.-L. (2003) "Our Island Story: Economic Development and the National Narrative in Singapore", in Abu Talib Ahmad and Tan Liok Ee, *New Terrains in Southeast Asian History.* Athens, Ohio: Ohio University Press.
Weis, Lois (1983) "Schooling and Cultural Production: A Comparison of Black and White Lived Culture", in M. Apple and L. Weis, eds., *Ideology and Practice in Schooling.* Philadelphia: Temple University Press, pp. 235–261.
Wilcox, Kathleen (1982) "Differential Socialization in the Classroom: Implications for Equal Opportunity", in George Spindler, *Doing the Ethnography of Schooling.* New York: Holt, Rinehart and Winston, pp. 268–309.
Wilder, William (1970) "Socialization and Social Structure in a Malay village", in Phillip Mayer, ed., *Socialization: The Approach from Social Anthropology.* London: Tavistock Publications, pp. 215–268.
Wilkinson, R. J. (1957) "Malay Customs and Beliefs", *Journal of the Royal Asiatic Society, Malayan Branch* 30:4.
Willis, Paul (1977) *Learning to Labour: How Working Class Kids Get Working Class Jobs.* Westmeand, England: Saxon House.
Wilson, Harold E. (1978) *Social Engineering in Singapore: Educational Policies and Social Change, 1819–1972.* Singapore: Singapore University Press.
Wilson, Peter J. (1967) *A Malay Village and Malaya: Social Values and Rural Development.* New Haven, CT: HRAF Press.
Yang Razali Kassim (1980) *Education and the Malays in Singapore: The Position, Perceptions and Responses of a Minority Community.* Unpublished academic exercise. Department of Political Science, University of Singapore.

THE CHINESE IN CONTEMPORARY MALAYSIA

Tong Chee Kiong

A description of who, or what, is a Chinese, and what constitutes Chineseness remains elusive. Wang (1999) notes that the Chineseness of Chinese is whatever went on among Chinese, so that, "there is nothing absolute about being Chinese." Goodman (1997: 18) described it as a "fragile identity [even] for the ethnic Chinese themselves." Clearly, the terms "Chinese" or "Chineseness" remain problematic categories that embody many dimensions and require further analysis. Moreover, studies of the relations between immigrant Chinese and host societies reveal contradictory findings. Some locate the ability of the Chinese to remain culturally distinct (Wilmott, quoted in Purcell, 1965; Gosling, 1983), while others point to the ability of the Chinese to assimilate into the host societies (Skinner, 1963; Amyot, 1972; Ossapan, 1979). Furthermore, sociological concepts such as assimilation, integration, and acculturation—terms developed by Western scholars to understand ethnic issues in the West—have been used ambiguously and inconsistently by others to make sense of the Chinese in Southeast Asia.

This chapter, drawing on fieldwork data collected in contemporary Malaysian society, has two main objectives. First, I seek to describe the ethnic identity of the Chinese in a multi-ethnic, pluralistic and modern nation-state. Who and what is a Chinese in Malaysia? What are the markers of Chineseness? How is this ethnic identity presented? How is ethnic identity invoked, negotiated and mediated? These questions are particularly important as an understanding of Chinese ethnic identity in Malaysia must take into account the influence of the state, the historical and sociopolitical context of Malaysian society and its unique ethnic composition, where over 47 percent of the population is Malay and 34 percent is Chinese; thus, this group constitutes a significant minority.

Ethnicity is no longer understood as a discrete phenomenon. It is a social process that involves mediation and transformation. As such, the issue is no longer whether the Chinese in Malaysia are assimilated or integrated, but in what context the Chinese identify and present themselves as Chinese. Second in this chapter, I seek to contribute to the current debates on ethnicity and ethnic relations. I will explore differential Chinese identity; that is, Chinese identity is heterogeneous and this is reflected in Chinese daily interactions with other ethnic groups. I suggest that such cultural contacts have not only created tension and conflict but, in the course of these interactions, have led to reciprocal influences between Chinese and Malay cultures.

The study of ethnicity has taken two opposing positions: primordialism and situationalism. Geertz is generally credited with the idea of a primordial sense of ethnicity (Jenkins, 1997: 44). Geertz believes that primordial ties or attachments are the basis of individual identity, and affect the formation of the nation-state. He advances the proposition that primordial attachments "stem from the "givens" . . . these congruities of blood, speech, customs, and so on, are seen to have an ineffable, and at times overpowering, coercive in and of themselves" (1963: 259). Similarly, Issacs argues that an ethnic group is "composed of . . . 'primordial affinities and attachments' . . . [that] a person . . . acquires at birth . . . [and] it is distinct from all other multiple and secondary identities . . . [that] people acquire." Thus, basic group identity comprises a "ready-made set of endowments and identifications which every individual shares with others at the moment of birth . . .", of which physical characteristics that make up the body and the name are two important diacritical markers.

Individuals, therefore, attribute "primordiality to the ties of religion, blood, race, language, religion and custom" (Hutchinson and Smith, 1996: 6). For the primordialists, these things are natural "givens" that cannot be negotiated or renounced. Ultimately, primordialists believe that what matters most is that these ties of blood, language and religion "are *seen* by the actors to be obligatory; that they are *seen* as natural" (Jenkins, 1997: 45). Sociologists extend the primordial position by arguing that the "wider kin-based groupings . . . . are bonded through mechanisms of . . . inclusive fit", and that ethnicity is simply extended forms of kinship ties (see Hutchinson and Smith, 1996; van de Berge, 1978).

The primordial approach to ethnicity has been criticized for presenting a model that is static, essentialized and lacking explanatory powers. Moreover, it tends to see an ethnic group as basically homogeneous. This is directly in contrast to the situational or instrumental approach of ethnic identity. This model of ethnicity emphasizes a degree of plasticity in ethnic identification and in the composition of ethnic groups (Jenkins, 1997: 44). One of the central themes of the approach is that individuals, or actors, are able to break away from their ethnic heritages and blend with another culture, or even create their own individual or group identities (Bhabha, 1990).

Barth (1969) argues that simply describing the content of a core culture does not allow one to understand the complexities of ethnic identity; hence, Barth seeks to redirect attention to the relations among groups and the ways culture is used to generate and preserve those relations. The two central notions of this approach are ethnic boundaries and social interaction (see Eller, 1999: 76). Thus, there is variability in the affirmation of identity, which is dependent on social situations (Okamura, 1981), and individual membership is related to values, interests, and motives that influence a person's behaviour in that situation. Identity is embedded in changeable social situations instead of in the unchanging attachments that often lie at the heart of primordialism (Cornell and Hartmann, 1998). In contrast to the primordialist view, situational ethnicity gives weight to the notion of choice and proactivity in determining a person's identity or ethnic group membership (Banks, 1996). The situational approach to ethnicity has often been criticized for its failure to take into account the actors' sense of the permanence of their ethnies, and for downplaying the affective dimensions of ethnicity (Hutchinson and Smith, 1996: 7).

I argue that the primordial and situational approaches need not be seen as mutually exclusive. From the actors' perspective, ethnic identity can be both primordial and situational at the same time. Using data from cases studies of the Chinese in Malaysia, I will argue that ethnic identity has both core and peripheral dimensions. At the core, ethnic identity is primordial, based on ascription and largely seen as central and permanent. At the periphery, ethnicity is open to negotiations, and while relevant, they are not regarded as necessary for ethnic identity. Here, the markers of identity, such as customs and religion, may be more variable—dependent on individual circumstances, the social situation, and the historical, institutional and environmental conditions relevant to the group or actor. In this paper, I will show that for the Chinese in Malaysia, attributes such as bloodline, phenotypical characteristics and language are regarded as core elements of Chinese identity. These are seen to be critical for in-group identification and for defining ethnic identity. Other attributes that are commonly associated with ethnic identity, such as language, customs festivals are seen as important but negotiable aspects of ethnic identity.

The Chinese in Malaysia: A Historical Overview

The unique ethnic composition of Malaysia makes it an interesting case study in ethnic relations. With the exception of Singapore, where the Chinese constitutes the majority, Malaysia is the only country where the immigrant Chinese makes up a significant community, over 34 percent of the population. In comparison, the Chinese in Thailand constitute only 10 percent of the population and in Indonesia, only 3 percent. This particular demographic distribution has had a significant impact on ethnic relations in Malaysia, not the least of which is the feeling among indigenous Malays that the Chinese will seize political power. The Malay distrust of Chinese economic power was, and still is, the main source of conflict between the two groups (Tan, 1982: 47). Similarly, given such a large voting bloc, politics in Malaysia has always been essentially communal and the government has, since independence, been a coalition of communal parties, with the Malay-based UMNO the dominant partner. A short history of Malaysia will help illuminate the factors that influence ethnic identity and ethnic relations in present-day Malaysia.

Although there is evidence of Chinese settlements in Malaysia in the fifteenth century (Yen, 2000), Chinese immigrants began moving to the Malay Peninsula in large numbers only in the nineteenth century (Freedman, 2000; Lee, 1998). They were driven by poverty and adverse conditions in China; namely, constant rebellion, floods, famine, and other social political calamities. They were drawn to better economic opportunities and socio-economic conditions in Southeast Asia, where British colonial expansion had created the demand for cheap labour. Most Chinese came from the southern provinces of Guangdong and Fujian, and spoke a multitude of dialects such as Hokkien, Teochew, Cantonese, Hakka and Hainanese. Many settled in the tin-rich states of Perak and Selangor, providing much of the labour, and later capital, for the tin mines. Others settled in the colonies of the Straits Settlements, Penang, Malacca and Singapore. Although subjected to harsh conditions and treatment during their voyage and arrival in Malaya, their numbers increased steadily, from 2069 in 1839 to 10,928 in 1850 (Ee, 1961). The Chinese population in

Malaya continued to grow due to large-scale migration and by 1911, there were 694,970 Chinese, constituting about 30 percent of the total population. By the mid-1950s, with the restrictive immigration policies after the war, the Chinese population had become fairly settled, with about 1.5 million Chinese, or about 37 percent of the population (Tey, 2002).

One of the features of British colonial rule was the "divide and rule" policy, wherein they segregated the local population based on racial categorization and "ethnic compartmentalization" (Stockwell, 1982: 55) such that each racial group performed a particular role or occupation in society. Significantly, this colonial legacy has had a strong impact on present-day ethnic relations in Malaysia, as it has in other Southeast Asian nation-states, because the "seeds of ethnic differentiation drawn along economic lines were . . . sown . . . by the British themselves" (Gambe, 1999: 77). Thus, upon independence in 1957, Malaysia was no more than the "construction of a departing colonial power" (Lian, 1997: 2), and one of the more prevalent issues that concerned the Chinese during that period was citizenship because many Chinese overseas, including those in Malaysia, had become "stateless" aliens because their citizenship status were "unclear" (see Suryadinata, 1985: 18–19). This also occurred at a time when nationalist sentiments among the Chinese overseas was becoming increasingly salient, and in Malaya, there was a strong desire to maintain their cultural identity that "stemmed primarily from powerful kinship ties and ethnicity" (Yen, 2000: 12).

The Federation of Malaya agreement in 1948 granted automatic citizenship to Malays, but not to non-Malays despite Malaya's *jus soli* citizenship policy (Tan, 2000). Citizenship for the Chinese was conditional and not a right, which implicitly marginalized the Chinese in Malaya and favoured the Malays, thus contributing to the emergence of a Chinese *ethnie*. Citizenship was "divisive and failed to cultivate a unifying nationality" (Lian, 1995: 96). The post-independent NEP (New Economic Policy) that was introduced in 1971 was supposed to achieve national unity through the proper distribution of wealth (Gomez, 2000). It was, however, arguably the final nail that cemented Malay *bumi* hegemony in all aspects of Malaysian life because it granted special concessions and privileges to Malays over all the other races (Tan, 2000). A new Malay middle class emerged and directly challenged the political and economic status of the Chinese, so much so that their position as citizens has become seriously eroded

(Lee, 1998; see also Suryadinata, 2000). The current state of ethnic relations in Malaysia has to be viewed against this background, taking into consideration that "both Malay and Chinese identities are influenced by the power relations between them and the national policies of the new state" (Tan, 2000: 448).

Being Chinese in Malaysia

Most of the Chinese informants in this study described their Chineseness in ascriptive terms. Phenotypical and genotypical (blood, bloodline) characteristics are often invoked in self-identification. To quote from some informants:

> I know I am Chinese by my skin colour. Yellow-skin, black hair, brown eyes. Tradition is man-made; it can change or be influenced. But not appearance. That does not change. Some Chinese are adopted by Indians, they speak Indian and may not consider themselves Chinese, but I think they are Chinese, because they look and are born of Chinese parents.
>
> I think the biological part comes first. I was born into a Chinese family, that is, a person whose parents are Chinese will be Chinese.
>
> You are Chinese because of your nature. You are born Chinese, your parents are Chinese, your roots are Chinese, and your blood is Chinese.

Informants refer to blood and bloodline, instead of cultural attributes, as the most important marker or criteria for ethnic identification. The emphasis on primordiality, rather than cultural attributes, as the central marker of identity is understandable. Living in close proximity to Indians and Malays, who are clearly of darker skin colour, phenotypical differences provide the first and most visible distinction from other ethnic groups. At another level, the use of primordial sentiments creates boundaries among groups, restricting the entry of outsiders and, to some extent, denying exit to insiders. As one informant noted,

> Many Indians in Malaysia are able to speak good Chinese and can act like Chinese. But, the blood itself is Indian. I will say, that no matter how, you can never change nature.

Informants emphasized that one cannot become Chinese, that one is born Chinese. In addition, a person who is Chinese will always be a Chinese, even if he or she does not speak the language, or practices another religion. Thus, at this level of discourse, identification is racial and is invoked to delineate the insider from the outsider, the "us" from the "them". Once a Chinese, always a Chinese, with or without the alleged cultural attributes of Chineseness, be it language, religion or customs. This clearly delineated boundary is reinforced by the data on intermarriage. The intermarriage rates in Malaysia, especially between the Chinese and Malays, is very low. Informants consider intermarriage to be undesirable and unacceptable. As one informant said,

> Chinese do not like to intermarry because they have to convert to Islam. Once you become a Muslim, your name will be changed, and your children later are also considered Muslims. Therefore, you become less and less Chinese in future.

> My parents will never agree to inter-ethnic marriage because of the burdens that every race carries; they are afraid this may corrupt the Chinese blood.

In fact, Chinese informants often describe inter-ethnic marriages in derogatory terms,

> Yes, the children will be *chup cheng* or mixed race. His blood will be *sia pun chi lai*, mixed-up. How can he be Chinese?

Thus, the informants maintain that children of mixed marriages cannot be considered Chinese. This emphasis on birth and blood implies categorical exclusion and exclusiveness, and is seen to contaminate the purity of Chinese blood. Almost all informants mentioned phenotypical characteristics and blood as the basis for ethnic identification. Other secondary attributes were also mentioned, but informants were quite adamant that the issue of blood was non-negotiable. As one informant puts it, "To me, skin colour and blood is number one, then there are traditions". Some of the more common indices mentioned are family names or Chinese name, Chinese values such as filial piety, Chinese festivals such as Chinese New year and *Qing Ming*, and traditions. When asked what makes them Chinese, some informants said,

> The way I was brought up, in a traditional Chinese family which observes a lot of Chinese tradition" *Qing Ming, bak chang* festivals. All Souls-Day. There are all Chinese traditions.

> I think the biological part comes first, being born of Chinese parents. Second is the practicing of Chinese culture. The food aspect, I think,

> is one thing that binds all Chinese. Food, I consider the most important. Certain Chinese traits, such as, family togetherness, practice of Chinese festivals, are also important. Religion will not define Chineseness. I would disqualify clothes, too. Chinese do not wear cheongsam anymore.

It is clear that while almost all informants agree on blood and parentage as defining characteristics of Chineseness, cultural attributes are more variable and negotiable. Some informants would insist that having a Chinese name is important; others do not think so. Some emphasize religion and customs, others argue that a Christian is still a Chinese. Still others point to the importance of the Chinese language while some claim that being English-educated and not knowing Mandarin does not make them any less Chinese.

The point is that these indices are not shared by all, or even by most Chinese in Malaysia, and are regarded as negotiable. Again, this view is reinforced by their attitude towards adopted children and children of intermarriage. One informant noted,

> For instance, if a Chinese adopts an Indian and he learns things Chinese. He may speak Mandarin, knows Chinese culture, have Chinese practices, but he still not Chinese (at this point, informant showed me his arm and pointed out its color). It is difficult to say who he is, to put it crudely; we call him *ban fun*, half-breed.

It can be argued that what may be considered "traditional" markers of ethnic identification (language, education, and religious affiliations) have lost their homogenizing influence among the Chinese in modern-day Malaysia. There is heterogeneity of religious beliefs and language competences that are now open to negotiation, interpretation and mediation, and are ambiguous rather than defining characteristics. Of course, the assumption that the Chinese community was once homogenous and is now heterogeneous may well be problematic. One can argue that the Chinese in Malaysia were never really homogenous to begin with. In the past, for example, the Chinese were divided along dialect, locality, regional and occupational lines. It is probably true that there were more factors holding the Chinese together in the past, factors such as territorial origin, historical consciousness and cultural identity, compared to present times, where it appears that only the principles of birth, blood and descent are of consequence. At another level, birth, blood and descent are more individual and family oriented rather than community-based. Thus, in terms of ethnic identification in Malaysia, it can be argued that there is greater reliance on family rather than on the community;

many informants place great emphasis on the family. There is also a great deal of cynicism that community and political organizations, such as the Malaysian Chinese Association—a junior partner in the Barisan National coalition government—truly represent the interests of the Chinese community as a whole.

I suggest that cultural attributes are not critical to the individual in his or her ethnic identification, and that different individuals—given different socialization experiences—draw on different attributes such as language, customs or religion to define their identity. Other than blood and descent, there is little agreement on what constitutes Chinese culture or identity.

Interestingly, while there is not much of a consensus in defining Chinese identity, there is a broad consensus on what constitutes the "outgroup". For the Chinese, the primordial sentiments of blood and descent form the basis for exclusion. Thus, a Chinese in Malaysia is Chinese because he is neither Malay nor Indian. Members of each of these races have different blood and look different. At the same time, something that surfaces in almost all the interviews is that a Chinese is not Malay because Malays are Muslim who cannot eat pork.

Religion and Food as Ethnic Markers

In Malaysia, religion and food become important markers for ethnic differentiation. In order to understand this, it is necessary to provide some background details. All ethnic Malays in Malaysia are Muslims. Religion was, and continues to be, a central issue in the relations among ethnic groups, and in how different groups react to the state. Islam is the official religion although the Constitution recognizes freedom of worship for other religions. In Malaysia, the ethnic identity of the Malays is equated with religious affiliation to Islam. In fact, Article 160 of the Federal Constitution states that a "Malay" is defined as a person who professes the religion of Islam, habitually speaks the Malay language, and conforms to Malay customs. Siddique (1981: 77) however, argues that the Constitutional definition of "Malayness" sets a "territorial boundary to the definition of Malay—hence an Indonesian who is Muslim, speaks Malay, and observes Malay customs would not be a Malay under the constitutional definition unless he fulfils the residence requirement . . .".

In Islam, like in Judaism, there are food prohibitions, or taboos. Food regarded as *halal* is deemed acceptable for consumption while some food is regarded as *haram*. While there are many types of food that are regarded as *haram*, the symbol of pork takes on special significance in that the Chinese eat pork often, while the Malays abhor it. Food thus takes on significance as a marker of differentiation. Informants, both Chinese and Malay, often refer to the notion of "makan sama tak makan sama", translated literally as "eat together and cannot eat together". Food restrictions mean that Chinese and Malays very often do not eat at the same table. For more fundamentalist Muslims, it is not simply the food but even the sharing of utensils that is taboo. In interviews with Chinese, the practice of not eating together often surfaces in discussions of ethnic relations.

> We eat in different restaurants. Malays don't usually eat with Chinese because they eat halal food. They even have different stalls in the same canteen.

> Yes, we take pork, they don't. When Malays come to your house, they will not touch your cups, plates, it is to that extent. We have to be careful with food. We cannot carelessly invite Malays for a meal. You also have to say things more carefully, for example, do not talk about pigs in front of Malays.

Barth (1969) suggests that ethnic boundaries, rather than the intrinsic culture within an ethnic group, are the key feature of ethnic identification. If ethnicity is only about the cultural attributes within an ethnic group, than it is unlikely that food, or the consumption of pork, can be invoked as a distinctive ethnic marker. In Malaysia, however, the consumption of pork is central to boundary maintenance; a Chinese consumes pork, as opposed to a Malay who does not. Tan (2000: 453) for example, notes that "eating pork is perceived by both Chinese and Malays as ethnically significant". Food consumption is a "cultural symbol" that draws the social boundary between the Malays and the Chinese. In fact, food is such a key symbol of ethnic differentiation that many Malays define the Chinese as "makan babi", that is, "people who eat pork".

Often, this distinction takes on political overtones. For example, when PAS, a fundamentalist Islamic political party won elections in the state of Kelantan, one of its proposals was to ban the sale of pork in the whole state. This caused uproar among the Chinese in the state as they viewed it as an attempt to impose Islamic values on non-Malays in the state. It should, however, be noted that other than the consumption of pork and *halal* food, a few informants suggested that food is a symbol of hybridity that has resulted in close cultural contact between the Malays and the Chinese.

> Food is the thing that unites all Malaysians. I feel at home eating Malay or Chinese food. The Malays also eat Chinese food, but they make sure it is *halal*. Malays eat chilli and *ikan bilis*. But now, we Chinese are eating more chillis too. It is all *champor* (mixed). We Chinese eat mushrooms, the Malays don't know how to eat mushrooms. Now, my Malay friend has learnt to eat Chinese food and guess what she says, *sedap* (delicious).

Even among these informants, however, there is acknowledgement that Muslims draw the line on the consumption of pork. Like food taboos, religion is a significant marker of ethnic boundaries. A Malay is a Malay because he is Muslim, a Chinese is a Chinese because he is not. There are, of course, some Chinese who have converted to Islam; however, these people are viewed with suspicion by both Malays and Chinese. They are said to have *masuk Malayu*, or "enter Malayness". Some Chinese used the term *jïp huan*, a Hokkien term that is extremely derogatory and can be literally translated, "to enter barbarism". People who become Muslims are regarded to be denying their culture but as expected, when asked whether they are still Chinese, the answer is affirmative, as they have Chinese blood and were born of Chinese parents. Among the Malays, they often question the motive for conversion, that is, they question if they have converted primarily for economic or other reasons.

It is important to emphasize that religion becomes a key symbol of differentiation partly because of its political overtones, rather than as something that is intrinsic in the religion. Politics in Malaysia, especially among the Malays, has religious overtones. For example, Islamic fundamentalist political parties such as PAS, have used the religion card to obtain votes. They propose to make the *Syariah* court the highest court of law in Malaysia and Islamic laws the primary source of Malaysian jurisprudence. More radical groups call for the implementation of Islamic law for the whole country, including to non-Muslims. PAS was able to win power in the state of Kelantan, and Trengganu in the last election, by championing Islam. This stance is very attractive to the Malays in these states who have strong roots in rural and village life. The ruling Malay political party, UMNO, has to meet this threat while simultaneously balancing the demands of Malay-Muslims and the rights of the 56 percent of the population made up of Chinese, Indians and other non-Malays. As Nagata (1995: 170) argues, "although Malaysia is not an Islamic state, Islam is the official religion, and an underpinning of the cultural and political dominance of the Malays". Siddique (1981: 80) suggests that "religion has been used to legitimate [sic] Malay political hegemony". In this sense, religious issues enter the daily life of the Chinese, at both the individual and communal levels. As one informant said,

> We are very conscious of politics. I talked about it since I was very young. Politics is ethnic based. My parents are in the civil service, they complain about the lack of promotion. We hear it at home. Even if you are top of your class, you can't go anywhere. There is a kind of anger that they (the Malays) have the easy way out.

What is evident from the interviews with informants is, at the same time, an attempt by many informants to separate the political and communal from personal life. At one level, in relation to politics, Malay special rights, Islam and pork, the Malays are conceptualized as a category. They are not viewed as people of flesh and blood, but rather, as a homogenized Other, an entity that discriminates against the Chinese, and a group to be wary of. In daily life and in interactions with other ethnic groups, however, various strategies are employed to deal with the business of daily life in a multiracial society. As some informants said,

> I can mix well with Malays. I can think like them and understand them. But when it come to core things, like religion, it is more difficult.

> With the Malays, I switch language to make the person feel welcome, to have a sense of kinship. Chinese hawkers use Malay to gain customers and in other business, it is the same. The Malay shopkeeper would use 'Ah Soh' or 'Ah Moi'. Even among professionals, we switch languages. Moreover, there are Malay expressions like *lepak*, loafing. It is a Malay word, but everyone knows what it means.

> I do enjoy mixing with Malays. I have to warm up to them. It took some time before they took me seriously. Because Malays are very communal, if you go out with them, eat with them, you can become close friends.

> My husband's brother's wife is Malay. My husband's brother, now he is a Muslim. At first, my mother-in-law didn't like it, but later; she found that the Malay was a kind-hearted girl. What matters most is the internal beauty; she is kind and helpful, so eventually, my mother-in-law permitted.

Most studies on ethnic relations in Malaysia tend to focus on the macro level, influenced by broader political issues involving the state and policies towards ethnic groups. From such a vantage point, one sees two homogenized and fundamentally essentialized groups in conflict with each other. For example, Tan (2000: 373) has sought to invoke the central role of the state in his analysis of the (mis)management of ethnic identities in Indonesia and Malaysia. He argues that "ethnicity is used as a means to mobilize the *bumi* majority", thus, cementing the domination of Malay majority rights over minority ones along ethnic lines under the guise of "state policy".

Such an analysis of ethnic relations and identity in Malaysia ignores individuals' subjective understanding of their identity and how they negotiate that identity in the discourse of everyday life. If we also examine the situation at the micro level, we see different interactional patterns that are based on personal inter-ethnic experiences. There are clearly those who express anger at the discrimination, whether it is the quota system for university places, inability to get promoted at the work place, or the 10–20 percent additional discounts that are given to Malays when they purchase homes. Others view the policies as necessary to raise the living standards of Malays and ensure ethnic harmony in Malaysia. Still others enjoy interacting with the Malays and have many Malay friends. Some are reticent about discussing sensitive ethnic problems in public, yet others intermarry. One informant sums it up, "Yes, there is discrimination at the national level, but in daily situations, I haven't come across any".

In the study of ethnic relations in Malaysia, it is, therefore, important to examine the problem from two separate perspectives—at the individual or micro level, where people go about strategizing the business of everyday life; and at the macro, national or political level, where ethnic relations are dealt with on a communal basis. I have argued elsewhere (Chan and Tong, 1995: 8) that any realistic model in studies of ethnic identity has to take into account the "plausibility of dynamic interactions as well as mutual and reciprocal influence" between the minority and majority groups, wherein the global, the national, the local, the macro, meso and micro all have to be considered as important variables in the maintenance or differentiation of ethnic identification (see also Tong and Chan, 2001). Analysing ethnic identity and ethnic relations of the Chinese in Malaysia is no different in the sense that micro and macro issues need to be considered in the analysis. This approach is also advocated by Shamsul

(1998: 20–21) in his "two social reality" approach to studying identity in Malaysia, although it is explained in a slightly different manner. He makes the distinction between the "authority-defined" (that is, macro) and "everyday-defined" (that is, micro) identities of people, arguing that the two social reality approach, which captures both the macro and micro levels, enables the analyst to listen to the "voices of the social actors . . . about their experience in contrast to the authority-defined one", so that a more balanced account is achieved. This will become clearer in the following discussion on language, education, and economic policies in Malaysia.

Language and Education

Language and educational issues are important in understanding ethnic identity and ethnic relations in Malaysia. During the colonial period, education was segregated along ethnic lines. English education was restricted to the upper class and urbanites, while Malay education was only available up to the elementary level and was provided mainly for rural Malays. The Chinese were left to fend for themselves and Chinese schools, set up by voluntary associations and clan groups, were oriented towards China, with their curriculum influenced by political developments in China. Similarly, Tamil schools were oriented towards India.

As British colonial rule ended, the first elected government of the Federation in 1955 proposed a National Education Policy. The basic aim was to foster national unity through a common educational system for all races and promote equal educational opportunities regardless of race or socio-economic status. The new educational policy proposed in the Razak Report, however, resulted in objections from some Chinese community groups, especially regarding the position of Chinese language and education. There was a perception in many quarters that Chinese vernacular education was not being safeguarded, especially among the "Chinese cultural nationalists", that is, the Chinese-educated elites, who generally saw education as one of the main channels for the promotion of a "pure" Chinese identity (Tan, 1997: 112). Moreover, after World War II, there was a general "reorientation away from China" by both the English educated and Chinese educated; most of them believed that as citizens of Malaya, they should be allowed to maintain their cultural identity through the preservation of the Chinese language (Lee, 1997: 84). As Tan (1997) has argued, Chinese Malaysians are very united as a community against state policies that discriminate against them as a group, such as quotas placed on Chinese entry to universities, and public sector employment. As such, the Chinese are extremely united about matters that concern their common and collective interests in the state.

In 1967, the National Language Bill was introduced to make Malay the sole official language. This was stipulated in the 1957 Federal Constitution, that "the national language shall be the Malay language" but it was provided in Article 152 that "for a period of ten years after Merdeka Day and thereafter until Parliament otherwise provides, the English language may be used in both Houses of Parliament, in the Legislative Assembly of every state, and for all other official purposes". Again, this led to objections from certain quarters of the Chinese population. The Chinese Guilds and Associations sent a memorandum to the Prime Minister demanding that Chinese be recognized as an official language. In the end, the 1967 National Language Bill accommodated some of the Chinese demands by affirming the right of the Federal and State governments to use the language of any other community for the translation of official documents or communications despite the stipulation of Malay as the national language. Conversely, this led to unhappiness among some Malay groups and several demonstrations were held. In 1970, English primary schools were converted to Malay-medium schools. By 1980, Malay became the sole medium of instruction in all secondary schools, although vernacular schools were still permitted at the primary level. Malay was also introduced as the medium of instruction at the university level.

Language and educational issues were and continue to be sources of tension and conflict among the different ethnic groups. As Tan (1982: 45) noted, "In Malaysia, many Chinese are still anxious about the eventual status of Chinese education. The increasing use of quotas to allocate scholarship and places of study in the university further creates uneasiness among the Chinese". Many Chinese also feel that a Malaysian education does not commensurate with economic opportunities because of the granting of preferential treatment for the *bumiputra* population.

While this view is borne out by some of the informants, the data actually show more varied responses. In fact, various strategies are used by the Chinese to deal with national educational policies. For example, while a majority of the Chinese now send their children to Malay-medium national schools, a significant 15 percent of Chinese parents have children in Chinese-medium schools who speak and read Chinese as a first language. Informants gave various reasons for this. Some said that a Chinese education is vital for the child to learn about Chinese culture. Others noted that because of the *bumiputra* policy, there are few opportunities for the Chinese in the Malaysian educational system. Some of these parents send the children overseas to Australia, the United Kingdom or Singapore for further education. Others prefer to send their children to English-medium private colleges. Overall, the vast majority of the Chinese send their children to Malay-language medium school, often due to economic considerations. Many parents, however, continue to provide some form of Chinese education. Some parents send their children for night classes in Chinese while others engage tutors to teach the children at home.

The same pattern is observed in language use. For those Chinese who attended Malay schools, they tend to use Malay in public or when dealing with Malays, both at work and in daily interactions. In the home, however, the language used is almost always Chinese, either Mandarin or dialects.

> Among my friends, I use Mandarin and Hokkien. At home we use Hokkien. I use Malay when I talk to Malays, or in school when I speak to my teachers.
>
> My education is in Malay, but I normally converse in English. My parents are multilingual; they speak Malay, English and Chinese. When we mix with Malays, we always use Malay, but at home, it is either English or Chinese.

It has been suggested that the adoption of the language of the dominant group and the extent of its use is often indicative of cultural assimilation, since language acquisition is accompanied by the adoption of cultural values as well as entry into the social institutions of the society. What the data suggest, however, is that the Chinese adopt different strategies when it comes to language and education. Some send their children to Malay schools, yet continue with the learning of Chinese at home, while others send their children to Chinese schools. In Malaysia, bilingualism among the Chinese is growing, with different languages used in different social situations. In the home environment, both Mandarin and dialects are frequently used, especially when communicating with parents or older relatives. Outside the home, when dealing with other Chinese, Mandarin is the common lingua franca. When dealing with Malay officials, when in school, or in daily interactions with other ethnic groups, including Malays and Indians, there is a need to use Malay.

There is a strong desire among many Chinese parents for their children to be exposed to some Chinese education. Yet, due to the problem of affordability, many send their children to Malay-medium schools. As one informant said, "After my generation, you have to know Malay to survive in Malaysia, that is why I send my children to Malay schools". Thus, the issue of language and education in Malaysia is constantly changing. In the struggle to come to terms with the changing political and global environment, language and education continues to be a contentious issue. For example, from interviews with some Malays, it surfaces that they do not regard the Chinese language as a threat to Malay society and culture. For them, the real challenge is the English language. In my interview with Malay respondents, many felt that the Chinese should be allowed to retain their language as it is their lingua franca. They felt, however, that the increasing emphasis on the English language will lead to greater numbers of young Malays speaking only English, thus, leading them to lose their cultural identity as Malays.

The Economy and Bumiputraism

Communal issues dominate Malaysian politics. From 1955 until the most recent elections in 2004, non-communal political parties have not had much success. The government itself, the Barisan Nasional, is a coalition of communal parties with UMNO, the Malaysian Chinese Association and the Malaysian Indian Congress as the dominant partners. In the opposition camp, PAS intends to turn Malaysia into an Islamic state, while the Democratic Action Party champions Chinese causes to gain political support from the community.[1]

[1] See Freedman (2000) and Kukreja (2002) for discussions on public discourse and how that public discourse is "ethnically entrenched". Lee (1998: 29), however, argues that because there is a significant proportion of "poor Chinese", several politicians in Malaysia have sought to present political issues along economic and class lines instead of communal ones.

Ingrained in national politics are the special rights of the Malays or *bumiputraism*, which refers to the special rights of the indigenous population, introduced after the racial riots of 1969 (Osman-Rani, 1990). In the past, and even today to some extent, the Malaysian economy is bifurcated along ethnic lines. The Chinese were dominant in the commercial sectors while the Malays, who were concentrated in rural villages, occupied the agricultural sector. While the Chinese were involved in the private sector, the Malays were concentrated in the civil service, police and military. This structural differentiation has often led to communal conflicts. The picture today, however, is not so clear. For example, an interesting development of the 2000 national elections was the perception that the ability to hold on to power by the then Prime Minister Mahathir and the National Front was due to overwhelming Chinese support, with Malay votes dropping drastically due to the incarceration of the former Deputy Prime Minister, Anwar Ibrahim, who enjoyed significant Malay support. Similarly, the commonly-held notion that the Chinese lived in urban areas, particularly in large cities such as Kuala Lumpur, Johore Bahru and Penang, and that the Malays lived in rural villages may be true in the past but is now no longer true. With rapid economic and urban development, many Malays have migrated to the cities. Arguably, even in the cities, there are still ethnic enclaves with areas such as Klang and Petaling Jaya predominantly Chinese while townships such as Shah Alam have more Malays. The rural–urban divide between the Malays and the Chinese has declined, with the exception of the states on the east coast.

The New Economic Policy (NEP) formulated after the 1969 race riots was to "eradicate poverty among all Malaysian and to restructure Malaysian society so that the identification of race with economic functions and geographical location is reduced and eventually eliminated" (Malaysia Plan, 1979: 7). Although Tan (1982: 44) is correct in arguing that instead of eradicating ethnic specialization, the use of race to restructure the distribution of resources has led to a reinforcement of racial differences, economic restructuring has led to the rise of a new class of Malay business elite in Malaysian society to compete with Chinese business owners. In my interviews with some of these businessmen, I sensed a new confidence among the Malay elite. Some, in fact, question the need to continue with the NEP; they commented that they can do just as well in business without special rights. The rise of this new elite has led to economic differentiation within the Malay community. For example, the 1974 peasant unrests in Baling were not directed against the Chinese, but against the Malay elites. Many poorer Malays resented the fact that a small group of Malays was becoming rich at the expense of other Malays. Thus, Cham (1975: 457) notes that in identifying the locus of political power in Malaysia, one has to be aware of class differences within Malay society. It is true that the Malays fill the leadership roles in the country; however, these are certainly not the ordinary Alis and Ahmads, but the Tuns, Tunkus, Datos and Tan Sris.

The Chinese response to the special rights has also been varied. Some informants feel that they are discriminated by the state. At the same time, many Chinese, especially businessmen, enter into complementary relationships with the Malay. Chinese businessmen, in order to protect their interests, have formed alliances with leading Malay businessmen and the political elite, who receive large remuneration packages by serving as directors in Chinese businesses. Chinese and Malay elites can be seen as subgroupings of different ethnic categories that assume complementary roles in the local environment (see Tong and Chan, 2000). Alternative strategies are adopted by the less well-off Chinese. For example, many become hawkers and owners of small businesses given the limited opportunities in the public sector.

Conclusion

Most studies on ethnic identity and ethnic relations in Malaysia have focused on the macro issues of national politics and inter-group relations at the communal level. The analysis centres on majority–minority relations. From such a perspective, the picture that emerges is one of discrimination and tension among ethnic groups. This analysis is not incorrect but because it is confined to public and political discourse, it fails to provide a full picture of ethnic identity and ethnic relations in Malaysia. For example, many studies mention that the Chinese in Malaysia feel discriminated in terms of education, thus, they send their children overseas for further education. In reality, those who send their children overseas to study constitute only one percent of the total Chinese population. The majority of Chinese continue to live in Malaysia, and have to deal with the business of living in a Malay-dominated society. As I have demonstrated in this chapter, some parents send their children to private Chinese schools in Malaysia. Others send them to Malay-medium schools, but engage tutors at home or pay for night classes in Chinese. Others prefer to send their children to English-medium schools. Some parents make it a point to speak to their children only in Chinese at home to ensure that they have a bilingual education. The Chinese, therefore, espouse different strategies in overcoming the problem of discrimination in education. This is the fundamental thrust of this paper—to examine how the Chinese go about the business of everyday life, studying the various strategies used, and their individual perceptions of life in a multiracial society where the Malays form the dominant group, both in population size and power.

The literature on ethnic identity and group identification has tended to pose a binary opposition between voluntary (choice) on the other hand and involuntary (birth) on the other, between ascriptive identity and instrumental identity. The data on Malaysia suggest that this is not mutually exclusive. Rather, it may be more useful to view it as a continuum. In this paper, I have demonstrated that ethnicity has both primordial and situational dimensions. For the Chinese in Malaysia, phenotypical and genotypical characteristics are the basis for ethnic differentiation. Skin and hair colour, blood and descent, are seen as the defining features of Chineseness; that is, identity is ascriptive. Living in a multi-ethnic environment, these ascriptive markers act as the basis of identifying the "insider", and as boundary markers to exclude the "outsider". Once this primary, core, and to a degree, emotive, marker of ethnicity is satisfied, the data suggest that a multiple and negotiable conception of ethnic identity is invoked. Here, the expressions of identity(ies) are more instrumental, individualistic, autonomous and peripheral; thus, cultural attributes, including language, customs, festivals and dress become negotiable and situational. There is a greater degree of freedom, heterogeneity and fluidity. They are important but are not critical for defining ethnic identity. Thus, at the core, physical attributes, blood and descent are seen as central, non-negotiable, and based on emotional attachments. At the periphery, ethnic identity is flexible, contested and instrumental. Here, people display different identities in different situations, but without denying the first premise of Chinese identity. The presentation of ethnicity is multiple and plural, more individualistic and voluntary. It is argued that for the Chinese in Malaysia, their ethnicity is not based on a common set of cultural or sentimental attachments. There is a rootedness based on the ascriptive marker of descent, but there are also expressions of identity that are linked to personal experiences, different socializations, situational and environmental factors, and subjective interpretations; these allow an individual to choose between alternative courses of action in defining their identity.

This chapter problematizes the notion of Chineseness and Malayness. It argues that the Chinese do not form a homogenous, singular group of people who share the same beliefs or responses to government policies. Instead, they are fragmented, and what is "Chinese" is continually defined and redefined. Similarly, and this is just as important an analytical concept, there is also no such thing as a "homogeneous" host society, that is, a homogeneous Malay. Just as there are many types of Chineseness, there are also many kinds of Malayness.

Another key idea that emerges from the empirical data has to do with the strategies adopted by both the Chinese and the host society in dealing with and managing cultural contacts. In Malaysia, we observe how the Chinese negotiate the business of everyday living by adopting various strategies such as bilingualism, differentiating between the private and public spheres (for example, speaking Chinese at home and Malay at work), or forging alliances with the Malay elite in business. Embedded within a web of interlocking forces and influences, ethnic actors constantly adjust their postures, strategies and identities. In the process of strategizing, ethnicity is invoked and negotiated in the host society. What happens is that the immigrants bring with them their parent culture, which shapes their initial behaviour. In the process of living and surviving in the new host environment, however, the structural conditions of the local context will significantly shape their long term adaptation patterns, or what Yancy (1976) calls "emergent ethnicity". Immigrant culture and identity are rarely transplanted wholesale but are reproduced and produced, thus creating strategic advantages and adoption. Thus, during cultural contact, it is important to study the processual, emergent and transformative features of ethnic identity. Again, it is important to emphasize that this process is not a one-way process of immigrants reinventing a new identity. We must also analyse the changes that occur in the host society due to the influx of immigrant cultures; there is a symbiotic relationship between the immigrant and host society.

In the case of the Chinese in Malaysia, we have to take cognizance of the fact that there is not a singular response from the Chinese, but a variety of strategies—at group and even individual levels—to state policies. Race and ethnicity dominate public and political discourse in Malaysia. At the macro level, the Malays view the Chinese as a "homogenous" group and as a racial category. This perception of homogeneity can be seen in the ethnic stereotypes that emerges, such as "all Chinese are rich", "all Chinese are businessmen and are rich", or "the Chinese are always eating". In reality, the data collected suggest that the Chinese in Malaysia are a heterogeneous and fragmented community divided by dialect, regional, religious and political differences. It should be noted that the Chinese also view the Malays as a racial category with equally stereotypical ideas. Economic relations are often also seen in ethnic terms. In order to gain a better understanding of ethnic relations in Malaysia, it is necessary to distinguish the macro from the micro level analyses. Clearly, perceptions at the macro-level, in relation to Chinese reactions to government policies, racial quotas and special rights for the Malays, affect the Chinese. These political, economic and communal issues filter down to the level of everyday life, as they must. Interviews with informants clearly demonstrate how ethnic differences between the Chinese and the Malays feature in the daily interaction between the groups. The everyday interactions between the Chinese and the Malays, however, do not simply reflect the political and economic relations of conflict and competition between the two groups. As some of the informants noted,

> As a whole, there is discrimination in the sense of government policies, for example, in the sense of educational policies. But in daily situations, I have not come across any discrimination.

> Only when the Malays are seen as a group do we think about ethnic discrimination, but as an individual, I have no problems. My best friend in school was a Malay.

At the micro-level, the exigencies of daily life necessitate various strategies in dealing with members of other ethnic groups, and with members of the same group. This ensures some coherence in the course of everyday existence, whether it is in social interactions with the Malays, looking after the educational needs of children, or eating daily meals with Malays. I argue that these strategies are mediated by personal circumstances, and environmental conditions.

There is a tendency in studies of ethnic relations in Malaysia to conflate macro and micro analyses. I hope to have demonstrated that by distinguishing between the two levels of analysis, a more nuanced understanding of relations between the Chinese and Malays in Malaysian society is possible.

REFERENCES

Amyot, J. (1972) *The Chinese and National Integration in Southeast Asia*, Institute of Asian Studies Monograph. Bangkok: Chulalongkorn University.

Banks, M. (1996) *Ethnicity: Anthropological Constructions*. London: Routledge.

Barth, F. (1969) *Ethnic Groups and Boundaries: The Social Organization of Cultural Difference* London: Allen and Unwin.

Cham B. N. (1975) "Class and Communal Conflict in Malaysia", *Journal of Contemporary Asia* 5 (4): 446–61.

Chan, K. B. and C. K. Tong, (1995) "Modelling Culture Contact and Chinese Ethnicity in Thailand", *Southeast Asian Journal of Social Science* 23 (1): 1–12.

Cornell, S. and Hartmann, D. (1998) *Ethnicity and Race: Making Identities in a Changing World*. London: Pine Forge Press.

Ee, J. (1961) "Chinese Migration to Singapore, 1896–1941", *Journal of Southeast Asian History* 2: 33–52.

Eller, J. D. (1999) *From Culture to Ethnicity to Conflict*. Ann Arbor: University of Michigan Press.

Geertz, C. (1963) "The Integrative Revolution: Primordial Sentiments and Civil Politics in the New States", in C. Geertz, *The Interpretation of Cultures*. New York: Basic Books, pp. 255–310.

Freedman, A. (2000) "Chinese Overseas Acculturation in Malaysia and the Effects of Government Policy and Institutions", in Teresita Ang See, ed., *Intercultural Relations, Cultural Transformation and Identity*. Manila: Kaisa-Angelo King Heritage Center, pp. 457–481.

Gambe, A. (2000) *Overseas Chinese Entrepreneurship and Capitalist Development in Southeast Asia*. New York: St. Martin's Press.

Gomez, E. T. (2000) "In Search of Patrons: Chinese Business Networking and Malay Political Patronage in Malaysia", in K. B. Chan, ed., *Chinese Business Networks*. Singapore: Prentice Hall, pp. 207–223.

Goodman, D. S. G. (1997) "The Ethnic Chinese in East and Southeast Asia: Local Insecurities and Regional Concerns", CAPS Papers No. 17, Chinese Council of Advanced Policy Studies.

Gosling, P. (1983) "Changing Chinese Identities in Southeast Asia: An Introductory Review", in P. Gosling and L. Lim, eds., *The Chinese in Southeast Asia*. Singapore: Maruzen Asia, pp. 1–29.

Hutchinson, J. and A. D. Smith (1996) "Introduction", in J. Hutchinson and A. D. Smith, eds. *Ethnicity*. Oxford: Oxford University Press, pp. 3–16.

Issacs, H. (1975) "Basic Group Identity: The Idols of the Tribe", in N. Glazer and D. Moynihan, eds. *Ethnicity: Theory and Experience*. Cambridge: Harvard University Press, pp. 29–52.

Jenkins, R. (1977) *Rethinking Ethnicity: Arguments and Explorations*. London: Sage.

Kukreja, S. (2002) "Political Hegemony, Popular Legitimacy and the Reconstruction of the Ethnic Divide in Malaysia: Some Observations", *Crossroads: An Interdisciplinary Journal of Southeast Asian Studies* 16 (1): pp. 19–48.

Lee, K. H. (1997) "Malaysian Chinese: Seeking Identity in Wawasan 2020", in L. Suryadinata, ed. *Ethnic Chinese as Southeast Asians*. Singapore: Institute of Southeast Asian Studies, pp. 72–107.

———. (1998) "The Political Position of the Chinese in Post-independence Malaysia", in L. C. Wang and G. W. Wang, eds., *The Chinese Diaspora: Selected Essays*. Volume 2. Singapore: Times Academic Press, pp. 28–49.

Lian, K. F. (1997) "Introduction: Ethnic Identity in Malaysia and Singapore", *Southeast Asian Journal of Social Science* 25 (2): 1–6.

———. (1995) "Migration and the Formation of Malaysia and Singapore", in R. Cohen, ed., *The Cambridge Survey of World Migration*. Cambridge: Cambridge University Press, pp. 392–396.

McAlister, J. T. (1973) *Southeast Asia: The Politics of National Integration*. New York: Random House.

Nagata, J. (1995) "Chinese Custom and Christian Culture: Implications for Chinese Identity in Malaysia", in L. Suryadinata, ed., *Southeast Asian Chinese: The Socio-Cultural Dimension*. Singapore: Times Academic Press, pp. 166–201.

Okamura, J. (1981) "Situational Ethnicity", *Ethnic and Racial Studies* 4 (4): 452–465.

Osman-Rani, H. (1990) "Economic Development and Ethnic Integration: The Malaysian Experience", *Sojourn* 5 (1): 1–34.

Ossapan, P. (1979) "The Chinese in Thailand", in L. Dhiravegin, ed., *Reader on Minorities in Thailand*. Bangkok: Phraephittaya.

Shamsul, A. B. (1998) "Debating about Ethnicity in Malaysia: A Discourse Analysis", in Z. Ibrahim, ed., *Cultural Contestations: Mediating Identities in a Changing Malaysian Society*. London: ASEAN Academic Press, pp. 17–50.

Skinner, G. W. (1963) "The Thailand Chinese: Assimilation in a Changing Society". Lecture presented at the Thai Council of Asia Society.

Siddique, S. (1981) "Some Aspects of Malay-Muslim Ethnicity in Peninsula Malaysia", *Contemporary Southeast Asia* 3 (1): 76–87.

Stockwell, A. J. (1982) "The White Man's Burden and Brown Humanity: Colonialism and Ethnicity in British Malaya", *Southeast Asian Journal of Social Science* 10 (1): 44–68.

Suryadinata, L. (1985) "Government Policies towards the Ethnic Chinese: A Comparison between Indonesia and Malaysia", *Southeast Asian Journal of Social Science* 13 (2): 15–28.

———. (2000) "Ethnic Chinese and the Nation-state in Southeast Asia", in Teresita Ang See, ed., *Intercultural Relations, Cultural Transformation and Identity*. Manila: Kaisa-Angelo King Heritage Center, pp. 308–327.

Tan C. B. (1982) "Ethnic Relations in Malaysia", in David Wu, ed., *Ethnic Relations and Ethnicity in a City State: Singapore*. Hong Kong: Maruzen Asia, pp. 37–61.

———. (1997) "Chinese Identities in Malaysia", *Southeast Asian Journal of Social Science* 25 (2): 103–116.

———. (2000) "Ethnic Identities and National Identities: Some Examples from Malaysia", *Identities* 6 (4): 441–480.

Tan, E. (2000) "Ghettoization of Citizen-Chinese?: State Management of Ethnic Chinese Minority in Indonesia and Malaysi,", in Teresita Ang See, ed., *Intercultural Relations, Cultural Transformation and Identity*. Manila: Kaisa-Angelo King Heritage Center, pp. 370–412.

Tey, N. P. (2002) "The Changing Demographic Situation of Malaysian Chinese", in L. Suryadinata, ed., *Ethnic Chinese in Singapore and Malaysia*. Singapore: Times Academic Press, pp. 45–66.

Tong, C. K. and K. B. Chan (2000) "Rethinking Assimilation and Ethnicity: The Chinese in Thailand", in Tong C. K. and K. B. Chan, eds., *Alternate Identities: The Chinese of Contemporary Thailand*. Singapore: Times Academic Press, Singapore, pp. 9–40.

———. (2001) "One Face, Many Masks: The Singularity and Plurality of Chinese Identity", *Diaspora* 10 (3): 361–390.

Van de Berghe (1978) "Race and Ethnicity: A Sociobiological Perspective", *Ethnic and Racial Studies* 1 (4): pp. 401–411.

Wang, G. W. (1999) "Chineseness: The Dilemmas of Place and Practice", in G. Hamilton, ed., *Cosmopolitan Capitalists: Hong Kong and the Chinese Diaspora at the End of the 20th Century*. Seattle: University of Washington Press, pp. 118–134.
Yao, S. (1987) "Ethnic Boundaries and Structural Differentiation: An Anthropological Analysis of the Straits Chinese in Nineteenth Century Singapore", *Sojourn* 2 (2): 209–230.
Yen, C. H. (2000) "Historical Background", in K. H. Lee and C. B. Tan, eds., *The Chinese in Malaysia*. Oxford: Oxford University Press, pp. 1–36.

THE POLITICAL AND ECONOMIC MARGINALIZATION OF TAMILS IN MALAYSIA*

Lian Kwen Fee

A substantial proportion of the Indian population in Malaysia is descended from low-caste South Indian Tamils of a peasant background. Landless and debt-ridden, they were virtual serfs of the landlords for whom they worked as farm labourers. Thousands migrated to Malaya in the late nineteenth and early twentieth centuries to work in rubber plantations and on public works, to escape a life of poverty and servitude. They were recruited in several ways—as indentured labour, by estate *kanganies*, or through a subsidized scheme organized by the government that guaranteed their repatriation. Fluctuations in the world demand for rubber and the limited-term basis on which such labour was employed ensured that these Tamil migrant workers could only be transient. Between 1925 and 1957, the number of returning migrants exceeded 80 percent of total immigration (Sandhu, 1969: 158). In the colonial economy, they constituted a captive labour force that earned the lowest wages among all ethnic groups, with practically no opportunity for alternative employment. The Depression of the early 1930s marked a decline in the flow of Indian migrants. With the Indian government's ban on assisted emigration in 1938 and the disruption caused by the Japanese Occupation, Indian immigration to the Peninsula virtually dried up. Those who remained in Malaya faced a period of uncertainty between 1950 and 1970. Restrictions on citizenship eligibility, their ignorance of procedures, the strength of ties with their relatives and villages in India, and uncertain economic opportunities in Malaya contributed to their anxiety about whether they should remain in Malaya or return to India.

In the post-independence years, various writers have documented the political and economic marginality of the South Indian population

* This chapter was previously published in *Asian Studies Review* 26: 3 (2002).

in Malaysia. In 1979, it was estimated that 60 to 70 percent of all Indian households lived below the poverty line of RM$700 (Insan, 1989: 2). A national study conducted by the government in 1973 (Murad, cited in Colletta, 1975: 89) concluded that rural children, especially those from the plantation environment, were underachievers and early leavers, and acquired jobs with low socio-economic status. Due to the small size of the Indian population and its geographic dispersion, its political representation both in parliament and in the government is weak (Snodgrass, 1980: 23). The Malayan Indian Congress (MIC) was only included in the ruling Alliance government on sufferance (Muzaffar, 1993; 220). In the first federal elections held in 1955, the Alliance could have easily won without MIC support. MIC candidates won in Malay majority constituencies only because of the help of the United Malays Organisation (UMNO), the dominant partner in the Alliance.

In this paper, I look into the possible reasons for the continued economic marginalization and political subordination of the Tamil community in Malaysia. The incorporation of the Tamil population into Malaysian society was, and continues to be, a protracted process compared to that of other immigrant communities such as the Chinese. The Tamils are at best only partially integrated. Historically, this may be attributed to their lower-caste background, their maintenance of strong ties with their villages of origin, their concentration within a plantation economy that blocks mobility through its labour practices and recruitment, and the essentially transient nature of migrant labour. A part-proletarian and part-peasant society has now been transformed into what may best be described as a "lumpenproletariat" in the major towns and cities of Peninsular Malaysia.

Burawoy's (1976) concept of a migrant labour system draws attention to the uncertain status and economic marginality of migrant workers, and the coincidence of race with economic function. One of the major foundations of British colonial rule and the colonial state in Malaya was the construction of an ethnic division of labour that served to reinforce the ethnic consciousness of the colonized population. This was given political expression after independence in the development of the consociational state, an arrangement that ensured the unequal sharing of power among ethnic communities. The formula of coalition rule was first adopted by the Alliance government after independence and was expanded into the Barisan Nasional after 1970. As the consociational state operates on the basis of communalism and patronage, the politicization of Malaysian society inevitably led to ethnic polarization. The MIC began as a political party led by North Indian professionals who were inspired by Indian nationalism and the fight for independence. The Tamilization of local Indian politics through the MIC in the mid-1950s and the appearance of caste politics in the 1970s are direct consequences of a consociational polity that both drives ethnicization and is, in turn, driven by it. The intended effect is the continued subordination of the South Indian population through patronage politics, first in the estates and now in urban squatter settlements.

The Migrant Labour System: Colonial and Post-Colonial Transformations

The Tamils are the dominant element in the Indian population of Malaysia. Their proportion varied from around 90 percent of the Indian population in the Peninsula in the 1920s to around 80 percent after World War II (Arasaratnam, 1979: 44–48), and has remained stable since. Many Tamils are of both working-class and lower-caste origin. The 1931 Census of Madras state recorded that more than one-third of the emigrants were from the untouchable caste (*Adi-dravidas*) and a conglomerate depressed caste, the former being landless labourers (Arasaratnam, 1979: 25). The remainder included higher-caste land-owning agriculturalists. Virtually indebted for life to the landlords who owned their labour, the only escape for the labourers was emigration (Sandhu, 1969: 40). To the British colonial administration and companies, low-caste South Indian peasants were most suited to the light repetitive tasks of plantation work (Sandhu, 1969: 56). They were malleable and easy to manage, and unlikely to pose the kind of problems the British were experiencing with the increasing number of Chinese in the Peninsula. Indeed, colonial officials believed that the growing Chinese influence could be checked by increasing Indian immigration (Sandhu, 1969: 58). Throughout the period in which Indian immigration to Malaya was supported, until the ban was imposed in 1938, South Indian labour was essentially transient. The average stay of the labourers prior to the 1930s was three to five years (Stenson, 1980: 24). During the prolonged depression of 1930–33, the Indian Immigration Fund was used for the first time to repatriate nearly a quarter of a million redundant labourers (Sandhu, 1969: 106).

The plantations did not attract the Malay peasant population, which was economically more self-sufficient and not inclined to work under regimented conditions. Neither were they successful in attracting the Chinese because the latter had alternative sources of livelihood, and if available for plantation work, they demanded higher wages for their labour. Hence, the stabilization of a cheap, expendable and transient Indian labour force was indispensable to its proletarianization. Selvaratnam (1984: 284) asserts that European plantations, with the support of the colonial administration, operated a coercive labour system aimed at total control over its workers in both work and non-work situations. One noteworthy feature of such a system of plantation labour, Selvaratnam continues, was that its part-coercive and part-paternalistic practices ensured that Tamil labour provided a captive workforce, with few opportunities to break out into alternative employment. The plantation houses provided Tamil migrants with housing, food, medical facilities and a rudimentary education in the vernacular, all of which served to reinforce their dependence on their employer.

In this early phase, Indian labour neither belonged to a wage-earning class nor was it permanently bonded slave labour. This is an issue that deserves some attention.

Baxstrom (2000: 65) describes the situation of Tamil workers in the plantations of colonial Malaya as that of peasant workers forced to survive in a system of wage labour. For the plantations to succeed, their labour needed to be forcibly extracted until they were fully proletarianized. On the other hand, Stoler (1995: 6) points to accounts of plantation systems throughout the world, including contemporary Southeast Asia, which argue that plantations have rarely reproduced the conditions for their existence by transforming a particular group into a fully-fledged proletariat. More commonly, this has been achieved by allowing or enforcing the self-sufficiency of these workers, through the allocation of land for subsistence cultivation. During the 1930s depression in Malaya, when many Tamils were unemployed or destitute, it was suggested that they be given plots to grow their own food. This was strongly opposed by the plantations, which preferred repatriation because of a fear that self-sufficiency would provide the workers with leverage in any future wage bargaining (Stenson, quoted in Ramachandran, 1994: 98). For the same reason, the appeals from the National Union of Plantation Workers (NUPW) to plantation managements to sell surplus land to estate workers of long service at reduced prices in the 1950s and 1960s were rejected. Colonial economic policy as well as the citizenship policy of the independent Alliance government as recently as the early 1970s simply worked against the incorporation of Tamil labour into Malaysian society. For this and other reasons that will be dealt with below, it is my contention that the concept of a migrant labour system is particularly useful in understanding the situation of Tamil labour in Malaysia.

By the mid-1920s the Chinese population showed clear signs of being a permanently settled community, as more women and the families of immigrants arrived, and as the proportion of local-born Chinese increased. The Indians, however, were less likely to settle in Malaya, for several reasons. First of all, it was easier, faster and less expensive for Indians to return to their homeland than it was for the Chinese to do so (Smith, 1964: 176). Secondly, political conditions in India and China encouraged the Indians to return home but deterred the Chinese from doing so. The depression in the 1930s drove more Indians back to India than Chinese to China, and independence in India in 1947 precipitated another exodus of Indians from Malaya (Smith, 1964: 182). The communist victory in the civil war in China in 1949 effectively eliminated the option for the Chinese in Malaya, particularly the China-born, to return to China. Thirdly, the overwhelming majority of the Indian population—more than 80 percent between 1911 and 1931—consisted of Tamils who were mainly employed in estate agriculture (Beeman, 1985:, 26). The Chinese were culturally and linguistically more diverse than the Indian population, and were involved in a wider range of occupations in not only urban but also rural areas. Ethnic and occupational diversity suggests that the Chinese were more likely to settle permanently in Malaya than were the Indians. Finally, in examining the census reports of the period, Beeman (1985: 40–41) found that among the estate population, the Indians had a higher proportion of females than the Chinese. Indian workers with families were unlikely to move off the estates in search of better working conditions, in contrast to Chinese workers who were male, single and highly mobile. They were, indeed, a captive labour force.

From the preceding discussion, it can be inferred that the Indian workforce, at least prior to World War II, constituted what Beeman (1985: 25) describes as a migrant labour system, whereas the Chinese workforce was on its way to becoming a permanently settled community in Malaya. Moreover, because the Indians were primarily involved in one sector of the economy—the plantation rubber industry, which neither Malays nor Chinese were interested in seeking employment in—and confined to rural enclaves, they did not pose a threat to the two major ethnic groups (Abraham, 1997: 150). They were regarded as a peripheral community that did not even have the potential to hold the balance of power. It is my view that in order to understand the position of the South Indian population in Malaysia today, the concept of a migrant labour system, first introduced by Burawoy (1976) and applied to Malaya by Beeman (1985), is worth revisiting.

In examining migrant workers in South Africa and the United States, Burawoy (1976: 1051) contends that the interest "is not how migrants adapt to the new environment but how structural, particularly political and legal, constraints make permanent 'integration' impossible. The issues are . . . enforced segregation through such 'total' institutions as the compound and labour camp and the corresponding persistence of race and ethnic differentiation". A migrant labour system does not encourage the integration of its workers in the society in which they are employed because of the inherent nature of its organization. For an economy to function, Burawoy (1976: 1051–53) argues, a labour force has to be maintained and renewed. Workers require support for their everyday subsistence, and when they leave or the industry expands, the vacancies have to be filled. Under normal circumstances, the maintenance and renewal functions are carried out in a common location and often by the same institutions. In the organization of migrant labour, however, the two processes take place in geographically separate locations and within separate institutions. On the one hand, the renewal function is made possible by remittances sent home by the productive workers. On the other, because migrant workers have no permanent legal or political status at their place of work, they are dependent on support from their families at home when the need arises, such as when they are laid off or disabled. An examination of the interaction between the organization of the separation of maintenance from renewal processes and the industry and state concerned, Burawoy (1976, 1054) submits, will throw light on relations among races, classes and class fractions.

A migrant labour system has two other ramifications for its workers (Burawoy, 1976: 1060). One is that migrant labour participation is incompatible with skilled employment for two reasons. First, it is not cost-effective to train a labour force with a high turnover; secondly, concentration in skilled occupations could result in the accumulation of power by certain groups—as in the case of the Chinese—making it difficult for employers to exercise control. The other ramification relates to the powerlessness of migrant labour. The state regards migrant workers as aliens without rights of citizenship. The lack of legal, political and civil status distinguishes such workers from domestic workers.

Moreover, a system of migrant labour in which racial characteristics coincide with particular occupations enhances and maintains the salience of ideology in the consciousness of the dominant and the dominated classes (Burawoy, 1976: 1061). Hence, behavioural characteristics attributed to participation in migrant employment are presented by the dominant ideology as racial traits. It is useful here to draw on Miles' work on the related processes of racial categorization and racialization. Racial categorization refers to the "process of delineation of group boundaries and of allocation of persons within those boundaries by primary reference to . . . inherent and/or biological (usually phenotypical) characteristics" (Miles, 1982: 157). It is an ideological process but has economic, political and ideological consequences. Racialization has the effect of subordinating a group to a materially and politically disadvantaged position, but it also elicits a political and ideological response from this group (Miles, 1982:, 185). "The response," Miles asserts, "is ideological in so far as those who are the object must construct a way of conceptualizing themselves and their circumstances. The response is political in so far as those who are the object negotiate a strategy by which to actively challenge their subordination". Later in this paper, I will discuss how the Indian population, Tamils in particular, came to be "racialized" by the politics of power sharing within the consociational state. By accepting a political accommodation within the structural constraints of the state, the Tamil community sought not to challenge, but to entrench, its subordination.

South Indians made up 75 percent of the total plantation labour force in Malaya in the pre-war years, and this figure declined to around 50 percent in 1947 (Arasaratnam, 1979: 38). A large majority worked on rubber plantations, and a few worked on coconut and oil palm estates. Since then, the proportion has hovered around 50 percent, the most recent figure being 46 percent in 1986. The exceptions were 1970 and 1975 when the proportion dropped to a low

40-something percent (Ramachandran, 1994: 85). These were the years following the race riots of May 1969, when under emergency rule, non-citizens were required to apply for work permits. Some 60,000 non-citizen Indian plantation workers, or 20 percent of the total Indian workforce in Peninsular Malaysia, were affected by this new rule (Ramachandran, 1994: 304).

In the years leading up to independence in 1957, citizenship laws were liberalized. Many Indians did not take up the opportunity to become citizens, partly because they wanted to keep their options open and partly through ignorance. It is estimated that in 1953, 46 percent of those Indians eligible for citizenship had not taken it up (Ratnam, 1967: 92–93). The introduction of work permits for non-citizens in 1969, as a solution to rural Malay unemployment, caused much distress and precipitated a political crisis in the Indian community. As a result of the uncertainty, some 60,000 Indians took advantage of the government repatriation programme and returned to India (Stenson, 1980: 206). Those who stayed and obtained work permits, Stenson notes, were permanently disadvantaged and lost whatever mobility they previously had.

As was the case with most migrant communities in the early years of settlement, sex ratios in the Indian community were lopsided. It was only in the 1930s that locally settled Indians began to contribute significantly to reproducing the labour force (Stenson, 1980: 21), and it was only in 1970 that the sex ratio was more or less balanced with 882 females to 1,000 males (Sidhu and Visswanathan, 1977: 25). In 1947, only 21 percent of the total Indian population was local-born, a figure that increased to more than 51 percent in 1947 and to more than 64 percent in 1957 (Hatley, 1969: 461). By 1970, this figure exceeded 81 percent (Sidhu and Visswanathan, 1977: 17). It may be inferred that by the 1950s, the Indian population relied on natural increase and was unaffected by migration flows. It was on its way to being a settled community from a demographic perspective; however, the political status and identity of the community in an independent Federation of Malaya remained ambiguous. It had neither the political influence nor the economic significance to influence negotiations prior to independence, which may have given it some assurance about its future.

Another significant development in the demographic transition of the Indian community was its urbanization. In 1931, more than 30 percent of the total Indian population was considered urban; in 1947 this figure was 39 percent, and it rose to 47 percent in 1957 (Hatley, 1969: 461; Arasaratnam, 1979: 42). As Arasaratnam notes, the drift to the towns had begun during the Depression when the Indians realized the uncertainty of employment on the plantations. The disruption of the economy in the war years accelerated the process. In the 1950s, British companies divested their investments in Malaya, resulting in the subdivision of the large estates. Between 1950 and 1967, around 18 percent of the total estate acreage was subdivided and sold to mainly smaller Asian owners, thus substantially reducing the required labour force. The switch from rubber to oil palm in the 1960s, which also required a smaller workforce, resulted in the retrenchment of Indian tappers. By then, too, the younger generation no longer perceived plantation work as providing an attractive future and was going in search of better educational and economic opportunities in the towns and cities. In the 1970s, Indian workers who were displaced by the introduction of the work permit but chose to remain in Malaysia were forced to migrate from the plantations to the urban areas in order to find work (Ramachandran, 1994; 304). The movement of Indian workers into urban squatter settlements that began in the 1950s as a consequence of subdivision accelerated in the 1970s after the riots of 1969, and continued as estates were sold off to developers for housing or industrial use in the 1980s. The social problems associated with plantation life (see Intisari, 1970)—large families living in overcrowded conditions, alcohol consumption, malnutrition, undereducated children who were forced to leave school for plantation labour—were simply transferred to the squatter settlements in the cities.

With the exception of the period 1921 to 1931, when the Indian proportion of the total population of Peninsular Malaysia was around 15 percent—a consequence of rapid immigration and economic prosperity—the figure remained at around 10 percent from 1947 until 1980. The Indian proportion of the population dipped to below 10 percent in 1991 (see Table 1), and is expected to decline to eight percent by 2021. Earlier in this paper, I referred to the political weakness of the Indians relative to the Malays and Chinese even during the time when the plantation rubber industry dominated the Malayan economy. The continuing decline of the Indian population will give it an even more marginal role in maintaining the balance of power between the two major ethnic communities. In 1957, more than 44 percent of the economically active population was engaged in plantation labour while another 20 percent was involved in urban labour, giving the Indian population a predominantly working-class character (Arasaratnam, 1982: 237). Since then, the proportion of Indians engaged in agriculture has steadily declined, with a corresponding increase in those involved in production, primarily in manufacturing where they are employed as production operators. In 1980, around 37 percent of Indians in Malaysia were involved in agriculture-related occupations and more than 31 percent were engaged in production; in 2000, the figures were around 15 percent and 40 percent, respectively (see Table 2), reflecting a reversal of the 1957 position. The working-class character of the Indian population, traditionally rural, has now become significantly urban and industrial.

Indian Political and Labour Organization

Colonial labour policy in Malaya was a reflection of the British perception of the appropriate social and economic roles of the races in the nineteenth century. Chinese labour was seen as independent and enterprising but difficult to supervise and inclined to be disorderly, particularly in view of the influential role of secret societies in the recruitment and organization of Chinese labour. Tamil labour, as British experience in India had shown, was easily manageable and suited to the regimented life of the estates. For this reason and because of the need to counterbalance the growing Chinese population, colonial officials were reluctant to support the official recruitment of Chinese labourers (Ramasamy, 1994: 20–23). Nevertheless, by 1931, 35 percent of estate labourers in the Federated Malay States were Chinese (Blythe, quoted in Ramasamy, 1994: 20). The main sources of Indian labour grievances throughout the colonial period were poor working conditions and low wages, and this was exacerbated by the wage disparity between the two ethnic groups, especially in the immediate postwar years. At different times, depending on economic conditions, Chinese labour was replaced by Indian labour and vice-versa to reduce costs (Leong, 1999: 45).

Table 1. Projected Population of Malaysian Citizens by Ethnic Group in Malaysia and Peninsular Malaysia, 1991–2021

Year	Bumiputera	Chinese	Indians	Total[a]
Malaysia				
Number ('000)				
1991	10,789	4,994	1,380	17,573
2001	14,198	5,641	1,609	21,930
2011	18,195	6,251	1,822	26,827
2021	22,179	6,725	2,036	31,559
Annual growth (%)				
1991–2001	2.75	1.22	1.53	2.21
2001–11	2.48	1.03	1.25	2.02
2011–21	1.98	0.73	1.11	1.62
Distribution (%)				
1991	61.4	28.4	7.9	100.00
2001	64.7	25.7	7.3	100.00
2011	67.8	23.3	6.8	100.00
2021	70.3	21.3	6.4	100.00
Peninsular Malaysia				
Number ('000)				
1991	8,434	4,251	1,380	14,475
2001	11,028	4,791	1,609	17,910
2011	14,043	5,297	1,822	21,720
2021	17,000	5,690	2,036	25,345
Annual growth (%)				
1991–01	2.68	1.20	1.53	2.13
2001–11	2.42	1.00	1.25	1.93
2011–21	1.91	0.72	1.11	1.54
Distribution (%)				
1991	58.3	29.4	9.5	100.00
2001	61.6	26.8	9.0	100.00
2011	64.7	24.4	8.4	100.0
2021	67.1	22.4	8.0	100.0

Source: Leete, 1996: 185.

Table 2. Employment of Indians by Occupation, 1980–2000

	1980			1985			1990			1995			2000		
OCCUPATIONAL GROUP	No. ('000)	% of total[1]	% of group[2]	No. ('000)	% of total	% of group	No. ('000)	% of total	% of group	No. ('000)	% of total	% of group	No. ('000)	% of total	% of group
Professional & Technical	29.7	10.3	6.8	36.7	8.7	7.4	44.9	7.7	7.9	55.4	7.0	8.8	77.5	7.6	10.1
Administrative & Managerial	2.5	4.9	0.6	6.6	5.1	1.3	6.5	4.0	1.1	12.3	4.8	1.9	21.6	5.5	2.8
Clerical	31.2	8.9	7.1	41.6	7.6	8.4	56.0	8.6	9.8	64.5	7.4	10.2	88.2	8.6	11.5
Sales	31.5	6.7	7.2	42.7	6.8	8.6	52.6	6.8	9.2	54.1	6.2	8.6	69.7	6.8	9.0
Services	41.8	10.0	9.5	64.6	10.1	13.1	73.4	9.5	12.9	72.4	8.2	11.5	93.3	8.5	12.1
Agricultural	163.9	8.8	37.3	140.9	8.2	28.5	138.3	7.3	24.2	111.6	6.9	17.7	116.5	6.9	15.1
Production	138.5	10.1	31.5	161.5	10.5	32.7	198.9	10.8	34.9	261.0	9.6	41.3	303.8	10.0	39.4
TOTAL	439.1	9.1	100.0	494.6	8.8	100.0	570.6	8.5	100.0	631.3	7.9	100.0	770.6	8.3	100.0

Source: Government of Malaysia, Fifth Malaysia Plan (1986); Sixth Malaysia Plan (1991); Seventh Malaysia Plan (1996); Eighth Malaysia Plan (2001). Kuala Lumpur: PNMB.

[1] Percentage of Indians of Total Malaysians Employed by Occupational Group.
[2] Percentage by Occupational Group of Total Indians Employed.

One significant organization to emerge in the local Indian community was the Adi Dravida Association, in 1929. It precipitated the formation of Tamil Reform associations in the towns in the 1930s. Led by the lower middle class of teachers, journalists, clerks and *kanganies*, the associations sought to eradicate caste abuse, improve the status of the lower castes and untouchables, dispel Brahmanic influence in Hindu society, and improve education and health (Ampalavanar, 1972: 219; Stenson, 1980: 78; Leong, 1999: 55). This movement, Ampalavanar (1972: 221) argues, represented the first instance when reformist efforts penetrated the isolation of Indian society in the estates, established urban–rural interaction, and awakened the consciousness of labourers. These links were later exploited by activists in trade union organization and were used to foment anti-colonial sentiment. Despite some success in social reform among Tamil labourers, Stenson (1980: 80) suggests that the movement's pre-occupation with Tamil culture, essentially an intra-ethnic issue, diverted it from the larger concerns such as the position of Indians in colonial Malaya (Ramachandran, 1994: 227).

In 1936, the Central Indian Association of Malaya (CIAM) was organized by middle-class, English-educated Malayalees and North Indians. Inspired by the nationalist movement in India, CIAM committed itself to looking after the interests of local Indians, giving priority to the plight of estate workers. It represented an important development in that it attempted to transcend communal loyalties within the Indian community (Ramachandran, 1994: 227–28). In the absence of grassroots organizations such as trade unions, the estate labourers accepted CIAM leadership, which showed a willingness to speak up for their grievances. CIAM, however, was treated with suspicion by the colonial government and was refused recognition. The latter regarded the organization as foreign influenced because of its close association with Indian nationalist leaders, and was wary of its aggressive stance in promoting Indian interests and the political rights and citizenship status of local Indians (Stenson, 1980: 45–46; Ramachandran, 1994: 228). Furthermore, CIAM played a significant role in persuading the British Indian government to ban the emigration of unskilled labour from India in 1938, a measure that did not go down well with the planters and colonial authorities in Malaya. In response, the colonial government sought to divide the Indian leadership by favouring conservative and Malayan-born Indians, and appointing Ceylon Tamils to government councils (Stenson, 1980:

47). In the end, the effectiveness of CIAM was limited by its English-educated, middle-class leadership of North Indians and Malayalees, who were unable to exert direct influence on the mainly Tamil-speaking labourers (Stenson, 1970: 26).

The first political movements to directly involve the Indian working class and provide them with organizational experience were the anti-British Indian Independence League (ILL) and the Indian National Army (INA), both sponsored by the Japanese during its occupation of Malaya (Jomo and Todd, 1994: 69; Ramachandran, 1994: 237). Although the movement was discredited after the war—its leaders intimidated and discriminated against by the British for collaborating with the Japanese—it created a political consciousness among Indian labour that was critical of the colonial administration, and provided its ranks with skills that were useful for trade union organization and activities after the war.

South Indian labour migration to Malaya was greatly reduced after 1938 and came to a halt during the Occupation. British attempts to revive the flow were met with strong local opposition, from both Indians and Malays (Stenson, 1980: 134). Contacts with India declined in the 1950s as the Indian population became permanently settled. The major source of labour unrest in the plantations in the immediate postwar years was low wages, which contributed to the poor living conditions of plantation workers (Ramachandran, 1994: 240–41). Despite the recovery of the rubber industry in 1947, there were only marginal increases in wages. The Chinese continued to be more highly paid, and this further fuelled Indian discontent. The plantation labourers in these years were organized into three main groupings (Ramachandran, 1994: 239). The largest following belonged to the communist-sponsored General Labour Union (later renamed the Pan-Malayan Federation of Trade Unions or PMFTU), dominated by the Chinese and active in the urban centres but later attracting many estate-based labour unions. The Federation was active in organizing strikes and other militant action against employers, creating a wave of industrial unrest both in the major urban centres and on the estates. For a brief period, a Chinese-Indian working-class alliance looked promising (Stenson, 1980: 107). The other organization that attracted a sizeable number of plantation workers was the Thondar Padai (Youth Corps), dedicated to improving the depressed conditions of Indian labourers and their families. Finally, plantation workers on the more isolated estates organized independent but moderate local unions.

Following the declaration of Emergency in 1948 and the ban on the Communist Party of Malaya, the Chinese-led unions collapsed as their pro-communist leaders went into hiding. During this period, attempts to organize Chinese unions were either discouraged or suppressed by the colonial authorities (Leong, 1999: 231). Few of the Indian union leaders identified with the objectives of the communist movement, and many questioned the communist tactics of using physical compulsion and organizing strikes for political rather than industrial reasons (Gamba, 1958: 287). The government renewed its efforts to reorganize the union movement, a task it had begun in 1946 with the appointment of a Trade Union Adviser to foster a moderate and pro-British labour organization. The colonial authorities were mindful of both British and international opinion that the suppression of union activity was unacceptable at a time when colonies were preparing for their eventual independence. The government's early attempts to penetrate the mass-based PMFTU had failed. Now, with the Chinese no longer in charge, it turned to the Indian leaders of the labour movement in the estates. The plantation unions were the logical focus for the Adviser (Ramasamy, 1994: 87) because they had a significant involvement in the PMFTU, the rubber industry was important to the interests of British capital, and the English-speaking leaders of these unions were considered to be relatively sympathetic to government concerns. In 1954, five unions, including several of the independent ones referred to earlier, amalgamated to form the National Union of Plantation Workers (NUPW). The leadership of the individual unions was opposed to left-wing influence, English-educated, and from middle or lower-middle class origins. None of the leaders were from the working class. Supported by the government, it was recognized as the sole representative of plantation workers by employers, and with a membership of around one-third of the total work force on the estates (Ramachandran, 1994: 253), the NUPW became the largest organization representing Indian labour.

The influence of the NUPW was limited, however, by its conservative approach. As a state-sponsored union, it shied away from taking on the government on political issues. The subdivision of estates in the late 1950s and the 1960s, noted above, not only caused job losses but also led to a decline in wages and conditions (Ramachandran, 1994: 260–61). The NUPW, thus, failed to protect the interests of Indian labour at a critical point. Instead, the Malayan Indian Congress

(MIC) led by Sambanthan proved more effective, with the help of urban middle-class businessmen, in establishing a company to buy up several estates. As the MIC initiative drew considerable support from estate workers, the NUPW felt threatened and its leadership criticized Sambanthan's efforts (Ramasamy, 1994: 108). Similarly, in 1969 when almost 24 percent of estate workers found themselves without citizenship status and jobless as a result of the introduction of work permits by the government, the NUPW was blamed for neglecting the political status of Indians and for not taking the initiative to have them registered as citizens (Ramachandran, 1994: 295). Any organization that was perceived to be a rival to the NUPW was, however, refused registration by the government. Under these conditions, an independent labour movement that could represent the interests of Indian labour failed to take root.

Stenson (1980: 137–38) identifies two reasons, one exogenous and the other endogenous, a working-class alliance failed to materialize at either the political or the industrial level. One was that the political mobilization of the Chinese and Indians in Malaya that was ignited by two separate nationalisms. A major strand of Chinese nationalism was the acceptance of Communist ideology, whereas radical Indian nationalism was more populist and syncretic. The other reason was that colonial policy compounded the existing racial division of labour. Indians and Chinese were employed in different jobs and at different wage rates; this made it impossible for the two ethnic groups to engage in collective bargaining. To these reasons, I would add a third. The appearance of incipient elements of class organization and class consciousness was quickly snuffed out through a process of depoliticization, effected by legislation to control the activities of unions and by co-option of prominent union leaders to create a moderate labour movement.

The Consociational State and the Politics of Subordination

To explain the ideological dominance of ethnicity in Malaysia, Brown (1994: 213–14) draws attention to the role played by colonialism and the post-colonial state. In the process of transforming local society into part of a world capitalist system, British colonialism created the ethnic division of labour in Malaya. The coincidence of race with economic function, Brown asserts, fostered the perception by the subordinated groups that it was their racial attributes that determined their class position. It may be added here that the maintenance of caste practices by the South Indian population helped to reinforce the inter-ethnic consciousness of the group in Malaysian society. In the process of decolonization, the postcolonial state saw the development of an alliance between state functionaries (drawn mainly from the Malay aristocracy) and the emergent commercial bourgeoisie (constituted predominantly by Chinese landowners and merchants) to take over power from the colonialists. The institutional form of such an alliance, which the departing colonial administration put into place, was that of the ethnically consociational state (Brown, 1994: 214). It is argued that in societies in which ethnic divisions are deeply entrenched, democracy is unworkable because political issues inevitably lead to ethnic polarization (Crouch, 1996: 152–53). In its place, there is a strong argument for the practice of a consociational democracy, in which significant ethnic communities are represented in the government, and decisions are reached by consensus. Further, the principle of proportionality should be observed in areas such as political representation, employment, education, and the disbursement of public funds. Within such a polity, Brown continues, "subordinate racial class fractions were persuaded to ally with dominant racial class fractions within patronage parties structured on avowedly ethnic communal lines". This political alliance found it to its advantage to maintain the existing ethnic division of labour. To this end, a major strategy it adopted was to employ ethnicity to maintain power. The consequence of a consociational arrangement is that the subordinate status of ethnic minorities is permanently entrenched. In the case of the Indians, who now constitute less than 10 percent of the population and are predicted to account for even less over the next 20 years (see Table 1), it is to the benefit of the incumbent political elite to support consociational politics.

Hence, by the time independence was achieved in 1957, all of the political parties that competed or co-operated for power were communally based in terms of their membership, ideologies and appeal (Brown, 1994: 216). The ideology of ethnicity came to dominate post-colonial Malaysia, but this does not preclude the significance of class interests. In particular, Brown reiterates:

> First, that colonialism engendered the emergence of racial-class groups which sought to organize themselves politically for the defence of their

> ethno-class interests. Second, that the colonial state promoted an ethnic ideology as the dominant paradigm for comprehending Malayan politics. Third, that the bourgeois racial-class groups were able to sustain their class dominance by employing this ethnic ideology to portray themselves as racial patrons (Brown, 1994: 216).

The Indians were a far more transient community than the Chinese in the 1940s, and this was reflected in the political leadership of the period. As noted earlier, the MIC was initially led by North Indian professionals and the better-educated Malayalees in the urban centres. Its politics was dominated by the unifying ideology of Indian nationalism and the struggle for independence. Local issues prior to 1946 were articulated only in reference to the politics of the homeland. Yet, the majority of Indians were Tamils who made up the backbone of plantation and urban labour; they naturally gravitated towards the trade unions that represented them. Local Indian leadership in the decade following the war was divided between those from a middle-class background with India-oriented political ambitions, and those who had the interests of local labour at heart. Unable to claim the support of the large labour population and with its loyalty called into question because of its political sympathies with India, the MIC was subjected to criticism from all sides, resulting in a change of leadership in the second half of the 1950s. "It was not," Arasaratnam (1982: 245) noted, "the challenge from the radicals or the leaders of labour that brought about major changes in the political leadership . . . The change came from a bid for power by the conservative traditionalists who went along neither with the dogmatic Indo-centric nationalism of the urban-based professionals nor with the exclusive championing of the cause of labour".

The new leadership avoided the Indo-centric nationalism of the past; neither did it appeal primarily to the interests of Tamil labour. Instead, it used traditionalist symbols such as Tamil language, culture and the arts, and Hinduism to mobilize Indian support (Arasaratnam, 1982: 246). Tamil culture and consciousness in South India had been given a boost more than a decade earlier through the Dravidian movement (Arasaratnam, 1979: 127), and the local leadership rode on the wave of this increasing ethnic consciousness. Looking to India for cultural and spiritual, rather than political, satisfaction was more acceptable to the Malay leadership and UMNO, which was poised to take over power in an independent Malaya.

The Tamilization of the MIC began in 1954 when Sambanthan, estate owner and graduate of Madras University, took over leadership of the MIC. Until then, the MIC leadership had been held by non-Tamils and professionals, who were fired more by ideology than race, and who were more willing to engage in non-communal politics. Sambanthan wasted no time in enrolling large numbers of Tamil estate labourers in the MIC. Many non-Tamils were purged from the party. With a strong working-class identity, the party attracted estate workers and small entrepreneurs who were seeking political and economic protection.

In the early years of the MIC and with the involvement of other ethno-linguistic groups within the Indian community, caste had little influence on the politics of the time (Ramasamy, 1984: 77–79). The Tamilization of the party in the mid-1950s did not immediately result in the introduction of caste politics. The MIC was admitted to the Alliance Party, which won every election between 1955 and 1969. Together with the Malayan Chinese Association (MCA) and led by UMNO, it formed the coalition government in those years. As Stenson (1980: 185–86) notes, it is misleading to regard the MIC as the unchallenged political representative of Indians. Its membership of 20,000 was only a fraction of the total adult Indian population of 300,000 in 1955. Working-class Indians in the major cities of Malaya supported the opposition such as the Labour Party and the Socialist Front. Lacking a strong political base, the MIC derived its influence from being a partner in the Alliance, later the Barisan Nasional government. As the numerically smallest of the ethnic communities and the weakest of the minority partners, it was completely dependent on UMNO support and largesse for its position. For this reason, the MIC was a party of personal patronage (Stenson, 1980: 194). Its weakness as a minority party in government is compounded by the absence of a strong Indian opposition party (Ampalavanar, 1993: 251). In contrast, the Chinese partner in the coalition (MCA) was more effective in wresting concessions from the government, partly because of the economic clout of the Chinese and partly because failure to grant such concessions would have strengthened the Chinese-based opposition, the Democratic Action Party.

In the first 10 years of the Alliance government after independence in 1957, many English-educated Indians benefitted from the Malayanization policy as they moved to senior positions in both the government service and the estate sector (Stenson, 1980: 198–99). Expanding educational opportunities also facilitated the upward mobility of urban Indian children. The Indian *petit bourgeois* such as merchants, moneylenders, land speculators and estate owners made fortunes. The expansion of Indian capital, however, was modest compared to that of the Chinese. Although the standard of living of Indian labour leaders improved, that of the mass of Indian labourers showed little improvement. The MIC under Sambanthan failed to reconcile the needs of labour with the political aspirations of the middle class (Amarjit Kaur, *The Star* 3 September 2001). The traditionalists and the lower-middle class consolidated their position within the party, while the middle-class professionals and intelligentsia moved away from it. Many considered that the party represented the interests of the Indian *petit bourgeois*, who stood to gain the most by adopting a conciliatory attitude towards UMNO (Willford, 1998: 231). As indicated earlier with regard to the role of the NUPW and the subdivision of estates, two divergent paths to leadership emerged among the Indians, one political and the other through a labour movement that eschewed political issues.

Caste politics within the MIC gradually evolved and came to a head in the 1970s with the death of Sambanthan, the MIC leader for two decades, in 1978. Caste sentiments were openly expressed in branch-level politicking throughout the country. The present leader of the MIC, Samy Vellu, built his support within the party through his work with Tamil drama groups and caste groups (Ampalavanar, 1993: 247), and is known for his organizational abilities. One consequence of his elevation, Ampalavanar notes, is the reinforcement of caste divisions within the MIC. In the 1980s, there were around 53 registered caste associations in Malaysia, many of them urban-based but with a large rural following (Lee and Rajoo, 1987: 393). Tamil schoolteachers, concerned with protecting caste interests and advancing caste status on an organized basis, took on a leading role in these associations. In 1988, the Vice-President of the MIC, Pandithan, challenged Samy Vellu for leadership of the party by championing the cause of the Adi Dravida or untouchables. Pandithan was sacked from the party and left to form the Indian Progressive Front (IPF), a direct consequence of caste politics. The IPF draws its support from lower-caste groups and symbolizes the very real caste divisions in Tamil society. Pandithan and the IPF are an effective rival for the MIC as the other parties in the ruling Barisan Nasional rely on them to organize support for their campaigns and elections. Most recently, the MIC opposed a move by the IPF to be admitted into the Barisan Nasional unless the IPF rejoined the MIC (*The Star*, 10 February 2001), an offer that was spurned by the IPF (*The New Straits Times*, 12 February 2001).

Conclusion

For virtually 50 years after their recruitment as plantation labour in Malaya at the end of the nineteenth century, Tamils lived within the constraints of a migrant labour system that was responsible for enforcing the segregation of the Tamil population from the rest of the populace through the organization of the labour camp and the colonial practice of racial division of labour. It also made it possible for the colonial government, in collusion with British capital, to only take responsibility for maintaining such a labour force, and not its reproduction. To this end, the government introduced a fund that ensured the repatriation of surplus labour and, through the supply of labour by the Indian Immigration Committee, determined wages mainly on the basis of individual subsistence with a small margin of savings. Wages were artificially depressed regardless of market influences, and the wages of Indian workers were maintained below those of Chinese workers. Although Indian labour migration to Malaya ceased after 1938 and the Tamil population was more permanently settled by the 1950s, the effect of the system was felt more than a decade after independence when thousands of Indians who had not taken up citizenship were repatriated after the race riots of 1969.

The racial division of labour maintained by the colonial government, which served as the basis of colonial labour policy, also led to the racialization of Malaysian society with its concomitant ideological and political consequences. As the object of racialization, the Tamil minority responded in several ways. First of all, Indian political activity during the Emergency was diverted towards the development of a race-based labour movement, and the movement's Indian leadership was carefully cultivated to the point where it clearly identified itself as apolitical. Second, as Willford (1998: 34) suggests, because of their relative economic and political weakness, cultural and religious activity has become the dominant expression of Tamil identity in Malaysia. One such activity, Thaipuism, a religious festival widely celebrated by working-class Hindu Tamils throughout the country and involving the fulfilment of religious vows, has become so significant that the MIC has sought to attract support by being overtly involved in it. Such religious activities have been described by Collins (1997: 103) as proto-political. Third, the Tamilization of the MIC occurred in the 1950s when Sambanthan assumed the leadership of the MIC. Fourth, caste interest in organized activity began in the 1930s and has been an underlying influence in local Indian politics since that time. It was Samy Vellu who first used it covertly and Pandithan who overtly capitalized on it to gain power.

The legacy of the departing colonial administration and its policy of racialization was the ethnically consociational state, the result of which has been to institutionalize unequal power-sharing among the three major ethnic groups in Malaysia—the Malays, Chinese and Indians—within the ruling Alliance government. State patronage of the political elites who represent the ethnic factions has resulted in piecemeal concessions by the dominant partner, UMNO, but the economically depressed Tamil population has gained little from such an arrangement. The expansion of the coalition government, the Barisan Nasional, to include political parties from the two states in East Malaysia in 1974 reduced the bargaining position of its Chinese and Indian partners (Crouch, 1996: 34), and further contributed to the marginalization of the Tamils.

REFERENCES

Abraham, C. E. R. (1997) *The Roots of Race Rrelations in Malaysia.* Kuala Lumpur: Insan.

Ampalavanar, R. (1972) "Class, Caste and Ethnicism among Urban Indians in Malaya, 1920–41", *Nusantara* 2: 209–36.

———. (1993) "The Contemporary Indian Political Elite in Malaysia", in K. S. Sandhu and A. Mani, eds. *Indian communities in Southeast Asia.* Singapore: Institute of Southeast Asian Studies, pp 237–65.

Arasaratnam, S. (1979) *Indians in Malaysia and Singapore.* Revised edition. Kuala Lumpur: Oxford University Press.

———. (1982) "Indian Society of Malaysia and its Leaders: Trends in Leadership and Ideology among Malaysian Indians, 1945–60", *Journal of Southeast Asian Studies* 13:2: 236–51.

Baxstrom, R. (2000) "Governmentality, Bio-power, and the Emergence of the Malayan-Tamil Subject on the Plantations of Colonial Malaya", *Crossroads* 14: 2: 49–78.

Beeman, M. A. (1985) *The Migrant Labour System: The Case of Malaysian Rubber Workers.* PhD thesis. University of Illinois, Urbana-Champaign.

Brown, D. (1994) *The State and Ethnic Politics in Southeast Asia.* London: Routledge.

Burawoy, M. (1976) "The Functions and Reproduction of Migrant Labour:

Comparative from Southern Africa and the United States", *American Journal of Sociology* 81: 5: 1050–87.
Colletta, N. J. (1975) "Malaysia's Forgotten People: Education, Cultural Identity and Socioeconomic Mobility among South Indian Plantation Workers", in J. Nagata, ed. *Pluralism in Malaysia: Myth and Reality. Contributions to Asian Studies.* Volume VII, pp. 87–112.
Collins, E. F. (1997) *Pierced by Murugan's Lance.* Dekalb: Northern Illinois University Press.
Crouch, H. (1996) *Government and Society in Malaysia.* Ithaca, NY: Cornell University Press.
Gamba, C. (1958) "Malayan Labour, Merdeka and after", *India Quarterly* July–September: 280–93.
Hatley, R. (1969) "The Overseas Indian in Southeast Asia: Burma, Malaysia, and Singapore", in R. O. Tilman, ed. *Man, State and Society in Contemporary Southeast Asia.* New York: Praeger Publishers, pp. 450–66.
Insan (1989) *Sucked Oranges: The Indian Poor in Malaysia.* Kuala Lumpur: Institut Analisa Sosial (Malaysia).
Intisari (1970) *Journal of the Malaysian .Sociological Research Institute* 3: 4.
Jain, R. K. (1970) *South Indians on the Plantation Frontier in Malaya.* Kuala Lumpur: University of Malaya Press.
Jomo, K. S. and P. Todd (1994) *Trade Unions and the State in Peninsular Malaysia.* Kuala Lumpur: Oxford University Press.
Kaur, Amarjit (2001) "For the Workers" *The Star*, 3 September.
Lee, R. and R. Rajoo (1987) "Sanskritization and Indian Ethnicity in Malaysia", *Modern Asian Studies* 21 (2): 389–415.
Leete, Richard (1996) *Malaysia's Demographic Transition—Rapid Development, Culture, and Politics.* Oxford University Press: Kuala Lumpur.
Leong, Y. F. (1999) *Labour and Trade Unionism in Colonial Malaya.* Penang: Universiti Sains Malaysia Press.
Miles, R. (1982) *Racism and Migrant Labour.* London: Routledge and Kegan Paul.
Muzaffar, C. (1993) "Political Marginalization in Malaysia", in K. S. Sandhu and A. Mani, eds. *Indian Communities in Southeast Asia.* Singapore: Times Academic Press and Institute of Southeast Asian Studies, pp. 211–36.
Ramachandran, S. (1994) *Indian Plantation Labour in Malaysia.* Kuala Lumpur: Majeed and Insan.
Ramasamy, P. (1994) *Plantation Labour, Unions, Capital, and the State in Peninsular Malaysia.* Kuala Lumpur: Oxford University Press.
Ramasamy, R. (1984) *Caste Consciousness among Indian Tamils in Malaysia.* Petalingjaya: Pelanduk.
Ratnam, K. J. (1967) *Communalism and the Political Process in Malaya.* Kuala Lumpur: University of Malaya Press.
Sandhu, K. (1969) *Indians in Malaya.* Cambridge: The University Press.
Stoler, A. L. (1995) *Capitalism and Confrontation in Sumatra's Plantation Belt, 1870–1979.* Second edition. Ann Arbor: The University of Michigan Press.
Selvaratnam, V. (1984) "South Indians on the Plantation Frontier: Malaysian Proletarians or Ethnic Indians?" *Development and Change* 15: 275–93.
Sidhu, M. S. and E. Visswanathan (1977) "Indians in Peninsular Malaysia", *The National Geographical Journal of India* 23 ( ): 17–25.
Smith, T. E. (1964) "Immigration and Permanent Settlement of Chinese and Indians in Malaya", in C. D. Cowan, ed. *The Economic Development of South East Asia.* London: George Allen and Unwin, pp. 174–85.
Snodgrass, D. R. (1980) *Inequality and Economic Development in Malaysia.* Kuala Lumpur: Oxford University Press.
Stenson, M. (1970) *Industrial Conflict in Malaya.* London: Oxford University Press.

———. (1980) *Class, Race and Colonialism in West Malaysia: The Indian Case*. St Lucia: University of Queensland Press.

Willford, A. C. (1998) "Cage of Freedom: The Politics of Tamil and Hindu Identity in Malaysia and Bangalore, South India". PhD thesis. University of California, San Diego.

CONSTRUCTING AND CONTESTING "SINGAPOREAN HINDUISM"

Vineeta Sinha

"Singaporean Hinduism" is a description that denotes a particular configuration of substantive elements that constitute what is labelled "Hinduism" among the migrant Hindu community in the island nation-state of Singapore. The diversity of the local Indian, Hindu population; the principle of secular, bureaucratic governance; and the multi-religiosity of social life here make it possible to speak of the making of "Singaporean Hinduism", which, not surprisingly, is a process that reflects multitude positions and, hence, disagreements about what constitutes "proper" Hinduism. While not adopting Vertovec's (1994) dichotomy of "Official Hinduism" and "popular Hinduism" uncritically, I do find in this a valuable analytical logic for analysing both elite and lay constructions of "Singaporean Hinduism" and the problematics associated with attempts to translate these into practice. In this paper, I begin with a critique of ahistorical, essentialist and reductionist interpretations and usages of such categories as "Hindu" and "Hinduism". While this appraisal is more than justifiable on scholarly grounds, the irony is that these terms can now no longer be expunged from the fabric of everyday custom and practice among Hindu communities, either in India or in the Disapora. Using ethnography from Singapore, I detail the various endeavours to formulate and delineate the outlines of "Singaporean Hinduism", and I consider the sociological implications these carry for the limits and possibilities of a "Hindu identity" in practice. In this paper, I argue that there are diverse, complex and contradictory modes of being Hindu in a secular, multi-ethnic and multi-religious Singapore while noting the tensions and anxieties that follow from such an assortment of religious styles.

Approaching "Hindu" and "Hinduism": Vacuous Terms?

In recent years, the category "Hinduism" has been critiqued on conceptual, epistemological and methodological grounds, thus making vacuous any claims of universal meanings (Sontheimer, 2001; Thapar, 1989; Weightman, 1985; Frykenberg, 1993; Smith, 1958). The etymology of the words "Hindu" and "Hinduism", and the manner of their usage suggest that they have a relatively short history and are of non-Indian origin. We know that the word "Hindu" and its various derivatives were primarily geographical terms used by Persians to characterize the inhabitants of "Hind"/"India" (Chaudhuri, 1979: 24). Despite the intellectual awareness and critique relating to the etymology and historical contingencies of the term, even in academic usage, it has not been adequately problematized. For evidence of its potency and popularity, one only needs to peruse the vast literature on social scientific accounts of religion, where it continues to be freely invoked without the reflexivity and caution that it surely deserves. In sociological and anthropological literature, the term is often used unquestioningly and invoked loosely as a short-hand and convenient description of complex "religious" scenarios, and it is also deemed to be self explanatory.

My own critique of the label is not of its linguistic description, but of the ways in which it has been conceptualized in the discourses of various disciplines. As we know, it is premised on a set of epistemological and methodological assumptions drawn from a particular mode of understanding "religion", grounded in experiences emanating from a Judeo-Christian tradition (Smith, 1958). Yet, an examination of the underlying conceptions and categories in which the term "Hinduism" is grounded, and a historicization of the concept has not culminated in a call for rejecting the terms "Hindu" or "Hinduism", although scholars have wondered if they are appropriate categories of sociological analysis. It is significant then that the designation of the religious life of a people as "Hinduism", "Vedism" and "Brahmanism" was the work of foreigners or non-Indians (Parrinder, 1971; Radhakrishnan, 1961). As there is no direct translation of the word "religion" in any of the Indian languages, some scholars have suggested that what is labelled "Hinduism" cannot be interpreted from the viewpoint of the European notion of religion (Sen, 1961; Chaudhuri, 1979). The transformation of the word "Hindu" from its geographical meaning to one with cultural and specifically religious overtones is historically interesting.

Given that the word "Hindu" has primarily territorial and ethnic connotations, it is essential and instructive to examine its popular and academic acceptance as a category with "religious" connotations.

Although these terms are used with great ease in discussions of Indian religion, tremendous variation and controversy exist over interpretations of a "Hindu" identity, and the religious and cultural phenomenon termed "Hinduism". Nonetheless, these labels continue to be commonly invoked, particularly in academic accounts, and are often assigned stereotypic, taken-for-granted meanings. There are, however, proponents of the view that the label "Hinduism", with its generic complex of meanings, is devoid of any heuristic value and, if anything, is misleading (Bowes, 1977; Pocock, 1973).

The Indological and sociological literature on Hinduism is vast and multifaceted. Despite this wide range of interpretations, it is possible to abstract from this body of writings a compilation of features that are seen to define "Hinduism". Most accounts of Hinduism begin by noting its "complexity" and "diversity" in rituals, beliefs and philosophical orientations. This variability is taken to reflect the tolerant, flexible and accommodating nature of the religion. Furthermore, the diffused and syncretic nature of Hinduism is seen to point to the absence of any exclusive central authority. Students of Indian religion have noted that the concept of dogma is lacking (Basham, 1954; Kinsley, 1982; Renou, 1953; Radhakrishnan, 1961), although some concepts (such as *dharma*, *karma* and *samsara*) are central to the daily lives of Hindus. The social structure of Indian society, a central feature of which is the presence of castes, is perceived to be intimately related to Hinduism.

Orientalist writings on India have tended to provide a textual and canonical reading of Hinduism, caste, and Indian society in general. There have been, however, anthropological and sociological accounts (both historical and contemporary) that point to the distance between official, literate views and what happens in practice (Radhakrishnan, 1961; Das, 1977). The present article is inspired by this literature in an effort to deconstruct categories (such as "Hindu" and "Hinduism") by demonstrating their dynamism in a real, empirical context: the modern, multicultural, multi-religious nation-state of Singapore.

Today, this rethinking exercise faces a number of challenges. Ironically, the most serious one comes from lay Hindus and non-scholars of Hinduism. Contemporary students of Hinduism cannot escape the fact that the terms "Hinduism" and "Hindu", far from being rejected, are now embraced and internalized among practitioners as labels of self-description, even as new meanings continue to be assigned to them. Although, the practitioners in question did not encapsulate their beliefs, rituals and philosophies either in the Judeo-Christian understanding of "religion" or in the generalized label "Hinduism", it is an imposition by outsiders. In fact, this self-conscious application of the labels in India by Indians to denote the religious life of Indians is a fairly recent practice. This process is also not a new one, but takes us back to at least the eighteenth century, when the term "Hinduism" was accepted by "natives" as one that denotes their "religion". There is a double problematic here, both in the acceptance of the Judeo-Christian notion of religion as well as its subsequent labelling. The intellectual argument—that the designation of a religious identity in the label "Hindu" and the use of "Hinduism" to denote a single, unified and coherent religious tradition are alien impositions and distortions of how religion has been understood, discussed and practised in the Indian subcontinent historically—now also has to contend with its easy adoption and acceptance by lay practitioners. The latter process legitimizes as valid and meaningful such categories as "Hindu" and "Hinduism". This is as true for Hindus in India as it is for those in the Diaspora.

Constructing "Singaporean Hinduism"

The awareness that words and labels have histories and that their meanings are themselves created requires us to rethink their unproblematic and taken-for-granted usage. In addition, this consciousness is further challenging in that it makes writing about a subject that requires the use of these terms an exceedingly difficult task, something I have experienced in efforts to write about Hinduism in Singapore. Thus, I commence with the important recognition that apart from the intellectual critique of the terms "Hindu" and "Hinduism" among scholars, they are nonetheless viewed as meaningful and valid categories that carry a range of nuances and interpretations for Hindus themselves. It is evident that, in particular, the term "Hinduism" has been claimed by believers/followers and accorded widespread legitimacy—a fact that contemporary students of Hinduism have to address. Beyond this adoption of the word, and the idea that it suitably portrays the "religion" of a people, there is little consensus among Hindus on what the term connotes; thus, its parameters remain ambiguous. The absence of a universally agreed upon "definition" of Hinduism, and its standing as a non-canonical religion without a singular notion of orthodoxy and orthopraxy renders it open to a range of readings and interpretations, both at the level of construction and practise. The sociological contribution of this paper is to demonstrate these twin processes within the nation-state of Singapore.

Given the history of Indian migration to the region, there co-exist similarities between Indian variants of Hinduism and those now in practice locally. Both the continuities with "tradition" as well as the departures can be identified in the practice of Hinduism in Singapore in the last 180 years. Despite the noted "empirical" resemblances with Hinduism "back home", expressions of "Singaporean Hinduism" must be viewed as the outcome of specific structural factors operating in Singapore society. The very labels "Hindu" and "Hinduism", although historically not generated within the Singapore context, are in regular use by local Hindus and are very real to them, framing both a discourse and practice of their religion. Thus, my interest lies in the labels "Hindu" and "Hinduism" as socially constructed, carrying specific meanings of contextual relevance. These have, in turn, produced specific modes of talking about Hinduism and further established particular ways of being "Hindu". The prevalence and acceptance of the term "Hinduism" among the local population is surprising only in so far as it has no direct translation in any of the Indian languages. Interestingly, I encountered no other term (in Tamil, Hindi or any other Indian language) used with as much frequency and popularity to carry the complex of rituals and beliefs implied in the label "Hinduism". In a very serious sense, a term coined by outsiders has been embraced and is now used for self-description. It is not without significance that over time, no label other than "Hinduism" has been proposed as an alternative for describing the religion of non-Christian and non-Muslim Indians in Malaya and Singapore. At different historical moments, however, and for a variety of reasons, such labels as "Sanatana Dharma", "Vedism", "Brahmanism", "Saivism", "Saiva Siddhanta", "Sanskritic Hinduism" and "Tamil Hinduism" have been suggested as accurate portrayals of specific strands of religiosity within the broader term. Yet, the label "Hinduism" as an overall, all-encompassing and unitary category has not been challenged and, certainly, calls have not been made for a more suitable substitute; it continues to be widely invoked, used and validated in practice. Most significantly, at the level of day-to-day usage, it is the label "Hinduism" that is more commonly used, both with

English-speaking Hindus and those for whom English is a secondary language. Today, in Singapore, the term "Hinduism" is not only a census category denoting a religion but is also a sign of individual religious identification and an important ethnographic category. Here, it is understood (by Hindus and non-Hindus alike) as one among numerous religious traditions, and named alongside others such as Christianity, Islam, Buddhism, Taoism, Sikhism and so forth. By extension, the word "Hindu" is used to signify and construct a particular religious and cultural identity—processes that in practice mix up racial, ethnic, cultural, nationalistic and linguistic traits.

Rather than speak of "Hinduism", I detail here how the label "Singaporean Hinduism" is constructed by a number of different, interested parties. It is not a term used by any of my informants but is a heuristic device that allows me to encapsulate the ways in which "Hinduism" is talked about and acted out in practice. Concretely, I have found it useful to see the category "Singaporean Hinduism" as a frame, and at any point in time what is included within its boundaries—both in terms of content and ideology—is conditional. This entails the drawing of boundaries around a named and labeled religious tradition as well as negotiating the substance within. I have suggested elsewhere (Sinha, 2003) that the phrase is an apt one for making sense of the manifold beliefs, rituals and ideologies prevalent in the local Hindu community. I approach this category as an abstraction, and a construction but with two important caveats.

First, that the phrase "Singaporean Hinduism" is not a singular, monolithic category. By no means does it represent an empirical reality "out there", fixed and unchanging in its manifestation, and that can be grasped objectively and definitively. As a heuristic device, it is an abstraction and a construction. In practice, while it may share a likeness with manifestations of Hinduism in other settings (both in the Diaspora and in India), its content and symbolic significance at any point in time are the outcome of a number of specific social, cultural and political forces working together, some emanating from within Singapore society and others impacting from the outside. The process of construction sees at work the agency of a number of parties, which includes lay Hindus as well as the leadership—administrative, bureaucratic, political and spiritual—within the local Hindu community.

Second, the combination of elements that make up "Hinduism" varies over time, and the actual shape is governed by a number of contextual factors. For instance, while today both *taipucam* and *timiti* are seen as quintessentially Hindu festivals and are valourized as essential features of local Hinduism, this was not always the case. About half a century ago, these festivals were viewed by reform-minded Indians and Hindus as primitive, superstitious rituals that fell outside the Hindu fold. In the 1950s, The Tamil Reform Association (TRA) of Malaya proposed a ban on these festivals. It is clear that such a call could not be made today and, if attempted, would not find too many supporters from within the local Hindu community, whose members see *taipucam* and *timiti* as distinctly Tamil festivals that have become both significant markers and prized symbols of a Tamil Hindu identity. Interestingly, these same events have been generalized sufficiently to mark Singapore's Hindu-ness, going beyond their original Tamil roots to embrace all Hindus here. Some internal factors that have shaped the category over time include the following: Singapore's multi-religiosity and multi-ethnicity, the minority status (both numerical and political) of Hinduism here, the socio-cultural profile of the migrant Hindu community, the self-perception as well as the general perception of Hinduism as a "tolerant, non-aggressive and non-proselytizing" religion, the de-politicization of the religious domain, the numerical dominance of a strongly evangelical Christian community, and the view that Hindus here are different from Hindus in India.

The Realm of Practice

The question of what constitutes a "Hindu identity" has inspired much academic discussion. Some scholars (both Indian and Western) have suggested that the acceptance of *Sruti* as "revelation of God" is incumbent upon a Hindu (Chaudhuri, 1979; Muller, 1882; Sen, 1961; Weber, 1958), drawing this from the *Vedas* and *Upanisad*—important texts from the vast corpus of sacred Hindu literature. At best, this is what my informants considered a "technical" definition of a Hindu, and one that is irrelevant and inapplicable to the Singapore context. To start with, a majority of my informants, when pressed, applied the label "Hindu" to denote their religious identity but were not familiar with Vedic literature or with other Hindu texts. Many challenged the ideas that belief in scriptures, and knowledge of texts or Hindu philosophy are defining features of a religious identity.

They ask, "Does this mean that an uneducated, illiterate person cannot be a Hindu?" Also, given the profile of the migrant Hindu community to Malaya in terms of class, caste and the largely South Indian Tamil population, it means that the Vedas and the Upanisads are not prioritized by the majority as the source for defining Hinduism.

Additionally, informants were not able to articulate the precise parameters of a Hindu identity, citing the notorious variation and flexibility of the "Hindu tradition" with regard to proper action or proper belief. In the absence of firm notions of orthodoxy and orthopraxy, they argued it was logical that there were no fixed answers about what makes a "Hindu". This rather inclusive and wide-ranging attitude in their religion, many felt, allows for a great deal of latitude and license to interpret and enact their religious identity. Thus, it was hardly surprising to find the mottled assortment of actual ritual practices my informants were engaged in subsumed under the rubric of "Hinduism" and a "Hindu identity". What is notable here is that at the level of participation and the enactment of one's religiosity or spirituality, the question of the descriptions used to denote one's "religion" and one's "religious identity" appear to be minor concerns, almost non-issues. My data reveal that what is deemed more crucial is what one *does* in practice in the name of religiosity. Here, it is clear that a variety of practices that could be defined as belonging to other "non-Hindu" religious traditions (for example, folk Taoism and Roman Catholicism) are easily and unproblematically embraced by those who call themselves "Hindu". What is sociologically interesting is that these individuals seem to be redefining these practices as part of their religious style, which cannot be denoted in affixing discrete labels such as Hindu, Taoist or Catholic.

As evidence of the very open-ended nature of the religion, I also encountered individuals who called themselves "Hindu" but felt that they were not required to "do anything" to demonstrate this. They referred to themselves as "non-practising Hindus" but were attached to the label as a marker of their ethnic and cultural leanings, though not its spiritual connotations. Some called themselves "born Hindu" or "nominal Hindu", without an accompanying set of disciplined religious activity that affirmed their "Hinduness". Thus, in contrast to those Hindus who had converted to other religious traditions, they did not see the need to change their religious identity, either for official or other more personal reasons. Clearly, individuals like these interpret the label in cultural terms and express an attachment to it as an ethnic and racial sign, even if they do not participate in the Hindu domain ritualistically and spiritually, except perhaps passively, and were Hindus by "default". Even so, this passivity contributes to the perpetuation and pervasiveness of the label locally, adds to its potency, and ensures its reproduction in the future. In the multi-religious context of Singapore, the possibility of religious conversion is real and quite common, and has led to fairly dramatic shifts in the religious profile of the population. During fieldwork, I encountered numerous Hindus who had become Christians and, in smaller numbers, Muslims. One pervasive sentiment among Singapore Hindus is the perceived openness, flexibility, and assimilative and accommodative nature of their religion. Additionally, Hindus are also prepared to rhetorically accord equality and sameness to all religions and religious identities. Yet, at the level of everyday life, both these ideas are challenged. This becomes evident particularly in instances of conversion out of Hinduism. I have argued previously, how in converting to another faith, a Singaporean Hindu is seen to be stepping outside permissible boundaries (Sinha, 1997). In this previous work, I had presented a scheme for classifying the body of Singaporean Hindus. Here, I want to focus instead on two categories: (1) those who are attached to the label "Hindu" as an autonomous religious identity and for whom this carries a set, restricted realm of religious activity; and (2) those who retain the term "Hindu" but do not see it as denoting a bounded and circumscribed identity, but who redefine its parameters, particularly through a wide range of ritual behaviour.

Students of Hinduism have generated an elaborate language for describing and analysing the complexities of the religion (particularly its manifestation in practice all across the Indian landscape), and have identified levels and varieties within the religion. A select illustrative list would include such dichotomies as "Sanskritic/non-Sanskritic" Hinduism, Brahmanic/non-Brahmanic Hinduism, "literate/non-literate" Hinduism, the "Great/Little" strands of Hinduism and the notion of "folk/popular/village" Hinduism. Researchers familiar with Hinduism in Diasporic settings have argued that while this terminology may today be applicable to the Indian context, the same cannot be said of Hindu domains in the Diaspora. According to Vertovec:

> Thus to continue to describe the variety of Hindu beliefs and practices amongst overseas Hindus in terms of 'Little' and 'Great' Traditions-even by way of an ideal-style continuum- would be for the most part an irrelevant exercise. Instead, it is suggested here that the notions 'official' and 'popular' religion may be more useful in describing strands or levels of Hinduism in places like these (2000: 41).
>
> 'Official' religion can be taken to mean a set of tenets, rites, proscriptions and prescriptions which are promulgated through some institutionalized framework . . . 'Popular' religion can be understood basically as beliefs and practices undertaken by lay believers: these include orthodox practices undertaken outside 'official' auspices (Vertovec 2000: 41).

Following this logic, Vertovec proposes the dichotomy of "Official Hinduism" and "Popular Hinduism" as being more relevant to theorizing expressions of Hinduism in the Diaspora. For the purposes of this paper, I find this schema to be useful in presenting data from Singapore Hindu domains. In this context, "Official Hinduism" refers to the various representations of Hinduism made through the initiative of the local Hindu leadership, constituted by Hindus who are generally the more literate, educated, professional, urban members of the community and who seem to be guided by a bureaucratic, rational and modern logic. "Popular Hinduism" refers to the daily practices of large numbers of lay Hindus whose religiosity translates variously (and is often at odds with an officially prescribed interpretation of Hinduism) within the multi-ethnic, multi-religious context of Singapore society. Not only are there competing and contrasting constructions of Hinduism here, but as would be expected, there are many ways of being Hindu on a day-to-day basis. At the level of practice, the category is not a homogeneous, monolithic one but is ethnographically complex. My discussion of the distance (and tussles) between popular and official modes of Hinduism reveals this diversity.

There is firm evidence that folk Hindu practices are appealing and continue among Singapore-born Hindus even today. Despite changes in the practice of day-to-day Hinduism over time, some features have, nonetheless, persisted. The ritual complex surrounding the veneration of local, household, village deities—a strong feature of folk Hinduism—is one such stable element that has remained and would be a constitutive element of "Popular Hinduism". This leaning towards village-based Hinduism is hardly surprising given the history of Indian and Hindu presence in British Malaya since the nineteenth century (Sandhu, 1969; Arasaratnam, 1970; Mani, 1977; Siddique and PuruShotam, 1982). We know that large numbers of Indians were brought in from Tamilnadu as cheap labour for estates and public works in British Malaya. Much of this labour was drawn from the lowest rungs of the Indian class and caste hierarchy, from the non-Brahmin, Adi-Dravida communities. Early religious practices included the veneration of village deities, and were evident in the establishment of places of worship and observance of rituals and festivals (Sandhu, 1969; Mialaret, 1969; Arasaratnam, 1970; Rajah, 1975). Therefore, the worship of *gram devata* (village deities) and more specifically, the *ciru devangal* and *kaaval deivam* (from Tamilnadu) were imported and grounded in the religious landscape of the Malay Peninsula. Today, the numerous shrines and temples, and the large numbers of devotees still adhering to dimensions of what would be labelled "folk" aspects of Hinduism hark back to Indian migration to Malaya. What is fascinating sociologically is the overwhelming evidence for the preferred attachment to the "old ways" (of folk Hinduism) among scores of Singaporean Hindus. In some cases, this is simply a continuation of ancestral practices and, thus, not surprising; more interestingly, in other cases it is a novel attraction to the gods and ritual practices of the Tamil country, and this is popular in the rubber estates of Malaya. The latter translates to the centrality of these specific features in these spaces: the privileging of mediums and trance sessions; the intimate, familiar, unmediated approach to deities (given the absence of a religious intermediary) the importance of *bhakti*, intuition, ecstatic devotion, emotion and religious experience; the offerings of non-vegetarian items, alcohol and *suruttu* to the deity; the absence of ritual procedures (*arccaanai*, *abishegam*, etc. and the chanting of *mantras* and *slokas*) in the act of worship; and valuing rituals of self-mortification.

Substantively, the domain of "Popular Hinduism" is a complex mixture of elements drawn from diverse local religious traditions, including elements from "Hinduism" defined broadly. By no means do its empirical boundaries replicate or even approximate what is understood as folk Hinduism "back home" in Tamilnadu. In Singapore, Popular Hinduism is striking for its robust and resilient religious syncretism. This entails a free and liberal use of deities, symbols and ritual practices associated with "other" religious traditions, foremost of which is a variety of religious/folk Taoism. Both the domestic Hindu domain and non-Agamic public spaces reveal the strong presence of deities and other religious paraphernalia from religious Taoism. Additionally, one sees in Hindu shrines religious altars typically recognized as part of a "Chinese temple"—ritual objects such as tall joss-sticks, large and small Chinese-style urns, floating oil candles, oranges, wooden pieces for seeking permission for four-digit numbers, together with deities from the vast Hindu pantheon. For example, paying reverence to Roman Catholic saints and attending the Novena service, according respect to Chinese deities such as Kuan Yin and Tua Peh Kong, frequenting tombs of Muslim saints, celebrating Vesak Day (viewed here as a Chinese Buddhist festival) and putting up a Christmas tree at home, all appear to constitute legitimate activities for local Hindus. Often, the presence of *keramat*(s), and Datuk gods completes the mixed but coherent and legitimate religious scene. The prominent presence of ethnic Chinese in these spaces, both as founders and devotees, is also hard to miss; and these numbers appear to be on the rise.

Expectedly, one also sees what the orthodox Hindu quarters would consider "indiscriminate borrowing" from all strands of Hinduism, without any concern for recognizing and maintaining boundaries and almost to the point of being irreverent. In my fieldwork, I was able to document, in practice, the truly hybrid nature of "Hinduism" in the co-presence under one roof of Vaisnavite, Saivite and Sakti dimensions (for instance, in having Hanuman, Ram, Murukan, Mariamman, Periyachee, Bhagvati and Kali together), the Brahmanic and non-Brahmanic elements (in the co-existence of Muneeswaran, Sanggali Karuppan, Madurai Veeran with Murukan, Ganesh and Vishnu),[1] and in conducting vegetarian and non-vegetarian prayers for respective deities on the same grounds, but with appropriate procedures and deference.

[1] The "Hindu" pantheon is vast and complex, a mixture of deities from the Sanskritic tradition and popular folklore and mythology. Regional specificities and variations add yet another dimension of complexity. In the Singapore context, one sees the prominence of gods from Tamilnadu. Deities like Muneeswaran, Sanggali Karuppan, Madurai Veeran are known as "village gods" and as *ellai kaaval deivam* (Tamil for "boundary, guardian gods"). The mother-goddess tradition is represented here through the popularity of Kaliamman, Mariamman and Periyachee amman. The "big gods" of the Saivite tradition (Siva, Murukan) and Vaisnavite tradition (Perumal, Visnu, Rama, Hanuman) also abound but are found only in the "proper" Agamic temples.

The presence of "non-Hindu" deities, whether in Hindu homes or in public spaces, is hardly new for Singapore. This has been documented to be the case for at least three to four decades (Nadarajah, 1990; Rajah, 1975; Sinha, 1988). Yet, I would argue that presently, the confluence of "folk" elements from Taoism and Hinduism is anthropologically significant. Such overlaps and alliances demand that we rethink the local dominant discourse on multi-religiosity and multi-ethnicity, which is defined by an assumption of essential and incompatible racial/ethnic and religious differences. On the basis of my data, I contend that there is little to choose between a variety of religious "Taoism" and "Hinduism" as practised in Singapore, if one removes the distinguishing lens of race. This clearly accounts for the ease and familiarity with which members of both communities easily participate in one another's ritual domains. These slices of ethnography allow me to argue for a "Singaporeanization" of Hindu practice in general and an "ethnicization" of Hindu identity in particular. All discussions of Hindu identity in the Singapore context necessarily lead to simultaneous narratives on Indian identity. My data show how Hinduism is reconstituted as an ethnic label through a *conflation* of Hindu and Indian identities. I have noted elsewhere that the terms "Indian" and "Hindu" in local discourse are used not only synonymously, but also interchangeably (Sinha, 1997, 2003). In Singapore, religions are ethnicized such that Hinduism is defined as an "Indian" religion and Islam as *a* "Malay" religion. Furthermore, a "Hindu" identity is seen to match "naturally" with an "Indian" one, both in official and lay discussions; here it is impossible to disentangle the two identities. This means that when one encounters the term "Indian", one cannot assume that it necessarily refers to an ethnic identity. Often, an invocation of the category "Indian" really signals a "Hindu" religious identity, the context of usage being crucial in determining the meanings that the terms carry. The complexities are conveyed in the following example, a conversation narrated to me by a colleague:

> Canteen Stall Owner: Hi! I have not seen you for a long time.
> Colleague: Yes. I was fasting.
> Canteen Stall Owner: Oh! I thought you were Indian!

In the context of this exchange, the term "Indian" is used by the stall owner to signal the assumed "Hindu" identity of my colleague, who has been re-defined as a "Muslim" given his observance of the fasting month. The various attempts at constructing official versions of Hinduism have the effect of essentializing the "CMIO"[2] classification, and freezing the messy and muddled socio-cultural and religious realities into homogeneous, monolithic racial and religious categories.

Official Hinduism

For reform-minded Singaporean lay Hindus as well as leaders of the Hindu community, the realm of trances, spirit-mediums, animal sacrifices, visiting Keramats, attending Novena, and the convergences with the Chinese Taoist ritual domain is alien but intriguing, and is obviously not part of "Official Hinduism". They were incredulous that "this kind of thing happens in Singapore" and that "people in Singapore still do all this." They were clearly non-participants in this domain, which for them was a spectacle to be observed, and those who did "this kind of thing" were clearly other-ed in being unlike them. Some even wondered if they should be considered "real" Hindus and if these practices were part of Hinduism. This ritual complex is clearly seen to be marginal to mainstream, orthodox, Agamized Hinduism and not one that finds official sanction and approval. From the perspective of official Hindu leadership, the production of a specific positive, public image of "Singaporean Hinduism" is a priority. I have often heard the sentiment that "what other Singaporeans think about our religion is important" and that, "We have to teach Singaporeans that Hinduism is not just about elaborate rituals but also has a history and rich philosophy". As I see it, the packaging of an acceptable face of Hinduism is as much for the self—the Hindu community (especially its younger members) as it is for others. As such, instances of "Popular Hindu" practices such as self-flagellation and animal sacrifices do not contribute to such a positive image. Reform-minded Hindus are clearly more comfortable with the kind of Hinduism they witness in the 24 registered Agamic temples on the island and the ritual complex therein, which is an important and dominant constituting element of "Official Hinduism".

[2] "CMIO" is an abbreviation of the "Chinese-Malay-Indian-Other" mode of differentiating and classifying the local population, popularized by the State but now pervasive in all societal domains.

It would be instructive to locate and document over time the emergence of "Official Hinduism" in Singapore, with a view to identifying the specific input from the various Hindu associations and institutions, as well as Hindu political leaders. While it is possible to reconstruct the role of such institutions as the Hindu Endowments Board and the Hindu Centre, the influence of Hindu politicians in shaping Hinduism is more difficult. This is due to a number of factors, including the governing principle of secularism and the careful separation of the religious and political domains in Singapore society. This does not imply that prominent Hindu politicians have no concrete input in constructions of "Official Hinduism". It is, rather, that their contributions occur through informal and, thus, less public routes, making it difficult to record their specific views. I turn now to the role of the institutional mechanisms.

Hinduism in Singapore operates within the institutional context provided by government-affiliated bodies—the Hindu Endowments Board (HEB) and the Hindu Advisory Board (HAB). These were early British colonial initiatives and can be dated to the early years of the twentieth century. The Hindu Endowments Board existed previously as part of the Mohammedan and Hindu Endowment Board (MHEB), created in 1905, but has existed separately since 1969. The Hindu Advisory Board was founded in 1915. The British government in Malaya had then justified the need for these two entities to ensure order and efficiency in the affairs of the local Hindu community, and in response to complaints of mismanagement of funds by the local Hindu and Muslim communities. The Mohammedan and Hindu Religious Charitable Endowments Bill was thus formalized in September 1905, and the colonial government set up the MHEB specifically to administer endowments and charities in the name of Muslim and Hindu communities. The second government-affiliated body, the Hindu Advisory Board, was set up in 1915 to advise the colonial government on matters pertaining to Hinduism in Malaya. The stated function of this board was to be responsible for all matters connected with Hindu worship and practice in Singapore. Today, membership of the HEB and the HAB is constituted entirely by local Hindus who are professionals, drawn primarily from the civil service as well as the private sector and business interests. The members of the two boards work closely together and are appointed for a term of three years by the Minster for Community Development and Sports (MCDS). Popular Hindu sentiment is that the members do not adequately represent the interests of the local Hindu community. Questions have also been explicitly raised about whether members of the two boards have sufficient knowledge of Hinduism to make decisions about the religion; indeed, they are often viewed as administrators and bureaucrats. Given the exclusive procedure of nomination, selection and appointment, these two bodies are further viewed as highly elitist and out of touch with popular, public opinion, not to mention being uninformed with regard to knowledge of Hindu affairs.

The HEB continues to administer the affairs and events of the four Hindu temples and oversees the two central festivals of the local Hindu community, *taipucam* and *timiti*, which have long been associated with the temples under the HEB jurisdiction. The remaining 20 registered temples on the island are privately managed by a community of devotees. In recent years, evidence indicates that the role of the HEB has become rather more generalized, diffused and extensive. Given the institutional location of the HEB and its perception by government authorities as well as members of other religious and cultural communities as "representing" the local Hindu community, the HEB, albeit unintentionally and through various statements, utterances and activities, has constructed a version of Hinduism for public consumption; in the process, it has defined what constitutes proper "Hinduism". Together with the HAB, it has both the legitimacy as well as the resources to construct and reproduce a version of local Hinduism that is officially sanctioned, that is, Vertovec's "Official Hinduism", itself as a syncretic mix of elements drawn from the various strands within Hinduism. Yet, the dominant strain here is what I would call an "Agamic"[3] brand of Saiva Siddhanta, emanating from Tamilnadu, carried in the Saiva Agamas and perpetuated in consecrated temples through the ritual labour of trained Brahmins as religious specialists. This, however, is mixed up with elements of what would be considered "folk" and "village" practices, such as the

[3] The word *agamas* literally means "that which has come down". The *Saiva Agamas* refer to a body of Saivite texts regarded by their adepts as revealed, to which the tantras and most.of the rituals of the major temples make reference, even today. It is constituted of mythological, ritual and philosophic material not contained in the Vedic texts. The Agamas, unlike the Vedas are accessible to women and non-Brahmins and are regarded by their followers as the "fifth Veda", that is, as divine revelation. The derivative term "Agamic" is used to signify a direct connection to the tradition carried in these texts, and may describe temples, rituals and philosophies.

popularity of mother-goddess worship and *kaaval deivam*, and the annual festivals of *tai pucam* and *timiti*, which are now institutionalized and officially sanctioned. After almost a century of management and administration, however, these festivals too have been transformed in fundamental ways. Some would argue that their ritual dimensions have been reshaped as well. Yet another source of input is from the various Saint/guru-based Hindu, reform movements such as Sai Baba, Sri Ramakrishna, Sri Aurobindo and Vivekananda. Expectedly, a dominant strain here is a reformist brand of Hinduism that highlights the rational, philosophical and scriptural aspects of this religious tradition and, more importantly, discourages the more ritualistic, superstitious, "primitive" and highly emotional elements of the same. The strong influence of English-educated, middle-class Hindus is evident in producing an officially sanctioned version of Hinduism. In this, one sees shades of what Tong (1992) has noted as the intellectualization and rationalization of religion in Singapore. Yet, constructions of "Official Hinduism" and "Popular Hinduism" are obviously class-related phenomena, as well as the outcome of state discourse on religion.

Much of what persists in Singapore in the name of "folk Hinduism", carried in the veneration of local cult deities, household deities and the accompanying ritual complex that sustains this domain, are not included in constructions of "Official Hinduism". This practice of offering meat, alcohol and intoxicants to deities; the reliance on spirit-mediums and trances; and the presentation of Hindu deities in their aggressive and malevolent manifestations would place this squarely in the second of Vertovec's dichotomy, the domain of "Popular Hinduism". This latter field fascinates educated, middle-class and upper-class Hindus, but also provokes critique and condemnation. The proponents of "Official Hinduism" are inspired to initiate "reform" but it is timely to remember that this is not necessarily rooted in an ideology to "Sanskritize"/"Brahmanize" Hinduism but is often grounded in a rather different thinking, that is, in the world of bureaucratic and administrative logic (Sinha, 2003). It is worth mentioning that, often, the agenda of these two ideologies conflate and overlap in complex ways that produce the "same" end-results vis-à-vis religious practices.

This authorized version of what Hinduism in Singapore should be is subject to a variety of administrative and disciplinary processes, necessary for sustaining its proper public image. The rallying call is for a specific kind of Hinduism appropriate for Singapore *in the present*, given its multi-ethnicity and multi-religiosity, and its citizenry who are professed to be modern, urban, rational, progressive and educated. These articulations have augmented the need for a version of Hinduism that is distanced from superstitious, primitive, overly ritualistic and emotional dimensions of the religion. I suggest that in this regulation (through the HEB, the HAB, the management committee of temples, and elites of the Hindu community) there is also carried a condensed view of what constitutes real, "proper" and legitimate Hinduism.

The concern with producing a respectable image of Hinduism relevant for modern Singapore is by no means new, but takes us back to at least the mid-twentieth century. This image was also intensified through reformist and modernist thinking in the post-independence period. For instance, it is notable that the year 1969 saw the inauguration of the "Singapore Hindus Religious and Cultural Seminar", on the theme of "Unity in Nation Building". This was followed by two seminars on the theme of "Religion and Community Service" and "Youth, Religion and Nation Building" in 1970 and 1971, respectively. As far as I could establish, this initiative, which was intended for annual seminars, was not successful beyond 1971. Another significant communal effort to raise social awareness about Hinduism can be dated to 1980, when the newly-formed Hindu Centre (Singapore) organized a seminar on "Religion and Moral Education in a Changing Society" and raised issues similar to those in previous seminars. Numerous other initiatives undertaken under the auspices of Hindu temples and associations can be cited to demonstrate that the Hindu community has been self-reflexive about the challenges and dilemmas it faces as a minority religion within a secular, modern and materialist context of the nation-state. Here are some concerns articulated in these discussions: the role of Hindu temples (not just places of worship but as centres of social service); the emphasis on explicit religious education of Hindus and allocation of requisite resources to achieve this; the institution of meditation and *bhajan* groups within temples to supplement daily worship and *puja* carried out therein; the need to reach out to younger members by forming youth groups in the temples; and encouragement of various types of social service and voluntary work among Hindus. Members of the Singapore Hindu community will agree that almost 25 years later, the agenda carry as much weight in the present. Although many of the proposals have been acted upon, leading to significant shifts within Hindu domains. One also observes areas of overlap and continuity over time at the discursive level, about the concerns of the local Hindu community. It is, indeed, striking that many of the "problems" and areas for action identified over the last few decades continue to be articulated by the local Hindu leadership today.

Concluding Remarks

Thus, at the level of practice, we have seen that there are many and diverse ways of being Hindu in Singapore, and not all of these modes involve Indian Hindus exclusively. The multiplicity of everyday Hinduism also includes numerous individuals of Chinese ethnicity who may consider themselves Taoist or Buddhist but who also engage in Hindu practices. Thus, there is no complete coincidence between Indian ethnicity and Hindu identity, and while conventionally (and officially) the latter is perceived to be an ethnic-religious identity, ethnographic variations challenge this reading. Despite efforts to organize, codify and delimit the Hindu realm, religious syncretism continues to be the norm. Not only does one witness the incorporation of elements from within different Hindu strands, but also easy borrowing from "non-Hindu" religious traditions. This mixing and matching produces a hybridization that enables diverse (and sometimes contradictory) components of ritual behaviour and thinking to co-exist. What is most remarkable is that what may be officially considered transgressive, deviant and illegitimate, is viewed as commonplace and normal from the perspective of ordinary practitioners. Singaporeans are used to the Census exercise of measuring the size of ethnic and religious populations, and while some get allocated to specific religious categories by default, many gravitate to religious affiliations not captured by official categories. Yet, in the realm of religious practice, ethnic and religious labels may mean little for those who are more concerned with "doing" religion and being religious, than calling themselves "Hindu" or "Taoist".

Officially, we see that the concern with producing the "right" image of Hinduism is elite-driven and occurs via the combined efforts of local Hindu leadership located in such spaces as the Agamic Hindu temples, the Hindu Endowments Board, the Hindu Advisory Board and the Hindu Centre. Within these institutional nexuses, there is an obvious concern with drawing boundaries and circumscribing what constitutes "real" Hinduism. This entails a conscious selection of what constitutes the legitimate aspects of the religion, and the rejection of others as "non-Hindu". Here, the respectability and public presentation of the religion, for the consumption of others, are priorities that require careful management and regulation. As we have seen, apart from the input of the local leadership, this construction could not be sustained if not for the strong support of lay Hindus, who act upon this interpretation as well.

Interestingly, the shape of authorized "Singaporean Hinduism" is not entirely textual and scripture-based, but is a fusion of disparate strands including Agamic, Vedic and "folk" elements. Yet, driven by bureaucratic, reformist and modernist agenda, official prescriptions continue to select and declare some rituals and festivals as "Hindu" and while denying others this status. To many Hindus, this selection process appears random and ad hoc, lacks any religious backing, and is motivated by administrative and political concerns. Therefore, tensions between "Popular" and "Official" Hinduism are to be expected and surface through contestations, the most recent being the closing down of the Muneeswaran Temple in Jalan Bena, Changi. While the two domains as constructions are distinct and separate, in practice, they are brought into close and uncomfortable contact through the ritual behaviour of those individuals whose interpretation of Hinduism is more inclusive rather than circumscribed. The possibility of these twin constructions of Hinduism and the contestations that follow do carry implications for the ways in which Hindu, Indian, Tamil and non-Tamil identities are thought about, constituted and enacted. For instance, local Tamil Hindus have proposed a return to the gods, saints, rituals and customs of the "Tamil country" and to sacred Hindu literature in Tamil. The rationale here is simply "because we are Tamil" and the attachment to "all things Tamil" is an affirmation and assertion of their Tamil identity. They lament the proclivity towards "Brahmanic" and "Sanskritic" ideology and practice they see in the Agamic temples, and would like to see "Tamil Hinduism" instituted in Singapore temples. On the other hand, those who are attracted to "Popular Hinduism" are less worried about exclusive definitions of their "ethnic" identities, largely because this domain draws a large number of non-Tamil, non-Indian and "non-Hindu" Singaporeans. Also, these individuals routinely engage in ritual practices that are viewed by the authorities as not just "un-Hindu", but also "un-Indian". Such sentiments and practices are disturbing in challenging the taken-for-granted limits of fields implied in the labels "Hindu" and "Indian" and, therefore, render their meanings uncertain. More importantly, they also complicate the natural conflation of Hindu and Indian identities.

In practice, there are many constructions of Hinduism and many modes of being Hindu. The categories seem to allow for considerable flexibility of interpretation in everyday life. The ethnographic material from Singapore strongly suggests that "religious identity" cannot be meaningfully viewed as an exclusive and immutable property of specific individuals. It is more viable to consider the "making" and "unmaking" of identities and communities. The data at hand demonstrate the central role of individual agency in making contextual and personally relevant religious choices, which produce alternative ways of conceptualizing a "Hindu" identity and translating this into practice. A sociological analysis further reveals that "Official Hinduism" does not reflect the diversity of practices and practitioners from the local Hindu community. Despite this difference of opinion, as yet, few structural constraints actively discourage or suppress these unconventional (but marginal) initiatives. The data presented here support the conclusion that while the labels "Hinduism" and "Hindu" are firmly entrenched in the everyday life of Singapore Hindus and are not likely to be rejected or replaced anytime soon, there is also nothing patently obvious, certain or transparent about their usage in specific ethnographic contexts.

REFERENCES

Arasaratnam, Sinnappah (1970) *Indians in Malaysia and Singapore.* Kuala Lumpur: Oxford University Press.

Basham, Arthur Llewellyn (1954) *The Wonder That Was India: A Survey of the History and Culture of the Indian Sub-continent before the Coming of the Muslims.* London: Sidgwick and Jackson.

Bharati, Aghenanda (1971) "Hinduism and Modernisation", in Robert F. Spencer, ed., *Religion and Change in Contemporary Asia.* Minneapolis: University of Minnesota Press, pp. 67–104.

Bowes, Pratima (1977) *The Hindu Religious Tradition: A Philosophical Approach.* London: Routledge and Paul.

Chaudhuri, N. C. (1979) *Hinduism.* London: Chotto and Windus.

Dalmia, Vasusha and Heinrich Von Stietencron (1995) *Representing Hinduism: The Construction of Religious Traditions and National Identity.* New Delhi: Sage Publications.

Das, Veena (1977) *Structure and Cognition: Aspects of Hindu Caste and Ritual.* New Delhi: Oxford University Press.

Frykenberg, Robert. E. (1993) "Constructions of Hinduism at the Nexus of History and Religion", *Journal of Interdisciplinary History* 23:523–50.
———. (2001) "The Emergence of Modern 'Hinduism' as a Concept and as an Institution: A Reappraisal with Special Reference to South India", in Gunther-Dietz Sontheimer and Hermann Kulke, ed. *Hinduism Reconsidered.* Delhi: Manohar Publishers, pp. 82–107.
Kinsley, D. (1982) *Hinduism.* Englewood Cliffs, NJ: Prentice Hall Inc.
Mani, A. (1977) "The Changing Caste-structure amongst Singapore Indians". Unpublished Masters thesis. Department of Sociology, National University of Singapore.
Mialaret, Jean-Pierre (1969) *Hinduism in Singapore: A Guide to the Temples in Singapore.* Singapore: Donald Moore.
Muller, Max, F. (1882) *Lectures on the Origin of Religion.* London: Longmans, Green & Co.
Nadarajah, Gunalan (1988) "Hinduism in the Domestic Setting". Unpublished Academic Exercise. Department of Sociology, National University of Singapore.
Parrinder, Edward Geoffrey (1971) *Dictionary of Non-Christian Religions.* Amersham: Hulton.
Pocock, David (1973) *Mind, Body and Wealth: A Study of Belief and Practice in an Indian Village.* Oxford: Basil Blackwell.
Radhakrishnan, Sarvapelli (1961) *The Hindu View of Life.* London: George Allen & Unwin Ltd.
Rajah, Ananda (1975) *The Ecological Study of Shrines.* Unpublished Academic Exercise. Department of Sociology, National University of Singapore.
Renou, L. (1953) *Religions of Ancient India.* London: The Athalone Press.
Sandhu, Kernial Singh (1969) *Indians in Malaya: Some Aspects of Their Immigration and Settlement Patterns (1786–1957).* London: Cambridge University Press.
Sen, M. K. (1961) *Hinduism.* Harmondswroth: Penguin Books.
Sharma, Arvind (1986) "What is Hinduism? A Sociological Approach", *Social Compass* 33 (2–3): 177–83.
Siddique, Sharon and Nirmala PuruShotam (1982) *Singapore's Little India: Past, Present and Future.* Singapore: Institute of Southeast Asian Studies.
Singapore Hindus Religious and Cultural Seminar Report (1969–1971) The Organising Committee, Third in Singapore Hindus Religious and Cultural Seminar-1971. Singapore.
Sinha, Vineeta (1988) "Hinduism in Singapore: A Sociological and Ethnographic Perspective". M. Soc. Sci. dissertation. Department of Sociology, National University of Singapore.
———. (1997) "Unpacking the Labels 'Hindu' & 'Hinduism' in Singapore", *Southeast Asian Journal of Social Science* 25(2): 139–60.
———. (2003) "Merging 'Different' Sacred Spaces: Enabling Religious Encounters through Pragmatic Utilization of Space?", *Contributions to Indian Sociology* n.s. 37(3): 459–94.
Smith, Wilfred Cantwell (1958) *The Meaning and End of Religion.* San Francisco: Harper & Row.
Sontheimer, Gunther D. (2001) "Hinduism: The Five Components and their Interaction", in Gunther-Dietz Sontheimer and Hermann Kulke, eds. *Hinduism Reconsidered.* Delhi: Manohar Publishers, pp. 305–324.
Srinivas, M. N. (1960) "Hinduism", *Encyclopaedia Brittanica* Vol. 11: 547–7.
Thapar, Romilla (1989) "Syndicated Hinduism", in *Hinduism Reconsidered,* Gunther-Dietz Sontheimer and Hermann Kulke, eds. Paperback edition in 2001. Delhi: Manohar Publishers, pp. 54–81.
Tong, Chee Kiong (1992) "The Rationalization of Religion", in Ban Kah Choon, Anne PAkir and Tong Chee Kiong, eds. *Imagining Singapore.* Singapore: Times Academic Press, pp. 00–00.

Vertovec, Steven (1994) "'Official' and 'Popular' Hinduism in Diaspora: Historical and Contemporary Trends in Surinam, Trinidad and Guyana", *Contributions to Indian Sociology New Series* 28(1): 123–47.

———. (2000) *The Hindu Diaspora: Comparative Patterns*. London & New York: Routledge.

Weber, Max (1958) *The Religion of India: The Sociology of Hinduism and Buddhism*. Trans. and ed. Hans Gerth and Don Martindale. New York: The Free Press, Macmillan Publishing Co.

Weightman, Simon (1985) "Hinduism", in John R. Hinnells, ed., *A Handbook of Living Religions*. Hardmonsworth: Penguin, pp. 261–309.

CHINESE AND MALAYS IN SINGAPORE: INCOMES, EDUCATION AND EMPLOYMENT, 1954–1995[1]

Lee Kiat Jin

Introduction

This essay examines the trajectory of the inequality between the Chinese and Malays in Singapore from 1954 to 1995. I focus on three aspects, specifically, incomes, education and employment. In 1995, the Chinese and Malays comprised respectively 78.7 percent and 13.9 percent of the resident population (Singapore Department of Statistics, 1996: 63–4). There are two pertinent components to the inquiry. First, I shall briefly review the principal contemporary literature regarding racial stratification in Singapore. Second, I shall document the transformations in the disparity between the Chinese and Malays. In the process, I shall verify present understandings and rectify fundamental misconceptions about the abovementioned.

Review of the Literature

There are three main propositions on the inequality between the Chinese and Malays in Singapore. The first and most prevalent thesis contends that the disparity had always been critical (for example, Bedlington, 1974; Betts, 1976; Clutterbuck, 1984; Chiew, 1987; Zoohri, 1987; Chiew, 1991). Accordingly, Chan (1971: 18) states that "(i)t is not without significance that past racial trouble in Singapore (except for the Maria Hertogh riots in 1950) were instigated by economic grievances". Similarly, Kassim (1974: 39) discerns that the economic plight of the Malays caused Singapore's worst racial riots in 1964.[2]

[1] An earlier version was presented at the Workshop for Contentious Politics at Columbia University in Fall 1998. I would also like to acknowledge Professor Charles Tilly for his incisive suggestions aimed at further improving the quality of this essay. In addition, I would like to thank Professor Michael Hanagan especially, for encouraging me to publish a rendition of the original paper.

[2] Contrary to popular perception, the racial riots in 1964 were the only major skirmishes between the Chinese and Malays in Singapore.

In a related second proposition, Vasil (1995) suggests that the weak standing of the Malays before 1959 remained stagnant or even declined until the 1980s. The Malay position has since improved significantly. On the contrary, the third thesis maintains that the standing of the Malays against the Chinese only deteriorated after 1959. Li (1989) exemplifies this perspective. Subsequently, Brown (1994), Lai (1995), and Rahim (1998) incorporate her analysis.

While evaluating the efficacy of these three propositions, I shall expound four basic points. First, the relative Malay income position only declined recently, specifically between 1966 and 1972. Second, in 1966, the educational inequality between the Chinese and Malays was minimal compared with the ensuing years. Third, as regards employment, it was the Malay lack of representation among the employers and its own account workers that previously defined its dissimilarity to the Chinese. During the later years, the Malays were under-represented among the administrators and managers. Finally, from 1973 onwards, there was a manifest lack of correspondence between the fluctuating income inequality, and the increasing educational and occupational disparities.

Household and Personal Incomes

As I mentioned earlier, the first and second theses postulate that the income inequality between the Chinese and Malays has always been acute. Yet, a little-known study conducted in 1953–4 challenges these propositions; previously, detailed statistics on the economic characteristics of the Chinese and Malays were unavailable. Goh (1958: 19) finds that 16 percent of the Chinese and five percent of the Malays lived in households with monthly personal incomes of $400 or more. These households were outside the scope of his study. Instead, the study concentrated on the remaining 83 percent of the population that lived in households earning less than $400.

Table 1 displays the contradiction between the perception that the Malays were economically impoverished and their favorable performance outside the higher end of the income distribution in 1954. Of particular interest is the comparison between the households headed by the local-born Malays and immigrant Chinese; they were the largest groups within their communities. Among the Malay household heads, 73.6 percent were born in Singapore or Malaya. Among

Table 1. Monthly Household and Personal Incomes, and Percentage of Households at the Poverty Line, 1954

	Monthly Household Income ($)			Monthly Personal Income ($)		Households at Poverty Line (per cent)			
	Lower Quartile	Median	Mean	Upper Quartile	Mean	Below 50%	Below 100%	Below 150%	Below 200%
Local-born Chinese	105	161	192	240	147	5.7	20.4	39.9	54.8
Immigrant Chinese	115	148	159	216	136	9.1	25.1	45.2	57.9
Local-born Malays	118	160	177	217	146	3.8	20.2	43.4	62.7
Immigrant Malays	94	119	141	166	110	3.8	34.4	59.4	76.3
Chinese	–	–	169	–	139	8.1	24.0	43.4	56.7
Malays	–	–	168	–	136	3.8	24.0	47.6	66.3

Source: Derived from Goh (1958: 26, 31, 87, 99, 135).

the Chinese, 70.1 percent were born outside Singapore or Malaya (Goh, 1958: 31).

In contrast to local-born Malays, immigrant Chinese were often assumed to be the most enterprising and prosperous section of Singapore's population. The local-born Malays, however, did better than the immigrant Chinese. This was true whether at the lower quartile household income, median household income, mean household income, or upper quartile household income. The discrepancies were especially striking with regards to their median and mean incomes. The median immigrant Chinese income was $148 per month in opposition to $160 for the local-born Malays; it was 92.5 percent of the local-born Malay income. Likewise, the mean immigrant Chinese income was $159, in contrast to $177 for the local-born Malays; thus, it was only 89.8 per cent of the local-born Malay income. Moreover, if we define below 100 percent of the poverty line as being relative poverty, then 25.1 percent of the immigrant Chinese households, as opposed to just 20.2 percent of the local-born Malays, were living in relative poverty. Similarly, if we delimit below 50 percent of the poverty line as absolute poverty, 9.1 percent of the immigrant Chinese, in contrast to merely 3.8 percent of the local-born Malays, were in absolute poverty.

As a whole, in 1954, the Malays fared as well as the Chinese apart from the upper end of the income scale. There were near parity with regard to mean household and personal incomes. The average Malay and Chinese household incomes were $168 and $169 per month, respectively; the Malay income was 99.4 percent of the Chinese income. At the same time, the respective mean Malay and Chinese personal incomes were $136 and $139 per month, with the Malay income at 97.8 percent of the Chinese income. Furthermore, the Malays did better than the Chinese at the bottom end of the income distribution. Compared with just 3.8 percent for the Malays, 8.1 percent of the Chinese households were living in absolute poverty; hence, this refutes the conception that the Malays have always been underprivileged.

In turn, Li (1989: 100–8) argues that the Malay household and personal income positions only worsened after 1959. She expressly stresses that between 1975 and 1980, the Malay personal income standing declined absolutely. Li (1989: 103) restricts her delineation to male workers as she professes that "the entry of large numbers of Malay females into low-paying manufacturing jobs in the late 1970s would . . . distort the comparison over the years".

Table 2. Employed Male Malays and Chinese by Monthly Income, 1975, 1978, 1980 (percent)

	Earning Less than $400 per Month		Earning More than $1,000 per Month	
	Malays	Chinese	Malays	Chinese
1975	62.6 (86.2)	67.1 (67.6)	0.8 (1.1)	7.0
1978	75.8	53.3	1.8	8.9
1980	64.1	41.8	2.7	12.9

Sources: Li, 1989:103; Singapore Ministry of Labour & National Statistical Commission 1975: 95.

Table 2 reports (and corrects) Li's data on the monthly incomes of male Malays and Chinese in 1975, 1978 and 1980. In 1975, according to Li, 62.6 percent of Malay men were earning less than $400 per month. By 1978, Li's figure had risen sharply to 75.8 percent, which purports the swift degeneration of the Malay position. In 1980, according to the same analysis, 64.1 percent of the Malay male working population earned less than $400. All together, in Li's data, a greater proportion of Malay men was earning $400 or less in 1980 than in 1975. Meanwhile, their Chinese peers made steady progress.

In 1975, 67.1 percent of Chinese men earned less than $400 while in 1978, the figure was 53.3 percent. By 1980, just 41.8 percent of male Chinese were earning less than $400. Li concludes, therefore, that the standing of Malay male workers declined absolutely between 1975 and 1980.

Employing the same primary source as Li, my figures in parentheses rectify her computation oversights and effectively diminish her allegations. In 1975, the ratio of the Malay male working population that earned less than $400 per month was 86.2 percent instead of 62.6 percent. Like their Chinese counterparts, Malay men made constant headway from 1975 to 1980. Contradictory to the assertions of Li (1989: 103), Brown (1994: 87) and Rahim (1998: 19–21), Malay male workers most certainly did not incur an absolute decrease in their position.

Table 3. Employed Male Chinese and Malays by Monthly Income, 1975, 1978, 1980 (percent)

	Chinese			Malays		
	1975	1978	1980	1975	1978	1980
Less than $200	23.8	15.7	11.4	23.7	15.7	8.9
$200–$399	43.9	37.6	30.4	62.5	60.0	55.2
$400–$599	16.8	25.1	28.2	10.0	16.2	23.5
$600–$799	5.7	8.7	11.8	1.8	4.5	7.0
$800–$999	2.8	4.1	5.2	0.9	1.8	2.7
$1,000–$1,499	4.1	5.6	7.4	0.7	1.4	1.9
$1,500 & More	2.9	3.2	5.6	0.4	0.4	0.8
Dissimilarity Index	18.6	22.4	24.8			

Sources: Singapore Ministry of Labour & National Statistical Commission, 1975:95; Singapore Ministry of Labour, 1979: 98; Singapore Ministry of Labour, 1981: 69.

Meanwhile, between 1975 and 1980, the Malay male working population did experience a very modest descent in its relative income standing. Table 3 shows that the Dissimilarity Index (DI) between the Chinese and Malay male income distributions increased marginally. The DI indicates the percentage in one scale that must be reclassified to make the two distributions identical. A DI of 0 denotes that the two scales are totally similar to each other. In contrast, a DI of 100 means that the two distributions are completely different from each other. For example, in 1975, 18.6 percent of the Malay or Chinese male population must be reordered to ensure that the

Malay and Chinese income scales are analogous to each other. Accordingly, in 1975, the DI between the Chinese and Malay male incomes was 18.6 points while in 1978, it was 22.4 points. By 1980, the DI between the Chinese and Malay male incomes had become 24.8 points.

Table 4. Employed Chinese and Malays by Monthly Income, 1966 (percent)

	Chinese	Malays
Less than $100	25.5	14.2
$100–$149	19.8	33.5
$150–$199	18.7	22.3
$200–$249	12.6	13.7
$250–$499	16.0	14.4
$500–$749	4.2	1.2
$750 and Over	3.2	0.7

Source: Derived from Rao & Ramakrishnan, 1980: 97.

I instead propound that it was between 1966 and 1972 that the comparative Malay personal and household income positions significantly declined. Table 4 portrays the Chinese and Malay monthly personal incomes in 1966. Like in 1954, the Chinese working population dominated both upper and lower ends of the income distribution. For instance, in 1966, 25.5 percent of the Chinese as opposed to 14.2 percent of the Malays were earning less than $100 per month. At the same time, compared with 1.9 percent for the Malays, 7.4 percent of Chinese were earning more than $500. Moreover, in 1966, the Chinese and Malay female participation rates in the labour force corresponded with those of 1954. In 1954, the proportion of the Chinese female working population was 27.0 percent of its male peer. For Malay women, it was 9.9 percent of their male counterparts (Goh, 1958: 26). In 1966, the ratio of Chinese female workers was 30.8 percent of their male peers. For the Malay female population, it was 8.5 percent of its male counterpart (Rao & Ramakrishnan, 1980: 96–7).

Table 5 suggests that the DI between the Chinese and Malay personal income scales fluctuated with a slight upward trend from 1972 to 1980. More significantly, as the overall DI between the Chinese and Malay incomes remained almost uniform, it also discloses that

Table 5. Employed Chinese and Malays by Monthly Income, 1972, 1974, 1975, 1978, 1980 (percent)

	Chinese					Malays				
	1972	1974	1975	1978	1980	1972	1974	1975	1978	1980
Less than $200	52.5	38.2	32.3	21.8	13.1	71.8	54.3	31.1	23.7	10.1
$200–$399	31.5	37.7	40.7	40.5	38.7	23.7	36.4	56.7	57.6	61.6
$400–$599	8.4	13.0	14.1	20.2	23.7	3.3	7.1	9.0	12.2	18.6
$600–$799	3.6	4.7	5.1	7.3	9.8	0.6	1.2	1.6	3.8	5.4
$800–$999	1.3	2.1	2.4	3.4	4.5	0.3	0.4	0.8	1.4	2.3
$1,000–$1,499	1.7	2.8	3.2	4.4	6.1	0.3	0.4	0.5	1.0	1.5
$1,500 & More	1.0	1.5	2.2	2.4	4.1	0	0.2	0.3	0.3	0.5
Dissimilarity Index	19.3	16.1	16.0	19.0	22.9					

Sources: Rao & Ramakrishnan, 1980: 109; Singapore Ministry of Labour & National Statistical Commission, 1974:93; Singapore Ministry of Labour & National Statistical Commission, 1975: 95; Singapore Ministry of Labour, 1979: 98; Singapore Ministry of Labour, 1981: 69.

the relative Malay standing had already declined by 1972. In 1972, 1974, 1975, 1978 and 1980, the respective DI between the Chinese and Malay incomes were 19.3, 16.1, 16.0, 19.0 and 22.9 points.

In addition, Table 5 demonstrates that in 1975, 1978 and 1980, the DI between the Chinese and Malay personal income distributions were alike those of their male segments at 16.0, 19.0 and 22.9 points, respectively. As outlined in Table 3, the respective DI for the Chinese and Malay male incomes were 18.6, 22.4 and 24.8 points. Contrary to the contention of Li, including the female workers in the inquiry did not seriously distort the comparison between the Chinese and Malay personal incomes.[3] On the contrary, it reduced the DI minimally.

Figure 1 proposes that the inequality between the mean Chinese and Malay household incomes declined from 1973 to 1980 but increased between 1980 and 1995. What is more important is that it also implies that the Malay household income position, in contrast to the Chinese position, had already degenerated by 1973. In 1973, the average Malay income was merely 67.3 percent of Chinese income, while in 1980, it advanced to 73.9 percent. In 1990, however, the mean Malay income decreased to 69.9 percent of

[3] This point does not apply to the mean Chinese and Malay household incomes because of the greater Chinese female participation rate in the labour force until 1980.

Figure 1. Malay and Chinese Households by Mean Monthly Income, 1973, 1980, 1990, 1995 (percent).

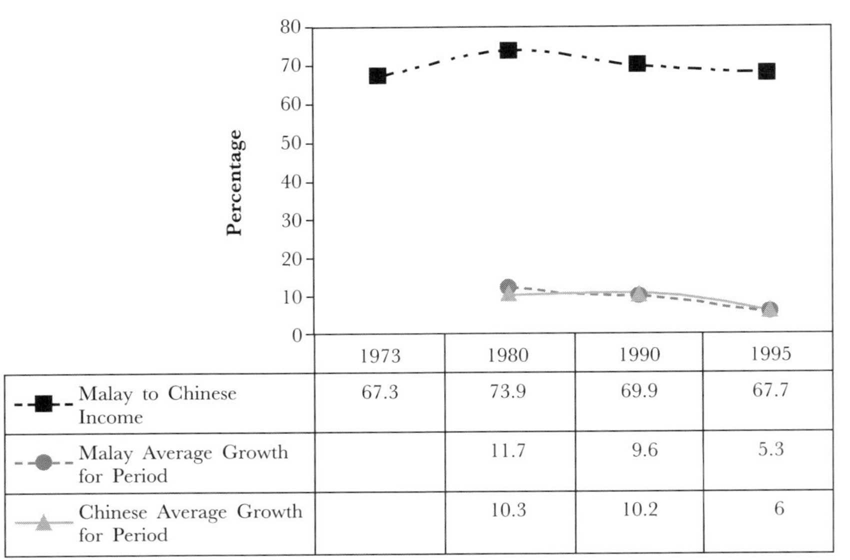

	1973	1980	1990	1995
Malay to Chinese Income	67.3	73.9	69.9	67.7
Malay Average Growth for Period		11.7	9.6	5.3
Chinese Average Growth for Period		10.3	10.2	6

Sources: Pang, 1982: 67; Singapore Department of Statistics, 1993: xiv; Singapore Department of Statistics, 1997: 19.

Chinese income. By 1995, it had fallen further to 67.7 percent of Chinese income. Accordingly, from 1973 to 1980, the average Malay income expanded 1.4 percent per annum more rapidly than the Chinese income. In contrast, between 1980 and 1990, the mean Chinese income increased 0.6 percent faster than Malay income. Likewise, from 1990 to 1995, the average Chinese income advanced more rapidly than the Malay income by 0.7 percent per annum.

Figure 2 indicates that the disparity between mean Chinese and Malay personal incomes expanded from 1966 to 1974 but fluctuated considerably without any distinct tendency between 1974 and 1995. It also establishes that the comparative Malay standing had already deteriorated by 1973. In 1966, the average Malay income was 83.9 percent of Chinese income. By 1973, it had declined to only 68.8 percent, and in 1974, the mean Malay income further descended to just 65.4 percent of Chinese income. In 1979, however, it improved to a 70.4 percent level, but in 1980, the average Malay income declined to 65.2 percent of the Chinese income. In 1990, it reverted

Figure 2. Employed Malays and Chinese by Mean Monthly Income, 1966,[4] 1973, 1974, 1979, 1980, 1990, 1995[5] (percent).

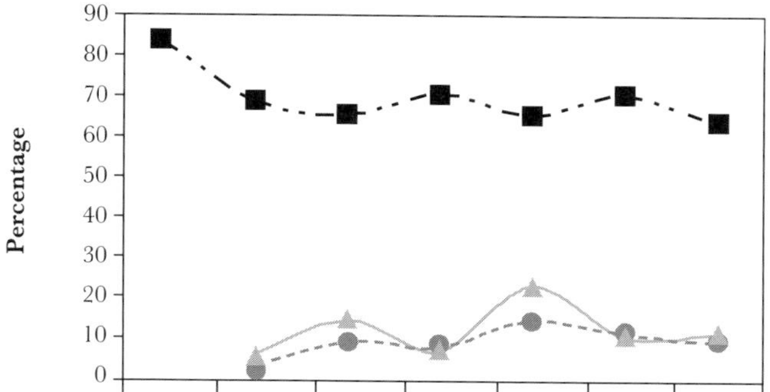

	1966	1973	1974	1979	1980	1990	1995
Malay to Chinese Income	83.9	68.8	65.4	70.4	65.2	70.1	63.3
Malay Average Growth for Period		2.2	8.3	7.7	13.5	10.5	8.3
Chinese Average Growth for Period		5.2	13.9	6.1	22.4	9.7	10.5

Percentage

Year

Sources: Pang, 1982: 67, 73), Singapore Department of Statistics, 1993: 17; Singapore Department of Statistics, 1996: 156–7.

to 70.1 percent while in 1995, the mean Malay income finally decreased to 63.3 percent of the Chinese income. Correspondingly, from 1966 to 1973, the average Chinese income increased 3 percent per annum faster than the Malay income. In addition, it advanced more rapidly by 5.6 percent between 1973 and 1974. On the other hand, from 1974 to 1979, the mean Malay income grew 1.6 percent

[4] There is a small discrepancy between the two sources of data regarding the mean Chinese and Malay monthly personal incomes in 1966. I utilize the figures from the more recent publication; however, the difference is insignificant. In Pang (1982: 67), the average Malay income was 81.3 percent of the Chinese income.

[5] The mean Malay and Chinese monthly personal incomes for 1995 are estimates of $1,560 and $2,465, respectively. For each intermediate income category, I presume its mid-point as its average. For the top class, emulating Rao & Ramakrishnan (1980: 21–2), I estimate its mean at 68.6 percent from its lower boundary (Inland Revenue Authority of Singapore, 1996: 68–9). For the lower category, I estimate its average at 50 percent from its upper boundary. In 1994, the mean of the bottom class was 56.9 percent from its upper boundary (Inland Revenue Authority of Singapore, 1995: 68–9). Similar data for 1995 and 1996 were unavailable.

Figure 3. Employed Malays and Chinese by Median Monthly Income, 1966, 1974, 1979, 1990, 1995 (percent).[6]

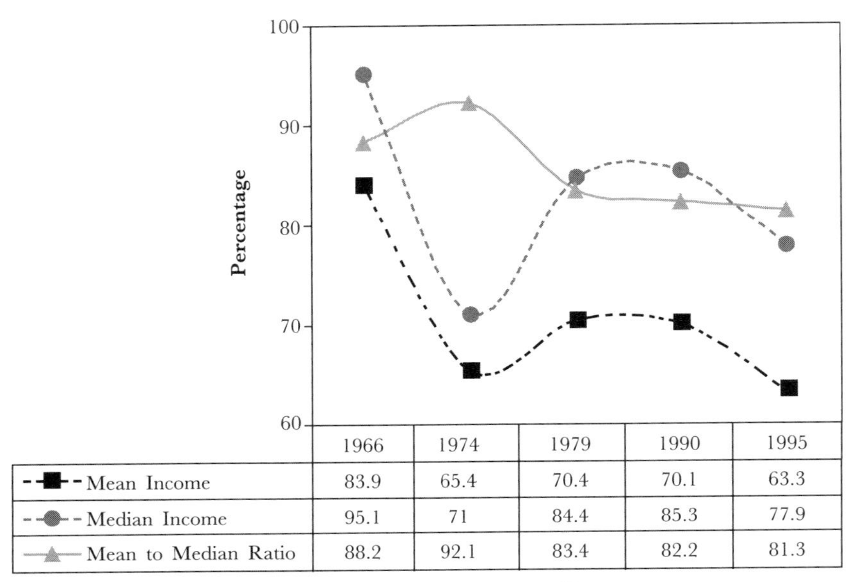

	1966	1974	1979	1990	1995
Mean Income	83.9	65.4	70.4	70.1	63.3
Median Income	95.1	71	84.4	85.3	77.9
Mean to Median Ratio	88.2	92.1	83.4	82.2	81.3

Sources: Derived from Figure 2; Rao & Ramakrishnan, 1980: 97; Singapore Ministry of Labour & National Statistical Commission, 1974: 93; Singapore Ministry of Labour, 1980: 99; Singapore Department of Statistics, 1996: 29.

faster than the Chinese income. In contrast, between 1979 and 1980, the average Chinese income expanded more rapidly by 8.9 percent. At the same time, the mean Malay income increased 0.8 percent faster than the Chinese income from 1980 to 1990. By comparison, between 1990 and 1995, the average Chinese income grew more rapidly by 2.2 percent per annum than the Malay income.

Figure 3 shows that the inequality between the median Chinese and Malay personal incomes increased from 1966 to 1974 but fluctuated without a trend between 1974 and 1995. It further affirms

[6] The median Malay and Chinese monthly personal incomes for 1966, 1974 and 1979 are estimates. In 1966, the respective Malay and Chinese incomes were $155 and $163. In 1974, they were $186 and $262, respectively. In 1979, the respective Malay and Chinese incomes were $303 and $359. Again, I presuppose an even distribution of individuals in each income category. For the intermediate classes, I assume their mid-points as their medians. For the Malay bottom category in 1974, I estimate its median at 40 percent from its upper boundary. Rao & Ramakrishnan (1980: 20) had previously approximated its mean at 37.2 percent from its upper boundary.

that the relative Malay position had already declined by 1974. In 1966, the median Malay income was 95.1 percent of the Chinese income. By 1974, however, it had descended to merely 71.0 percent. In contrast, in 1979, the median Malay income advanced to 84.4 percent of the Chinese income and in 1990, it grew minimally to 85.3 percent. At the same time, in 1995, the median Malay income eventually decreased to 77.9 percent of the Chinese income.

Furthermore, Figure 3 conveys the consistent reduction of the mean to median ratio in spite of the fluctuating personal income disparities between the Chinese and Malays from 1974 to 1995. This firmly suggests that the discrepancy between the Chinese and Malay personal incomes was shifting towards the higher end of income distribution. While the mean income depicts the simple average, the median income is in the 50th percentile of all earnings. Thus, the median income is much less susceptible than the mean income to a large variation in remuneration, particularly at the top end of the income scale. An increase in the mean Malay income or the median Chinese income will cause the mean to median ratio to expand, which indicates that the divergence between the Chinese and Malays transpired towards the bottom half of the income distribution scale. Conversely, an increase in the mean Chinese income or the median Malay income will induce the ratio to fall, denoting that the Chinese and Malay dissimilarity took place at the upper end of the income scale. Between 1966 and 1974, the mean to median ratio grew from 88.2 points to 92.1 points, which infers that the Chinese and Malay difference expanded towards the lower half of the income distribution scale. By contrast, in 1979, the ratio declined to 83.4 points. In 1990, it fell further to 82.2 points. By 1995, the mean to median ratio had eventually descended to 81.3 points. These suggest that between 1974 and 1995, the Chinese and Malay discrepancy steadily increased at the top end of the income scale.

Education

The genesis of Malay under-achievement in education has been well examined (Ahmat, 1973; Gopinathan, 1974; Zoohri, 1987). Yet, Table 6 demonstrates that in 1966, inequality between the Chinese and Malays was not at all immense. For instance, 1.6 percent of the Chinese and 0.4 percent of the Malays had completed their university or college education. At the same time, compared with 7.7 percent for the Chinese, 3.6 percent of the Malays were secondary school graduates. In addition, 31.8 percent of the Chinese and 34.3 percent of the Malays had concluded their primary education. Further, 58.9 percent of the Chinese as opposed to 61.7 percent of the Malays did not have primary school education.

Table 6. Chinese and Malay Non-Student Population Aged 10 Years and Over by Highest Qualification Attained, 1966, 1980, 1990, 1995 (percent)

	Chinese				Malays			
	1966[7]	1980	1990	1995	1966	1980	1990	1995
University	1.6	2.4	5.1	8.2	0.4	0.2	0.6	0.9
Upper Secondary	–	6.0	10.9	17.3	–	2.4	4.4	9.9
Secondary	7.7	12.5	24.4	26.2	3.6	11.7	25.8	33.2
Primary/ Incomplete Secondary	31.8	42.5	27.7	24.8	34.3	51.2	38.5	32.6
No Formal Education/ Incomplete Primary	58.9	36.6	31.9	23.5	61.7	34.5	30.7	23.4
Dissimilarity Index	5.3	8.7	12.2	14.8				

Sources: Singapore Ministry of National Development, 1967: 63–4; Singapore Department of Statistics, 1993: xvi; Singapore Department of Statistics, 1996: 74–7.

Table 6 also discloses that from 1966 to 1995, the comparative Malay educational standing continually declined. In 1966, the DI between the Chinese and Malay educational scales was only 5.3 points. In 1980 and 1990, however, they were at 8.7 points and 12.2 points, respectively. By 1995, the DI between the Chinese and Malay attainments had expanded to 14.8 points. The increasingly dissimilar percentages of Chinese and Malays who had completed their university education elucidated the descent of the Malay position. Between 1980 and 1995, while the overall Chinese university graduate population steadily advanced from 2.4 points to 8.2 points, the Malays grew from 0.2 point to just 0.9 points.

Table 7 and Table 8 display the remarkable increases in educational disparity between the Chinese and Malays from the oldest to youngest age groups. To facilitate comparisons, I have included the periods during which each cohort began its primary education. For

[7] In Singapore Ministry of National Development (1967), the "University" category consists of both university and college graduates.

Table 8, I have also confined my investigation to the upper age group of 60–64 years and the lower age cohort of 25–29 years. Beyond 60–64 years, natural mortality becomes an increasingly important factor. At the same time, many of those below 25–29 years have yet to complete their education.

Table 7. Chinese and Malay Non-Student 35–54 Age Cohort by Highest Qualification Attained and Commencement of Primary Education, 1966 (percent)

	Chinese	Malays
	1919–38	
University/College	1.5	0.4
Secondary	5.2	2.4
Primary/ Incomplete Secondary	17.5	19.4
No Formal Education/ Incomplete Primary	75.8	77.8
Dissimilarity Index	3.9	

Source: Singapore Ministry of National Development, 1967: 63–4.

Table 8. Chinese (C) and Malay (M) Non-Student Population Age Cohorts by Highest Qualification Attained and Commencement of Primary Education, 1995 (percent)

	University		Upper Secondary		Secondary		Primary/ Incomplete Secondary		No Formal Education/ Incomplete Primary		Dissimilarity Index
	C	M	C	M	C	M	C	M	C	M	
60–64 1938–42	1.9	0	4.2	0.8	8.8	3.5	22.0	22.3	63.1	73.4	10.6
55–59 1943–7	3.0	0.4	7.9	2.2	14.2	7.5	28.1	32.0	46.8	57.9	15.0
50–54 1948–52	4.1	0.6	9.7	2.9	19.0	13.6	29.5	39.2	37.7	43.7	15.7
45–49 1953–7	5.6	0.6	11.8	4.6	25.8	27.2	32.9	40.6	23.9	27.0	12.2
40–44 1958–62	7.0	0.6	13.3	7.4	31.3	36.5	33.9	41.1	14.5	14.4	12.4
35–39 1963–7	9.1	1.0	17.7	9.3	32.5	41.0	29.9	39.0	10.8	9.7	17.6
30–34 1968–72	13.6	1.3	20.0	10.4	33.5	44.9	25.7	36.0	7.2	7.4	21.9
25–29 1973–7	19.1	2.5	29.5	17.2	30.4	44.8	16.1	28.5	4.9	7.0	28.9

Source: Singapore Department of Statistics, 1996: 74–7.

With respect to the generation that started its primary school education from 1919 to 1938, the DI between the Chinese and Malay distributions was just 3.9 points. In distinct contrast, the DI for the five age groups that began their primary education from 1938 onwards was much larger. With regard to the cohorts of 60–64, 55–59, 50–54, 45–49 and 40–44 years in 1995, they fluctuated at 10.6, 15.0, 15.7, 12.2 and 12.4 points, respectively. Since 1963, the DI between the Chinese and Malay attainments had started to increase. Concerning the groups of 35–39, 30–34, and 25–29 years, they were 17.6, 21.9, and 28.9 points, respectively. Interestingly, the last cohort that had the highest DI was also the first whole group to undergo the new educational policy implemented in 1979 after the 1978 Goh Report sanctioned the elaborate tracking of students to reduce educational wastage.

As I noted previously, the growing Malay under-representation among the university graduate population epitomized its relative educational decline. For example, pertaining to the 40–44 years cohort in 1995, seven percent of the Chinese and 0.6 percent of the Malays had graduated from university. With regards to the age group of 35–39, they were 9.1 percent and 1.0 percent, respectively. About the 30–34 years cohort, 13.6 percent of the Chinese as opposed to only 1.3 percent of the Malays were university graduates, and with regard to the group of 25–29 years, in contrast to 19.1 percent for the Chinese, just 2.5 percent of the Malays had concluded university education.

In addition, Table 8 reveals that in 1995, there was no Malay university graduate in the 60–64 years cohort. This insinuates the substantial emigration of the tiny Malay educational elite, in all likelihood to Malaysia. Except for brief anecdotes, there has been no contemporary account of this phenomenon. In Rahim (1998: 253), the then Minister of Environment and Malay/Muslim Affairs, Ahmad Mattar, inadvertently divulged the departure of Malay graduates in the Singapore Civil Service for Malaysia in the early 1970s.

The DI in educational attainments between the Chinese and Malay age groups of 35–39, 30–34 and 25–29 years was greater than the overall DI of 14.8 points for the Chinese and Malays in 1995. Excluding an altogether unanticipated contraction in the educational discrepancies among the younger cohorts presently in school, coupled with the progressive passing of the elder groups with much smaller dissimilarities, the current tendency towards increasing inequality will unquestionably endure into the immediate future.

Employment

Plenty of attention has been accorded to the critical Chinese dominance over the Malays in entrepreneurship. For example, Li (1989: 106–8) speculates that it is an important cause of inequality between the Chinese and Malays after 1959. Elsewhere, Chiew (1987: 79, 81) and Chiew (1991: 148–51) claim the same but on very different premises.

Table 9. Chinese and Malay Workers Aged 10 Years and Over by Employment Status, 1957, 1966, 1970, 1980, 1990 (percent)

	Chinese					Malays				
	1957	1966	1970	1980	1990	1957	1966	1970	1980	1990
Employers	4.2	4.1	3.1	4.5	3.7	0.2	0.3	0.3	0.3	0.7
Own account workers	20.8	17.8	19.3	12.7	8.1	6.4	6.2	6.1	3.4	2.4
Unpaid family workers	6.8	5.4	4.5	3.1	1.3	0.7	0.6	0.5	0.5	0.3
Employees	68.2	72.7	73.1	79.7	86.9	92.7	92.9	93.1	95.8	96.6
Dissimilarity Index	24.5	20.2	20.0	16.1	9.7					

Sources: Singapore Department of Statistics, 1964: 181–2; Singapore Ministry of National Development, 1967: 97–8; Singapore Department of Statistics, 1973b: 69–70; Singapore Department of Statistics, 1993: xvi.

On the contrary, Table 9 shows that between 1957 and 1990, the DI between the Chinese and Malay employment status steadily declined. In 1957, 1966, 1970, 1980 and 1990, they were 24.5, 20.2, 20.0, 16.1 and 9.7 points, respectively.

Meanwhile, the Chinese prevalence in enterprise as measured by employers and own account workers constantly decreased. While the overall proportion of the Chinese working population who were employers fluctuated slightly downwards from 4.2 percent in 1957 to 3.7 percent in 1990, the Malay number increased marginally from 0.2 percent to 0.7 percent. Between 1957 and 1990, however, the Chinese own account worker figures diminished significantly. In 1957, 20.8 percent of the Chinese were own account workers while in 1966, it was 17.8 percent. In 1970, the Chinese own account workers grew minimally to 19.3 percent. In contrast, just 12.7 percent of the Chinese were own account workers in 1980. By 1990, the percentage of the Chinese own account workers had fallen to only 8.1 points. Conversely, from 1957 to 1990, Chinese employees expanded rapidly. In 1957, 1966, 1970, 1980 and 1990, they comprised 68.2, 72.7, 73.1, 79.7 and 86.9 percent of the Chinese working population, respectively. To recapitulate, the Chinese and Malay employment status had become increasingly similar between 1957 and 1990.

Table 10. Chinese and Malay Workers Aged 10 Years and Over by Occupation, 1957, 1966, 1970, 1980, 1990, 1995 (percent)[8]

	Chinese						Malays					
	1957	1966	1970	1980	1990	1995	1957	1966	1970	1980	1990	1995
Professional & Technical	4.4	6.5	8.4	12.2	17.3	24.6	2.9	4.5	5.6	6.0	9.7	15.3
Administrative & Managerial	1.5	1.8	1.7	6.8	10.0	12.7	0.5	0.4	0.3	0.7	1.1	1.6
Clerical	9.3	11.9	12.7	14.9	13.8	13.7	12.1	12.1	13.4	9.9	15.4	18.1
Sales	20.9	17.8	17.7	–	–	–	3.2	3.0	4.2	–	–	–
Services	15.5	19.8	11.6	–	–	–	29.3	35.6	23.6	–	–	–
Sales & Services	–	–	–	15.2	14.5	13.6	–	–	–	12.0	14.0	13.2
Agriculture & Fishery	8.8	4.2	4.3	1.8	0.3	0.1	9.9	3.2	5.3	1.0	0.3	0.0
Production & Related	39.6	38.0	40.1	42.8	39.7	30.5	42.1	41.2	43.4	67.8	57.0	48.4
Not Classified	0	0.0	3.5	6.3	4.4	4.8	0	0.0	4.2	2.6	2.5	3.4
Dissimilarity Index	20.2	19.2	17.7	25.0	18.9	22.3						

Sources: Singapore Department of Statistics, 1964: 220–33; Singapore Ministry of National Development, 1967: 142–3; Singapore Department of Statistics, 1973a: 197; Singapore Department of Statistics, 1993: xvii; Singapore Department of Statistics, 1996: 140.

Table 10 portrays that the DI between the Chinese and Malay occupational scales decreased from 1957 to 1970 but fluctuated without a trend between 1970 and 1995. Closer inspection as presented in Figure 4, however, reveals a consistent tendency towards greater Malay under-representation within two occupational groups from 1957 to 1995. They were the professional and technical workers, and the administrative and managerial workers.

In 1957, the dissimilarity between Chinese and Malay representation among the professionals and technicians was just 1.5 points, while in 1966, the difference was 2.0 points. In 1970, the divergence between the Chinese and Malays grew to 2.8 points. In 1980, it further increased to 6.2 points. In 1990, the dissimilarity between the

[8] Note the different occupational classification systems adopted for 1957, 1966 and 1970, in opposition to 1980, 1990 and 1995.

Figure 4. Chinese and Malay Professional & Technical, and Administrative & Managerial Workers, 1957, 1966, 1970, 1980,[9] 1990, 1995 (percent).

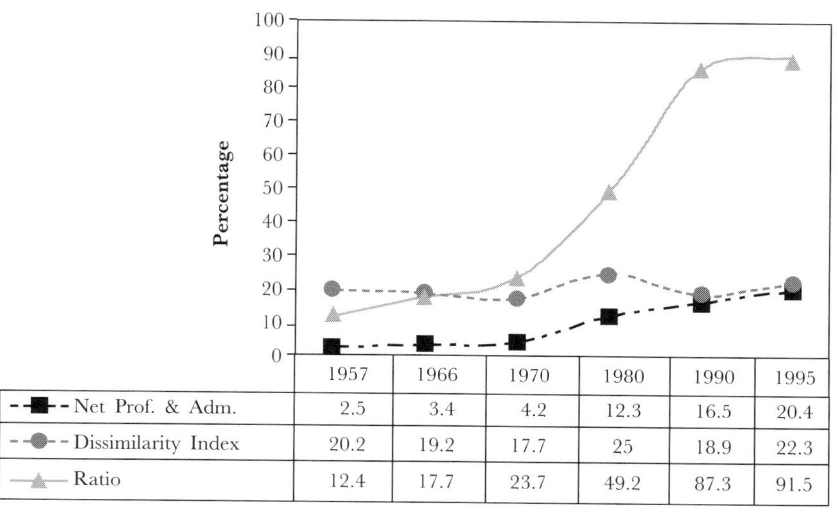

	1957	1966	1970	1980	1990	1995
Net Prof. & Adm.	2.5	3.4	4.2	12.3	16.5	20.4
Dissimilarity Index	20.2	19.2	17.7	25	18.9	22.3
Ratio	12.4	17.7	23.7	49.2	87.3	91.5

Source: Derived from Table 10.

Chinese and Malays advanced to 7.6 points. By 1995, the discrepancy between the Chinese and Malays among the professionals and technicians had expanded to 9.3 points.

With respect to the smaller administrative and managerial occupational group, the contrast between Chinese and Malay representation was even more compelling. In 1957, the difference was merely 1 point. In both 1966 and 1970, it was 1.4 points. In 1980, the divergence between the Chinese and Malays increased to 6.1 points. In 1990, it further advanced to 8.9 points. By 1995, the disparity

[9] The current classification system overstates the Malay under-representation among the professional and technical workers, and administrative and managerial workers. In the previous system, in 1980, the Malays were under-represented by 4.2 percent as opposed to 6.2 percent among the professionals and technicians. With regard to the administrators and managers, it was 4.6 percent instead of 6.1 percent. At the same time, the DI between the Chinese and Malay occupational distributions was 24.4 points as compared with 25.0 points. In addition, the administrators and professionals comprised 36.1 percent as opposed to 49.2 percent of the DI between the Chinese and Malays (Singapore Department of Statistics, 1981: 66; Singapore Department of Statistics, 1993: xvii). Nevertheless, the point about the increasing Malay under-representation among the professionals and administrators is entirely valid.

between the Chinese and Malays among the administrators and managers had reached 11.1 points.

Figure 4 also indicates that from 1957 to 1995, the discrepancy between the Chinese and Malays among the professionals and administrators constituted a constantly increasing proportion of the DI between their occupational scales. For instance, in 1957, the professionals and administrators comprised 12.4 percent of the differences between the Chinese and Malays. In 1966, the ratio grew to 17.7 percent. In 1970, the professionals and administrators composed 23.7 percent of the dissimilarities between the Chinese and Malays while in 1980, the percentage advanced to 49.2 points. In 1990, the professionals and administrators constituted 87.3 percent of the discrepancies. By 1995, the professionals and administrators accounted for 91.5 percent of the DI between Chinese and Malay jobs.

Conclusion

Now I shall reiterate the primary findings of this essay as regards the inequality between the Chinese and the Malays. As I stated at the outset, the first thesis claims that the disparity had always been critical. At the same time, a related second proposition argues that the comparative Malay position before 1959 remained stagnant or had even deteriorated until the 1980s; yet, the Malay standing has since advanced significantly. In contrast, the third thesis maintains that the position of the Malays compared to that of the Chinese only degenerated after 1959. The first and second propositions are inconsistent with the results of this inquiry. Conversely, the third thesis is more consistent with the findings of this investigation, but with some important corrections.

This paper demonstrates that the overall incomes, education and employment of the Chinese and Malays became increasingly unequal from 1954 to 1995. Contrary to the prevalent perception, in 1954, the Malays did as well as the Chinese outside the higher end of the income distribution. Between 1966 and 1972, however, their relative standing declined seriously. Subsequently, the Malay personal income position fluctuated significantly without a distinct trend. Meanwhile, its household income standing improved from 1973 to 1980 but decreased between 1980 and 1995. At the same time, the comparative Malay educational position deteriorated persistently. In

1966, the discrepancy between the Chinese and Malay accomplishments was not at all severe. Indeed, it was quite negligible when contrasted against the remarkable increases among the younger age cohorts in later years. The growing Malay under-representation among the university graduate population elucidated its educational descent. With respect to employment, it was the lack of Malay representation among employers and own account workers that previously demarcated them from the Chinese. Contradictory to the common viewpoint, the Malays were not critically under-represented among the professional and administrative elite in 1957. It was only subsequently that the disparity between the Chinese and Malays grew increasingly critical.

The loss of the Malay occupational niches within the former colonial economy partially accounted for the degeneration of its income standing from 1966 to 1972. For example, the new Singapore state precluded the Malays from the police and military forces. At the same time, the impending British withdrawal relinquished numerous service jobs. Likewise, the decreasing importance of the immigrant Chinese market could be attributed to an industrialization process that was overwhelmingly dominated by the state and international capital. The imperatives of the new political economy also created many professional and administrative positions. Similarly, the growing discrepancy between the Chinese and Malay educational achievements might be attributed to the offspring of the immigrant Chinese, who prevailed over the rapidly expanding technical fields such as engineering.

The abovementioned denote that counter to the general standpoint, educational and occupational attainments are indeed highly segmented. Further, there was the evident lack of correspondence between the fluctuating personal income inequality from 1974 to 1995, and the persisting Chinese ascent regarding education and employment. High educational qualifications seemed to confer professional and administrative stature, but not significantly greater incomes. Yet, during the same period, the fundamental change in the income difference between the Chinese and Malays transpired towards the upper end rather than the lower half of the income scale. After all, income levels may ultimately depend upon the appropriate ties embedded in the social milieu, and reinforced through specific educational and career trajectories. Accordingly, further research should be conducted about the mechanisms through which the differential possession of material goods—such as income—and symbolic goods that manifest power, prestige and clientele—like education and jobs—by the English-speaking, Chinese-speaking and Malay-speaking directly and indirectly affect their segmented educational and occupational accomplishments (Lee, forthcoming).

REFERENCES

Ahmat, Sharom (1973) "University Education in Singapore: The Dilemma of the Malay-medium Educated", in Yip Yat Hoong, ed., *Development of Higher Education in Southeast Asia: Problems and Issues*. Singapore: Regional Institute of Higher Education and Development, pp. 161–84.

Bedlington, Stanley (1974) "The Singapore Malay Community: The Politics of State Integration". Ph.D. thesis in Political Science. Cornell University.

Betts, Russell (1976) "Multiculturalism, Meritocracy and the Malays of Singapore". Ph.D. thesis in Political Science. Massachusetts Institute of Technology.

Brown, David (1994) *The State and Ethnic Politics in South-East Asia*. London: Routledge.

Chan, Heng Chee (1971) *The Politics of Survival 1965–1967*. Singapore: Oxford University Press.

Chiew, Seen Kong (1987) "Ethnicity, Economic Development and Occupational Change in Singapore, 1957–1980". *Akademika* 30(1): 73–89.

———. (1991) "Ethnic Stratification", in Stella Quah, Chiew Seen Kong, Ko Yiu Chung and Sharon Lee Mengchee, eds., *Social Class in Singapore*. Singapore: Times Academic Press, pp. 138–82.

Clutterbuck, Richard (1984) *Conflict and Violence in Singapore and Malaysia, 1945–1983*. Singapore: Graham Brash.

Goh, Keng Swee (1958) *Urban Incomes & Housing: A Report on the Social Survey of Singapore, 1953–54*. Singapore: Government Printing Office.

Gopinathan, Saravanan (1974) *Towards a National System of Education in Singapore, 1945–1973*. Singapore: Oxford University Press.

Inland Revenue Authority of Singapore (1995) *Inland Revenue Authority of Singapore, Annual Report 1994*. Singapore: Inland Revenue Authority of Singapore.

———. (1996) *Inland Revenue Authority of Singapore, Annual Report 1995*. Singapore: Inland Revenue Authority of Singapore.

Kassim, Ismail (1974) *Problems of Elite Cohesion: A Perspective from a Minority Community*. Singapore: Singapore University Press.

Lai, Ah Eng (1995) *Meanings in Multiethnicity: A Case-study of Ethnicity and Ethnic Relations in Singapore*. Kuala Lumpur: Oxford University Press.

Lee, Kiat Jin (forthcoming) "Linguistic Categories, Education, and Occupations in Singapore, 1945–1996". Ph.D. thesis in Sociology. New School for Social Research.

Li, Tania (1989) *Malays in Singapore: Culture, Economy, and Ideology*. Singapore: Oxford University Press.

Pang, Eng Fong (1982) *Education, Manpower & Development in Singapore*. Singapore: Singapore University Press.

Rahim, Lily (1998) *The Singapore Dilemma: The Political and Educational Marginality of the Malay Community*. Kuala Lumpur: Oxford University Press.

Rao, Bhanoji & M. Ramakrishnan (1980) *Income Inequality in Singapore: Impact of Economic Growth and Structural Change 1966–1975*. Singapore: Singapore University Press.

Singapore Department of Statistics (1964) *Report on the Census of Population 1957*. Singapore: Government Printer.

———. (1973a) *Report on the Census of Population 1970, Singapore Volume I*. Singapore: Government Printer.

———. (1973b) *Report on the Census of Population 1970, Singapore Volume II*. Singapore: Government Printer.

———. (1981) *Census of Population 1980, Singapore: Economic Characteristics*. Singapore: Department of Statistics.

———. (1992) *Singapore Census of Population 1990: Households and Housing*. Singapore: SNP Publishers.

———. (1993) *Singapore Census of Population 1990: Economic Characteristics*. Singapore: SNP Publishers.

———. (1996) *General Household Survey 1995: Socio-Demographic and Economic Characteristics*. Singapore: Department of Statistics.

———. (1997) *General Household Survey 1995: Transport Mode, Households and Housing Characteristics*. Singapore: Department of Statistics.

Singapore Ministry of Labour & National Statistical Commission (1974) *Report on the Labor Force Survey of Singapore 1974*. Singapore: Ministry of Labour & National Statistical Commission.

———. (1975) *Report on the Labor Force Survey of Singapore 1975*. Singapore: Ministry of Labour & National Statistical Commission.

Singapore Ministry of Labour (1979) *Report on the Labor Force Survey of Singapore 1978*. Singapore: Ministry of Labour.

———. (1980) *Report on the Labor Force Survey of Singapore 1979*. Singapore: Ministry of Labour.

———. (1981) *Report on the Labor Force Survey of Singapore 1980*. Singapore: Ministry of Labour.

Singapore Ministry of National Development (1967) *Singapore Sample Household Survey, 1966 Report No. 1*. Singapore: Government Printer.

Vasil, Raj (1995) *Asianising Singapore: The PAP's Management of Ethnicity*. Singapore: Heinemann Asia.

Zoohri, Wan (1987) "Socio-Economic Problems of the Malays in Singapore". *Sojourn* 2(2): 178–208.

POST-INDEPENDENCE EDUCATIONAL CHANGE, IDENTITY AND *HUAXIAOSHENG* INTELLECTUALS IN SINGAPORE: A CASE STUDY OF CHINESE LANGUAGE TEACHERS*

Sai Siew Yee

> Sometimes, whenever I walk within the city centre, sprawling with numerous skyscrapers, bustling with endless streams of cars and people, a desolate loneliness would creep stealthily into my heart. Thus, I slowly realize this is a desolate city, with too many putrefying wounds. One of them is this status of the *Huaxiaosheng*.
>
> (Zhang Hui, 1992: 219)

Zhang Hui discussed his social condition as a *Huaxiaosheng* or Chinese-educated person in his epilogue, "My Status". The themes of helplessness, ridicule and much sorrow brought about by his identification with the status of a *Huaxiaosheng* were highlighted and rendered "problematic". The idea of the "status of a *Huaxiaosheng*" seems to embody, then, a larger sense of identity. Identity is a slippery and, often, a "problematic" concept. Any analysis of identity should encompass an examination of the sociohistorical context of the group concerned while bearing in mind that identity is a creative reflection of the group and its members (Lian, 1982: 42).

Based on the data collected in the fieldwork I undertook between October 1994 and January 1995,[1] this article explores the impact of educational change on the identity of the *Huaxiaosheng* or Chinese-educated as an *analytical* social category. By focusing on this specific group of *Huaxiaosheng* intellectuals; namely, Chinese language teachers[2]

* Previously published in *Southeast Asian Journal of Social Sciences* 25: 2 (1997), under the imprint Times Academic Press by Marshall Cavendish International.

[1] The primary method of data collection was through loosely-structured, face-to-face interviews based on an interview guide. I also used documents, mainly the literary sources found in the body of work known as the "Literature of the Wounded". For the definition and the attributes of this body of literature, please refer to note 12.

[2] I have identified three subgroups of Chinese language teachers. They are, first, those who are currently teaching Mandarin as a second language; second, those who used to teach it while teaching another subject like Geography, Art, History, Mathematics or Biology in English, referred to as "converted" teachers; and, finally, those who have already left the profession and are currently engaged in other vocations like business and journalism.

who felt the direct impact of these changes most intensely, like fish caught in a net, this article seeks to capture the transformation of identity across generations. The fluid sense of identity is defined by the social location of individuals embedded within the larger social category of *Huaxiaosheng*, which is generation-specific. A generation shares a "common location in the social and historical process, thereby limiting them to a specific range of potential experience, predisposing them [to] a certain characteristic mode of thought and experience, . . . a characteristic type of historically relevant action". Thus, a "concrete bond" is "created between members of a generation" due to their exposure to the "social and intellectual symptoms of a process of dynamic destabilization". The generation phenomenon is, thus, a "particular kind of identity, embracing related age-groups in a historical-social process" (Mannheim, 1952: 290–92, 303–6). Identity is ultimately tied to the individual's biography, in this case, educational experiences in a particular medium and a specific social-historical configuration. In addition, the "status" of the Chinese-educated is partially concerned with ethnic identification. Educational experiences in a particular medium, in this case, Chinese education, influence ethnic identity. This group of Chinese-educated intellectuals who belong to the larger social category of *Huaxiaosheng* is a creation of a particular sociohistorical configuration.

The Making of the Huaxiaosheng *as a Social Category*

It is pertinent to commence with a historical narrative of Chinese education in Singapore. It should be noted from the beginning that the most significant development since 1965 is the institution of national bilingual education by 1987, in which English became the principal medium of instruction and Mandarin, the "second language" for students of Chinese descent.

Chinese education in Singapore dates back to the early nineteenth century. These early Chinese schools were private and voluntary institutions known as *yi xue*. They were established to meet the concerns of the early immigrants that their descendants who were living in a foreign land for extended periods and lacking in influences from "Chinese traditional ethics and morals" would gradually forget their origins. The development of *yi xue* throughout the nineteenth century was ignored by the British colonial government. The curriculum of these early Chinese schools centred on the inculcation of "traditional thinking and ethics", in addition to teaching the basics of letter-writing and arithmetic (Cui, 1994: 150–55).

In the colonial and post-war periods, the vernacular educational system was compartmentalized into four streams—English, Mandarin, Malay and Tamil—that catered to the major ethnic groups (Doraisamy, 1969: 34–35). With the founding of the Republic of China in 1911, modern Chinese vernacular schools rapidly expanded. Under the influence of the Chinese reformists and revolutionaries who visited Southeast Asia, the local Chinese enthusiastically established many Chinese schools (Ang, 1994: 315; Cui, 1994: 156), which came to dominate the vernacular educational system. The curriculum reflected that of China, stressing Chinese culture, patriotism and Chinese nationalism. Teachers were recruited from China and textbooks, which were mainly imported from China, espoused love for the homeland (Cui, 1994: 157–65; Doraisamy, 1969: 85). Such a development could be largely attributed to the rise of "revolutionary nationalism" in China between 1900 and 1912 (Yen, 1995: 215–16).

In 1917, local Chinese schools switched to using Mandarin as the medium of instruction after the success of the National Language Movement in China. With the advent of the May Fourth Movement in 1919, local textbooks, which were largely Chinese classics, were replaced by textbooks written in vernacular Mandarin (Wang, 1970: 155; Cui, 1994: 164). Consequently, the potential role of Mandarin as the "political and cultural symbol for overseas Chinese" was highlighted (Murray in Hill and Lian, 1995: 71). Although there was a movement to rewrite textbooks in Chinese in the 1930s, there still existed a strong link between Chinese education of the 1940s in Singapore and a patriotic nationalism centred on China. At the secondary level, textbooks continued to come directly from China, just as with English education, for which the textbooks came from England. Teachers continued to be recruited from China (Borthwick, 1988: 39–43). Even in the early 1950s, Chinese education had a China-centred curriculum of Chinese nationalism and Chinese culture (Franke, 1965: 187). The association of Chinese education in Singapore and Malaya with China's nationalism meant the continual orientation towards the nation-state of China and identification with its political destiny by a generation of the Chinese-educated (Hill and Lian, 1995: 71).[3]

[3] The conflicting political ideologies between the nationalists and the Communists

Chinese education suffered a temporary setback during the Japanese Occupation. After liberation, Chinese schools sprang up all over the island to meet the unprecedented post-war demand for education (Doraisamy, 1969: 90). When the colonial authorities returned, they were committed to decolonization and the establishment of a Malayan nation. A new, predominantly English-medium national education, stressing a Malayan consciousness, was needed in order to pave the way for Singapore's eventual unification with the Malayan Union. This had an impact on the existence of Chinese schools.[4] The "monolingual Chinese teachers" were alarmed at the prospect of their eventual elimination in an educational system in which English was to be dominant (Doraisamy, 1969: 91–92).

During the pre-war decades, a bifurcation between English-medium education and other streams had already developed. In the post-war years, the British authorities believed that English education and the learning of English were equivalent to loyalty to Singapore, and that the nation's interests "would be best served by an English-educated élite" (Gopinathan, 1974: 8–9). Hence, the British authorities attempted to nurture an English-educated Chinese leadership in preparation for the eventual independence of Malaya. The 1950 pro-Malay Barnes Report, released by the colonial government, delineated a national education system in which there would only be Malay or English primary schools and English post-primary schools. This created widespread fears among the Chinese community about the survival of the Chinese language and culture, which had been nurtured by the Chinese schools (Hill and Lian, 1995: 73). As a consequence, there was agitation by dissatisfied Chinese middle school students over the colonial educational policy towards Chinese schools.[5] The headlines

in the mainland found their way into the hearts and minds of the Chinese-educated in Singapore and Malaya (Hill and Lian, 1995: 71).

[4] In 1947, the colonial government proposed a Ten-Year Programme of Education, in which universal free education in the mother tongue was to be chosen by parents for their children. Selected pupils of vernacular schools, however, were to be channelled off after their third year to train intensively for free in the English medium. Chinese schools interpreted the easy transfer to English schools as a threat to their existence (Doraisamy, 1969: 91–92).

[5] English schools were built by the colonial government in places where Chinese schools were located and by charging lower fees, drew many Chinese school students away (Wang, 1970: 165).

in and after 1954 were dominated by reports of student agitation (Doraisamy, 1969: 92). There was also a subsequent burst of Communist activities in Chinese schools following the defeat of the Japanese in Malaya and the creation of Communist China in 1949 (Yeo, 1973: 185, 194, in Hill and Lian, 1995: 74–75). Chinese education in the 1950s was associated with anti-colonialism and Communist ideals.

In response to student unrest in Chinese schools, a committee was established to look into Chinese education in 1956, and this resulted in the All Party Report on Chinese Education. This marked the beginning of bilingual education. It gave parity of treatment to the four language streams, stressing a common, nationally-oriented curriculum, bilingual education for primary schools and trilingual education for secondary schools. English was made the second language in the Chinese schools while Mandarin, Malay and Tamil were the second languages in English schools (Kwok, 1995: 227). In effect, bilingual education in 1956 implicitly referred to English and a second language. It meant that English was to be the neutral, utilitarian language while the choice of second language was left to parents (Hill and Lian, 1995: 80). Anxious parents quickly developed a pragmatic attitude towards their children's education. Enrolment in English schools soon began to exceed that of Chinese schools (Doraisamy, 1969: 97). Interest in Chinese education declined and this was perceived as a crisis by the Chinese community.[6]

[6] The community's leaders were galvanized into commissioning a report to account for the phenomenon in 1962. This report, commissioned by the Singapore Chinese Chamber of Commerce, examined the reasons behind the decline and attributed it to: (1) the future prospects of Chinese school graduates, be it the furthering of education or employment, were obstructed—a higher standard of English was needed to gain admission to universities such as the University of Malaya and the colonial government paid special attention to the English language; (2) there was a favourable bias in educational policies towards the English-stream; and (3) parents did not understand the importance of "mother tongue" education (*Nanyang Wenzhai*, [1963] 4(11): 17–18).

The report culminated in a concerted campaign mounted to promote mother tongue education. This movement to save Chinese education through a monthly campaign was co-ordinated by the Chinese Chamber of Commerce, together with three other major educational organizations. Several activities were undertaken during this campaign, such as the conducting of family visits by Chinese schoolteachers. There was an effective media campaign mounted through the radio, Rediffusion and the Chinese press to appeal to the general public to put emphasis on the "mother tongue" (Guo, 1965: 31–32; *Nanyang Wenzhai*, [1965] 6(10): 27).

After Singapore's independence in 1965, the enrolment in Chinese primary schools declined steadily compared with that in English schools. Between 1959 and 1978, the proportion of total school enrolment in the Chinese-medium decreased from 45.9 percent to 11.2 percent (Goh et al., 1979). Declining primary school enrolment was mirrored in the declining enrolment at Nanyang University, commonly known as "Nanda" (Li, 1994: 96). By the 1970s, Chinese education had declined further, with continuously falling enrolments at the primary school level, and the merger of Nanda with the English-medium Singapore University to form the National University of Singapore in 1980. In the early 1970s, however, Mandarin continued to be the medium of instruction and was taught as a subject in some Chinese schools. Mathematics and Science were taught in English while Social Studies was taught in Mandarin. Chinese schools favoured a higher proportionate increase in their exposure time to English compared with that given to the second languages in English schools. An analysis of falling enrolment in Chinese schools and increased exposure time to English in Chinese schools indicates that more parents believed that an English education would give their children better career prospects (Goh et al., 1979).

Currently, both English and Mandarin are offered at Special Assistance Plan (SAP) schools and at selected secondary schools at the first language level. The plan to convert nine established Chinese-medium secondary schools into bilingual institutions was initiated in 1980. They were set up ostensibly to preserve the character of Chinese schools and to counter criticism that the Ministry of Education (MOE) was indifferent to the decline in the standard of Mandarin (Gopinathan, 1994: 78). This took place amid the development of English as the common language for government, commerce and administration, leading to a change in the attitude to language use among Singaporeans (Ang, 1994: 318–19). In effect, there was a change in the status of English language; in tandem with the rise of bilingual education was the rising status of English (Pakir, 1992).

By 1987, the switch to a national bilingual education system in which English was to be the principal medium of education became official (Gopinathan, 1994: 87). Hence, Chinese education was dramatically transformed and reduced to a subject possessing only second language status. There was a simultaneous conversion from Mandarin to English as the main medium of instruction. Under this new system, which had stabilized by the 1990s, Mandarin as a second language was placed under a continual second language policy (Ang, 1994: 320–28).[7]

Significantly, the social categories of the *Huaxiaosheng* and *Yingxiaosheng* (English-educated) emerged with the development of a vernacular education system. The two categories appeared as a consequence of their specific experiences within the respective streams, exhibiting differences in language use, cultural orientation, political affiliation and social status (Kwok, 1995: 223). Hence, by 1965, the *Huaxiaosheng* formed a recognizable social category. Members were oriented politically and culturally towards China while the *Yingxiaosheng* were partial to the colonial government and "Occidental" values. The longer one was educated in the Chinese stream, the more intense was one's degree of identification with being a member of the Chinese-educated community (Borthwick, 1988: 42). According to Lau (1992: 20), the *Huaxiaosheng* were largely monolingual in Mandarin, with a different world view and different value systems and ideals from those of the *Yingxiaosheng* (Lau, 1992: 20). Engaging in mutual stereotyping, the *Huaxiaosheng* tended to despise the *Yingxiaosheng*, calling them *ermaozi*,[8] while seeing them as arrogant, open, modernized, Westernized and lazy. With equal contempt, the *Yingxiaosheng* called the *Huaxiaosheng* *shibushi*[9] or "stupid Chinese". They regarded *Huaxiaosheng* as narrow-minded, conservative, chauvinistic, politicized and hard-working (Lau, 1994).

How might the social situation of the *Huaxiaosheng* be characterized? Using Chinese language teachers as a case in point,[10] Lau described Chinese-educated intellectuals (*Huawenzhishifenzi*) as possessing

---

[7] Some of the measures of the Second Language Policy between the 1970s and 1990s, included the promotion of the use of *hanyu pinyin* and simplified Chinese characters in 1973, compilation of lists of Chinese characters, the development of instructional materials such as textbooks and the setting up of Special Assistance Programmes. There was also the setting up of the Chinese Language Review Committee in 1992 by the MOE to review the current teaching and learning of Mandarin as a second language (Ang, 1994: 320–28).

[8] This term refers to "deculturalized slaves of the Westerners".

[9] Literally, this term means "'yes' and 'no'", but as figurative speech, it is a term meant to mimic the way *Huaxiaosheng* speak Mandarin and, thus, serves to mock them.

[10] Lau sees Chinese language teachers as one of the three social groups of Chinese-educated intellectuals. Chinese-educated intellectuals are active in the educational, professional and artistic spheres (Lau, 1992: 20). Li similarly notes that the group of Chinese-educated intellectuals are dispersed in the political, academic, educational, journalistic, cultural and business/industrial circles (Li, 1994: 48).

certain traits such as harbouring a deep love for Mandarin and Chinese culture. They hoped bilingual education could be given equal emphasis, since they could not bear to see Singapore become a monolingual English-speaking society. They saw themselves as inheritors of Chinese cultural traditions because they had been influenced by Chinese school traditions, which impressed upon them mainstream Confucianist thinking and principles of morality. They had a sense of mission and a concern for the larger society. Yet, change in an education system in which fluency in the English language was respected and Mandarin was lowly regarded, even despised, had displaced them. They were disadvantaged in career promotion because of their English language handicap, and they felt discriminated against. As a group within the category of *Huaxiaosheng*, Chinese language teachers felt frustrated, demoralized, prone to a sense of setbacks and finally became the "silent majority" (Lau, 1992: 22–27; Lau, 1994). The decline in the status of Chinese education profoundly affected the *Huaxiaosheng* emotionally and psychologically, rendering their identity "problematic". The gradual but continual attenuation of Chinese education in post-independence Singapore implies that the economic and modernization process in Singapore is "English-driven" (Gopinathan, 1994: 74). Those who are handicapped in English will be unable to gain access to valuable knowledge and skills, much less participate in the economy and modernization. They will be left out of the mainstream economically, socially and occupationally, and become a minority group.

Post-Independence Educational Change: The Place of Chinese Language Teachers

As a consequence of political changes and educational developments in Singapore over the past 50 years, the *Huaxiaosheng* have become a social minority. In particular, Chinese language teachers have borne the full impact of these changes. In the data collected, there is a discernible pattern among older teachers above 35 years of age; they collectively feel discriminated against by mainstream English-speaking society, in terms of their common perception that the social status of Chinese language teachers is very low relative to that of the English teachers. Madam Meng put it bluntly:

> Chinese language teachers, in this present educational system, they aren't in the mainstream. They are in the marginal stream. Since they are in the marginal stream, of course, in terms of positioning, they aren't given as much emphasis as those in the mainstream . . . Because Mandarin isn't used in the administration, the working language has become English, of course, we can only stand aside, right?

These people also feel they are despised and talk of feeling like second-class citizens. Ms Ke used a poignant analogy of Chinese language teachers as being "adopted children":

> I also feel that Chinese teachers are being despised by other people. The MOE does look down upon Chinese education . . . [they] treat Chinese teachers as if they are second-class citizens. As if the English teachers are their only life and blood and we Chinese teachers are only their adopted children.

Such a self-perception seems to be accompanied by a similar view of the low status of Mandarin via the lack of emphasis given to it in the school curriculum of the past.[11]

Moreover, they also feel they have been singled out for discriminatory treatment because of their poor command of English. They are unable to access the higher echelons of the school administration since English is the dominant working language in society. By extension, it is also the language of administration in schools. Thus, most of the older teachers believe that their chances of promotion are low, and that they have already been passed over because of their language handicap. Mr Xing captured the mentality of being discriminated against in the world of work succinctly:

> Basically, there's a low chance of being promoted. This recent promotion exercise has upset me for quite a while . . . I feel this is unfair to us. One of the reasons for this disparity basically is . . . I am still a Chinese-medium-based [teacher]. The ability to use the language [English] still isn't good enough . . . So those from a Chinese-medium school background are disadvantaged . . . This recent promotion exercise, a lot of Chinese language teachers didn't get anything basically. This is our state.

[11] This view, however, seems to have dissipated recently. Presently, they feel that there has been a rise in the status of Mandarin as seen from the Government's recent emphasis on the language. Many attribute this to the opening up of China's economy.

The perceived discrimination in work is reinforced in the larger occupational structure. Some informants spoke of the difficulties of finding employment as Nanda graduates because of their English language handicap and the negative societal perception that they were "second-rate". Miss You and Mr Yong expressed these sentiments respectively:

> For example, [Nanda graduates] working as clerks and factory supervisors . . . because it wasn't easy to find a job then. Then, there was the additional element of language. We were quite disadvantaged.
>
> In our generation, when Nanda graduates came out, they were different from the Singapore University graduates in terms of status . . . They said at that time that Nanda graduates were adopted children while Singapore University graduates were the real biological children.

Significantly, they identify themselves as "pure" (*chun*) or "traditional" (*chuantong*) *Huaxiaosheng*. They constitute an identifiable social category by locating themselves in a dichotomous world view vis-á-vis the *Yingxiaosheng* category. This is reflected by the perceived existence of a language divide between them and the *Yingxiaosheng* when I queried them on whether they perceived differences between a Chinese language teacher and an English language teacher. As Mr Liang said:

> In the past, it was quite natural because if you were a *Huaxiaosheng*, you would speak in Mandarin, and if you were from English schools, you would speak English of course.

There is a common pattern of perceiving the *Huaxiaosheng* and *Yingxiaosheng* distinction among the older *Huaxiaosheng* teachers. They tend to talk about the "character" (*xingge*) of the *Huaxiaosheng* as if these people have a distinctive cultural orientation, value system, personality profile and behavioural style, as opposed to the "character" of the *Yingxiaosheng*. Miss Ke described the perceived difference in cultural orientation while Mr Liang spoke of perceived differences in terms of values, character and behaviour, respectively:

> They're more inclined towards the West whereas we're more inclined towards the East. Moreover, there are differences in the handling of interpersonal relations. They're more Westernized.
>
> In terms of values, there's a big difference. They're more individualistic whereas when we handle matters, we tend to consider . . . other people's feelings. We aren't so direct and are more subtle. This is the style of those from a purely Chinese-educated background.

As such, a mentality of "us" versus "them" seen in terms of perceived differences implies a lack of mutual understanding. It helps to reinforce the idea that "they", the *Yingxiaosheng*, harbour a prejudice against "us", the *Huaxiaosheng*. Mr Yang implied that the prejudices of the "pure" English-educated resulted from their refusal to enter into the cultural world of the Chinese-educated:

> There's a small number of teachers, those purely from the English-educated background. They harbour a prejudice against us . . . First they look at you with jaundiced eyes. Their perceptions and your perceptions are different . . . I feel that such perceptions are a type of cultural ignorance.

The older *Huaxiaosheng* teachers are monolingual, proficient only in Mandarin. This language orientation is seen in the cultural and ethnic sentiment they associate with Mandarin and by extension, Chinese culture, as expressed by Mr Bing:

> I believe this isn't chauvinism or whatever. Just like what we are emphasizing now. You're a Chinese, you know your own mother tongue. I feel this is abiding by the natural laws of heaven and earth, right? Because this is your mother tongue, your language.

To them, the mother tongue functions as a crucial avenue in preserving one's "roots", a metaphor they often employ to refer to "Chinese cultural traditions". Such sentiments attached to the mother tongue imply that it is a preserver and repository of cultural traditions and a signifier of ethnicity. The function of the mother tongue and the sentiments attached to it were expressed by Madam Zen and Miss Ke respectively as follows:

> Actually, learning Mandarin is to allow people to know our traditions, know our roots.
>
> You should know who you are and your own mother tongue. Those are your roots. You're born a Chinese. If you don't know Mandarin, you will feel very ashamed.

They also maintain an inseparable and intimate link between language and culture. Language refers to the medium of instruction in education, which functions simultaneously as a mother tongue. Mr Chi expressed these sentiments thus:

> They cannot be separated. Once you have mastered a language, within it, there's a deep sense of our thinking. It's all inside the words . . . Language and culture cannot be separated.

The empathy these older teachers have developed with Mandarin is partly a consequence of reaction–formation. As a minority and feeling deprived by their Chinese-medium education, the older *Huaxiaosheng* teachers constitute a powerless in-group that takes pride in their stigmatization by the powerful out-group. In a posture of counter-defence, these teachers maintain the inseparable linkage between one's mother tongue and one's "roots" in moral terms (Tong and Chan, 1994: 21), claiming shame in not knowing Mandarin. The older teachers are oriented towards "Chinese culture" (*zhonghuawenhua*) and Eastern traditions (*dongfang chuantong*), as implied in their sentiments about Mandarin as a mother tongue. They also believe they have a cultural responsibility in transmitting Chinese culture to their students when asked about their role in the educational system. Mr Sheng articulated his role eloquently:

> We're like the torchbearers of culture. We want this fire to be passed down . . . Once it fizzles out, everything will be gone.

Located as a social minority and effectively displaced from the English-speaking mainstream, whether it is in the world of teaching or administration, their experiences of cultural displacement are described in powerful analogies of being overwhelmed and finding themselves locked into a frustrating, passive silence. As Madam Ling put it:

> I have this feeling. Our feeling is that in our English-medium school, there's already a big group of English teachers. Then, the entire administration, the entire daily communication, must be done in English. Unless Chinese-medium schoolteachers are good in English . . . this environment disallows them to speak freely . . . Chinese language teachers can only struggle in their own little corner.

Such experiences of displacement have resulted in a sense of not belonging to the school community. They cope with the dislocation apparently by silently and passively accepting their "strange environment", by becoming "immune to it". Mr Feng expressed the lack of a sense of belonging and Madam Meng, her acceptance, respectively:

> Usually, we've this feeling we're being despised and being pushed out . . . This is natural when you're in this kind of school and working environment for communication problems do occur . . . so, you don't seem to be a member of this community. You have no sense of belonging.
>
> You see, now when we walk along the streets, how many signs are in Mandarin? . . . Why is it we slowly see our environment becoming stranger and stranger to us? . . . This is a very uncomfortable feeling. Initially, it was really bitter. Now, I'm already immune to it after time has gone by.

For most, their feelings of being displaced by educational change have made them cling to the past. They adopt a traditionalist world view in which Mandarin is the inevitable mother tongue of all ethnic Chinese, and a cultural world view that is rooted in "Eastern cultural traditions" as opposed to the *Yingxiaosheng's* "Westernized cultural orientation". Unable to locate themselves in the present system of bilingual education, they choose to rely on the past as seen in their presumed sense of mission and cultural responsibility. It is an attempt to interpret their role in an educational system which gives them little recognition.

Chinese Language Teachers: The Older Generation

Their experience of displacement expresses itself in a disjointed self-identity, partially ethnic. This sense of displacement is very much tied to the sense of their identity, defined by their social location in terms of generation.

Teachers who are within the age brackets of the late 30s and the late 50s or older belong to the older generation because they were either in their teenage years or young adulthood in the pre-independence decades. These were the years when Chinese education thrived. Consequently, this older generation experienced the full impact of its gradual attenuation in the post-independence decades when they were reaching full adulthood. The older generation of teachers constitutes related age groups sharing a particular identity. They are "pure" *Huaxiaosheng* since they share a common location in terms of having received a Chinese-medium education in the pre-independence era. Their self-identity is inextricably linked to and framed in Chinese education. This was echoed by Mr Rong, who attempted to explicate his identity in terms of his Chinese school experiences:

> We *Huaxiaosheng*, of course, refer to those who are purely educated in the Chinese-medium. Even after you've graduated, your identity is still a *Huaxiaosheng* . . . For example, you can't call those students from the nine SAP schools *Huaxiaosheng*, right? . . . A true *Huaxiaosheng* is: they've received a pure Chinese-medium education. They had been nurtured in an integrated Chinese education system . . . In terms of thinking and all other respects, they have their own system . . . They have no chance to come into contact with those things from the English-stream. In our generation, all subjects were taught in Mandarin; so normally, in school and most of the habits of daily life, the language used, etc., they all derived from Chinese-medium education.

My informants had an amazingly uniform way of discussing how Chinese education had inculcated in them principles of morality and value systems, which shaped their behaviour. Their entire world view had been influenced by it. Chinese education had given them a bearing in life and had helped to locate them in the Chinese world spiritually. Madam Ling and Mr Yang discussed how Chinese education had influenced them respectively:

> Personally, I feel that in the areas of character, cultivation and morality, Chinese-medium education has given us a guideline when it comes to behaviour and thinking.
>
> My entire spiritual support is still Mandarin. I read many works in English about Western philosophy and politics . . . but my entire point of reference, my bearings are still located within Mandarin.

Chinese education had given them a sense of cultural location or belonging and helped them identify themselves as ethnic Chinese. Madam Meng explicitly expressed this sense of cultural location or belonging and by extension, her ethnicity:

> I feel the influence is very great. Because I had attended Chinese schools, I single-mindedly try to be a pure Chinese. I think my roots are in the 5,000 years of Chinese culture. I feel there's a strong sense of belonging . . . I feel a sense of joy that my parents had sent me to Chinese schools. Because at least there's something I can identify with. My roots are there. I feel, as a person, there's a sense of direction. It can give me a bearing, right? I belong to this culture, this ethnic group. I'm very clear and I'm very proud. I won't lose my way.

The perceived influences derived from their social location in the common experience of Chinese education predispose them to a certain characteristic mode of thought, feeling and behaviour as a *Huaxiaosheng*. An analysis of their discourse illustrates their tendency to speak of the *Huaxiaosheng* behaving in a certain style and possessing a distinctive *Huaxiaosheng* personality. They locate their educational experiences vis-à-vis the *Yingxiaosheng*. As older *Huaxiaosheng*, they perceive themselves as being endowed with a particular world view oriented towards "traditional Chinese culture", seen largely as "Confucianist" in nature. Mr Deng pointed out:

> Especially for the Chinese schools of our time, we're rather influenced by the traditional modes of thought from China . . . The main ones are, of course, Confucianism, Taoism and Buddhism. These schools of thought form what we call the traditional Chinese modes of thought but the mainstream is, of course, Confucianism . . . For example, in

> terms of interpersonal relationships, the Chinese emphasize the collectivity and blending into it, being not that individualistic. We approach problems from the interests of the larger body . . . For instance, the traditional Chinese-educated person doesn't make obvious one's achievements. We do things quietly . . . Our generation don't do things this way because we feel this doesn't accord with the traditional way of thought . . . This example I've raised shows that there's a gaping difference between a Chinese-educated and an English-educated.

Thus, Chinese-educated intellectuals perceived the dramatic educational change in the post-independence era to a national, bilingual educational system as a painful crisis. They felt the gradual attenuation of Chinese education in intensely emotional terms for what was at stake then was the personal identity of the older generation of teachers as "pure" *Huaxiaosheng*. These intellectuals responded with the "*baogen*" (preserving roots) mentality. Their reactions ranged from initial sorrow and anger to a more withdrawn passivity later, when change was read as inevitable (Li, 1994). Likewise, the responses of my informants towards such a change, regardless of whether they were Chinese language teachers or "converted" teachers, ranged from pain (*tongku*), a sense of setback (*cuozhegan*) and disappointment (*shiwang*) to one of passive, resigned acceptance of inevitable change (*wukenaihe*). Madam Meng, Mr Feng and Mr Qing expressed these sentiments, respectively:

> It's painfully heart-rending, very painfully heart-rending.
>
> It has become such that the things which you should teach have disappeared . . . You've to teach something new. Naturally, you'll feel a sense of set-back . . . that is to say, how should I put it? It was unbearable . . . You can imagine this as a very complicated psychological process. Of course, you can't help but feel extremely disappointed. Sometimes, you'll also suddenly feel that there is no future for the language of the Chinese entirely, at least in Singapore. This feeling isn't strictly personal because our feelings are ultimately not restricted to individuals. Sometimes, we'll worry it will disappear, right? . . . Of course, we feel this sense of loss, this sense of not knowing what to do, of helplessness.
>
> When the situation has developed to the present stage, you've to accept it . . . To put it simply, "Knowing that something is inevitable, you remain resigned to it and calmly accept your fate."

Hence, the biographies of the older teachers reveal a "deepest pain" that forms the "concrete bond", that "active or passive experience" of being similarly located in a common, pre-independence Chinese education and participating "in the common destiny" of its gradual attenuation. This makes them the *Huaxiaosheng* "generation as an actuality". Moreover, their typical response to the bilingual policy is that it harbours an "imbalance" (*piancha*). In their parlance, this means that there has been an overwhelming emphasis on English, with Mandarin as a somewhat isolated and insignificant subject.

Given the cultural and ethnic symbolisms associated with Chinese-medium education, it means that "it is foolish to believe that we can ever completely divorce language, culture and education from the passions with which people jealously guard their personal identities", as Lee noted somewhat ironically (Kwok, 1995; Goh et al., 1979: iv). The consequent attempt to divorce or negate them means that the world of the past, in which the older teachers were educated, is no longer salient in the present context of national education. The *Huaxiaosheng* identity is, in a way, a ruptured identity, framed by a discontinuous Chinese educational experience. This dislocated, ruptured *Huaxiaosheng* identity was captured most poignantly by Mr Rung through the powerful metaphor of "severing of roots":

> Personally, I feel this is the first time change in the academic system has brought about an impact upon me as a *Huaxiaosheng*, because I've become the extinct batch. It's like saying, my identity, my value, suddenly it has been cut off halfway, or in the future, I can't find my roots, my origins any more. This is just like my school . . . and those public schools later, which had been made to become irrelevant and were closed down. It's the same situation, that is, as if we've lost some of our roots.

Despite its present "ruptured" manifestation, the *Huaxiaosheng* identity is still present in the links it draws on its educational past as is illustrated by the psychological pain in their biographies. This inability to forget results in an attempt to evince the "purity" of their *Huaxiaosheng* identity and articulate a "mythologized" Chinese education by evoking the benign influences it has conferred upon them. Such an identity can be read as an attempt on their part to maintain a sense of dignity in the face of an English-speaking world.

The Special Intra-Generational Case of Bianliu Jiayuan: *"Converted" Teachers*

The dramatic impact of post-independence educational change is depicted fully in the experiences of the "converted" teachers. The emergence of such teachers was a direct consequence of a ruptured teaching experience caused by the process of "conversion" to the English-stream. Converted teachers are a special case among the older generation of *Huaxiaosheng* teachers. Originally from the Chinese stream, they had to change to become teachers in the English stream. Converted teachers only emerged after Mandarin became a second language (Zhang, 1990a: 16–17) in the 1980s. A prominent Chinese language journalist, Liu Pei Fang (1994), characterized the situation of these teachers as follows:

> In the transitional period during the 80s, . . . some Chinese-stream teachers, during the process of conversion [changing from teaching in Mandarin to teaching in English], resigned. Some left the profession, and there were even some who had gone insane or committed suicide because they could not take the pressure.

This special group of teachers from the older generation within the *Huaxiaosheng* category was forced to cope with radical changes in their lives after undergoing six months of language training before returning to teach subjects like Geography, Art, History, Mathematics and Science in English. These included inadequate training, which caused fear and embarrassment. There was also the commonly embarrassing problem of classroom control, for students laughed at their English pronunciation. Moreover, there were the problems of pressure from school authorities such as other teachers from the English-educated background or the principals or the general public, who blamed them for a lower standard of English. Miss Chen pointed out one of the practical problems of conversion vehemently, calling such teachers the "sacrificed ones":

> Sometimes, you can hear some teachers saying, or other people tell me, "Ei, I've heard on the bus from a certain teacher that this school's English results aren't good because their Chinese language teachers speak only Mandarin to them." Moreover, there are many converted teachers, you know; so the English standard is lowered. Putting the blame on us . . . I believe our batch is unhappy. We're the sacrificed ones . . . We're unhappy . . . because we struggle like this, yet we're still being scolded by others.

The personal biographies of converted teachers register the additional dimension of psychological pain and "spiritual torment". In a sense, their ruptured *Huaxiaosheng* identity conflates with their identity as converted teachers to form a double layer of compressed dislocation. Madam Lian reacted emotionally to her bitter experiences of conversion, breaking down in the midst of articulating her painful experiences. Enduring these silently, she drew strength from her membership in the *Huaxiaosheng* category:

> Being sent to the Language Proficiency Centre (LPC) for English lessons was very bitter . . . I felt it was really difficult to bear. (*Informant's voice began to waver and broke down.*) So, I memorized my lessons. It was very arduous . . . Thinking about it, it's difficult to bear. Now thinking about it, I feel it might be because of my Chinese education that I refused to submit. I told myself it's not my fault . . . That's how I eked it out . . . So, a lot of us who were converted in this way suffered of course. There was unhappiness and complaints, but we still accept [this]. The Chinese-educated will just bear things silently.

Chinese Language Teachers: The Younger Generation

The social location of the younger generation of Chinese language teachers is markedly different. These teachers are between the age range of the early 20s and the early 30s. They are the products of either an evolving or an institutionalized bilingual education system in the 1980s. Some of them are SAP school graduates. They were in their teens when bilingual education was instituted. Being located socially in the common experience of bilingualism in schools, they are generally more competent in English compared with their older colleagues. Most encounter no problems in reading, speaking or writing in English. Unlike the older teachers, they do not perceive discrimination in issues such as promotion. Thus, they do not perceive themselves as a discriminated minority. They are more confident about their chances of promotion, which are seen as being related to work performance rather than English language ability, as expressed by Mr Neng:

> I feel they're evaluating you on your willingness to work, not your background . . . Although I've been teaching for only half a year, the school seems to value me now. So, from here, I say it's not because of your language standard, your English is poor, so the Principal doesn't give you the promotion.

Yet, their responses to the status of Chinese language teachers are mixed. Some younger teachers feel that such teachers generally enjoy a low status while others believe that they are still important. Unlike the older teachers, the younger teachers do not carry a strong sense of cultural responsibility in their perception of their role as Chinese language teachers. Mrs Shen expressed this:

> I feel because you're teaching a language, you'll definitely influence the development of your students' characters, whether you're a Chinese language or an English Language Teacher . . . If you have the attitude of being a torchbearer of culture when teaching, it's very painful! . . . You'll have to shoulder such a heavy responsibility . . . I fell I do have the responsibility but I don't want to see it as being too heavy.

Indeed, the older teachers perceive the "cultural sentiments" of the younger teachers to be "weaker".

Significantly, some of the younger teachers replicate the sentiments of the older teachers in that they still see a difference between a *Huaxiaosheng* and a *Yingxiaosheng*. There is a similar tendency to perceive the *Huaxiaosheng* as a person exhibiting certain character traits mentioned earlier. As Mr Neng expressed it:

> Actually, I feel those *Yingxiaosheng* are generally more open in their thinking. We say they aren't concerned with details . . . Sometimes, I feel that. I've already said they have a sense of superiority, so you'll feel that when these people speak, they'll say things forcefully and their demeanour, arrogant. So, you feel "They despise you . . ." I feel that it's because a *Huaxiaosheng* is more modest and polite.

Mr Neng also commented on the prejudice existing between the *Huaxiaosheng* and the *Yingxiaosheng*:

> Personally, I feel it's very difficult for me to get along with them . . . It's very difficult for us to communicate our thinking and opinions. Some people might have this way of looking at you, as those "Chinese-educated". They have this image of the Chinese-educated as antiques. Actually, this is not so . . . There exists mutual prejudice so that there's no room for mutual interaction.

As for some of the younger teachers, they prefer to locate themselves vis-à-vis the *Yingxiaosheng*. With others, any perceived sense of discrimination from the *Yingxiaosheng* is lacking even though they tend to discuss the two social categories in terms of stereotypes informed by their subjective experiences. Mrs Mei put it aptly:

> I feel those Chinese-educated basically are more traditional and conservative . . . Those English educated generally are like Westerners. They're relatively more individualistic, putting more emphasis on liberty and are more frank . . . My views . . . are more subjective.

The difference responses of the younger teachers are directly related to their self-identification. Those who share the perception of discrimination against *Huaxiaosheng* of the older generation tend to identify themselves as atypical or "impure" *Huaxiaosheng*. This subgroup within the younger generation stands at one end of a continuum. At the other end is a group whose members identify themselves either as the *Yingxiaosheng* or as the "bilingual-educated". Their varying self-identities are the consequence of a common experience within a developing or developed bilingual education system in the post-independence period. It is an experience which recognizes the place of both English and Mandarin in Singapore.

The subgroup of younger teachers in their late 20s who prefer to identify themselves as "impure" *Huaxiaosheng* is indicative of a dilution of the *Huaxiaosheng* identity. Mr Neng identified himself as an "impure" *Huaxiaosheng*:

> I'm originally a *Huaxiaosheng*, although I'm from a SAP school, because all SAP schools are Chinese schools . . . But we're from the transitional period, so we've changed in terms of quality. Because in the past, what's meant by *Huaxiaosheng is* that they're relatively purer. They had studied Science and Mathematics in Mandarin . . . We studied Mandarin as first language, but other subjects were still taught in English . . . We're not pure *Huaxiaosheng*.

Yet, this identification tag does not necessarily mean acceptance by the older generation of teachers. For the "impure" *Huaxiaosheng* teachers, Mandarin and English, perceived as cultural signifiers of the East and West respectively in their world view, are firmly located in their bilingual educational experiences. As such, it is not surprising that the younger teachers readily affirm and positively recognize the bilingual policy. Mr Neng said:

> I feel I'm special in this way. I'm receiving a Chinese-medium education, but at the same time, I'm in contact with things from the West. So, from here, you can have a comparison . . . I feel this [bilingual] policy is really worth considering, because to know one more language is always good . . . To raise an example from my own case, I feel I've benefited from it.

Teachers in their early 30s, who identify themselves as "pure" *Huaxiaosheng*, tend to dismiss the seemingly inextricable connection between receiving a Chinese education and an affinity with "Chineseness" or "Chinese cultural traditions". This is in stark contrast with the older teachers, who perceive Chinese education as an influence framing one's ethnicity and cultural belonging. As articulated by Mr Heng:

> Right. I'm still a purely Chinese-educated person . . . But taken as a whole, Chinese-medium education . . . I think it depends on the individual. It's very difficult to say how this has moulded a person's character. For me, I like Literature, Chinese History and culture. Basically, it has nothing to do with being Chinese-educated. I can't explain why. It's my personal experience.

The dilution of the *Huaxiaosheng* identity occurs in that they acknowledge that English and Mandarin have a place in their educational experiences. This was acknowledged by Mrs Shen:

> When I was studying, I wasn't affected in my primary school examination, but when I was in secondary school, I was affected. There was a rule that you must score a 1, 2 or 3 in your "O" levels for English before you could gain admission to a Junior College.

Significantly, the declining enrolment in Chinese schools in later years did not elicit any emotional responses from these two groups of younger teachers. Any sentiments were expressed mildly. Mrs Xuan conveyed her emotions:

> I don't feel particularly strongly about it. I feel it's a pity but I won't feel very strongly about it, saying this shouldn't be done.

Ms Yen did not feel anything at all, saying:

> Frankly speaking, at that time, I didn't feel anything. In '84, I was only about 10 years old!

In marked contrast to the *Huaxiaosheng* identity stands the *Yingxiaosheng* identity. One informant, Ms Weng, aged 24 years, identified herself as an *Yingxiaosheng*, despite a double Chinese major at university:

> I'm an *Yingxiaosheng* . . . Before university, I was in touch with relatively more English. But after entering university . . . everything was in Mandarin.

Significantly, a new identity emerges in contrast to the *Huaxiaosheng* identity when the subgroup comprising those in their early 20s and 30s identify themselves as the "bilingual-educated". Usually, they have a SAP school background. Mrs Mei summed up their subgroup identity:

> Being bilingual-educated (*shou shuangyu jiaoyu*), it becomes such that when you look at problems, I believe it's more neutral.

Among this subgroup, on the one hand, the inextricable connections between Chinese education, ethnicity and orientation towards Chinese cultural traditions made by the older teachers are dismissed; on the other hand, the place of English and Mandarin as first languages in their bilingual experience is positively affirmed, providing a "balanced" way of viewing matters. Mr Cong and Mrs Mei expressed these sentiments, respectively:

> Maybe in the eyes of the previous generation of *Huaxiaosheng*, this is very sacrilegious: I feel Mandarin happens to be the language I handle competently . . . If I happen to be born a Japanese or French, even if I don't know any Mandarin, I don't feel this is regrettable in any way. Being a Chinese doesn't mean you must know whatever . . . I feel this identification isn't important.
>
> If you're bilingual-educated, you've a certain knowledge of Mandarin and a certain level of mastery of English too. You can perhaps be more balanced, not tilt to either side.

More significantly, in their world views, it is only because they perceive themselves as being more culturally objective that some of them claim to be intermediaries between two cultural worlds. Such a cultural orientation sets them apart from the monocultural and "traditionalist" orientation expressed by the older teachers. Mr Cong put it aptly:

> Of course, I feel this educational background is an advantage . . . that is, I can see things from two worlds simultaneously . . . In this way, if you put it nicely, you can gather the double advantages from the two cultures . . . Sometimes, I feel I understand some of the sentimental ties of the *Huaxiaosheng* and those of the *Yingxiaosheng* too . . . I'm [from] two worlds . . . Ah, flitting [between the two worlds], right.

The dramatic switch to a national, English-centred bilingual education system as a major societal transformation has led to the dominance of English and produced a generation of "receptive bilinguals" (Pakir, 1993: 81).

Conclusion

Members of the older generation of teachers take pride in their identity as "pure" *Huaxiaosheng*. That pride, is exhibited in their sentiments about Chinese-medium education, language and culture, coupled with the hurt, pain and indignity articulated in their personal biographies. The social condition of the older *Huaxiaosheng* generation must be understood and empathized with within a specific sociohistorical context of decolonization and the subsequent independence of Singapore as a nation-state from Malaysia. In the historical narrative of independence, the theme of the survival of a small city-state predominates. One of the manifestations of the "problem of survival" and the "need to succeed" is the transformation of education as the sole means of equipping Singaporeans with jobs. As the "language of commerce, science and technology", English came to be equated with "the language of survival" (Chew, 1976). Such an ideological belief in the prowess of the English language led to the institutionalization of the bilingual educational policy and the gradual attenuation of Chinese education. In the process, the older generation of the Chinese-educated was effectively displaced from the English-speaking mainstream. The phenomenon of the Chinese-educated as a "lost generation" cut across racial and ethnic boundaries (George, 1997). The Malay-educated (and the Tamil-educated), sharing the same generational location, were similarly affected by the gradual attenuation of vernacular education and post-independence educational change (Ahmat, 1973, in Hill and Lian, 1995: 83–84).

The *Huaxiaosheng* "status" of the older generation is complicated by the question of ethnicity, in this case, the sense of "Chineseness". The links between education, language and identity that led the older teachers to evince a "pure" *Huaxiaosheng* identity seem to correlate with a conception of Chinese ethnicity that is primordial. The primordialist school posits an ascriptive nature to ethnicity "based on blood ties, shared descent, a particular language and culture". Ethnicity, argue De Vos and Romanucci-Ross, is "a past-oriented form of identity embedded in the cultural heritage of the individual and group" (De Vos and Romanucci-Ross, 1982: 63, in Khoo, 1990: 5–6). Such an essentialist and primordial notion of ethnicity points to the question of "Where are you from?" where one is rooted. The point of anchorage for the ethnic individual is the need to locate himself or herself spiritually and culturally in an original, "pure" and, therefore, "authentic" "Chinese" cultural domain, the source of which is found in "China". The "purity" of a *Huaxiaosheng* as a signifier of the "East", of "Chineseness", begs the presence of an alibi of what Rey Chow termed the "prescribed otherness" (Ang, 1973: 9). This "otherness" is imagined to be the "*Yingxiaosheng*", a signifier of all things "Western".

For the younger generation of teachers, however, ethnic identity seems to be less essentialist and more relativized. The strong sense of "pure Chineseness" pregnant in the identity of "pure" *Huaxiaosheng* has been diluted by varying degrees of knowledge of English as the bilingual policy is being implemented. Their self-acknowledged lack of "typicality" or "impurity" is a position of ambiguity, of a reluctance to anchor themselves in the "Chinese education" of the past, which did not form a part of their educational experiences. Yet, at the same time, they are in contact with the "West", signified by the English language. For those who identify themselves as "bilingual-educated", the ambiguities of being caught somewhere in between English and Mandarin, which constitute the cultural signifiers of "East" and the "West", are even more pronounced. This self-positioning of being "cultural intermediaries", of "in-between-ness", is a position that attempts to creatively balance between "where you are from" and "where you are at" (Ang, 1973: 13) "Chineseness", for them, becomes an attempt at creating hybridity. It is a syncretic construction of a new, hybrid identity in dialectical conjunction with their local experiences of bilingualism in Singapore. The space for "Chineseness" is thus opened up. Ethnicity becomes a constant process of (re)invention and (re)negotiation.

The "Chineseness" of the younger generation needs to be further explored. Suffice it to say, if English-knowing bilingualism is the major sociolinguistic phenomenon created by a bilingual educational system that subsequently produces "receptive bilinguals", to what extent does the younger generation of Chinese in Singapore embrace the labels *of Huaxiaosheng* or *Yingxiaosheng* as part *of* their "Chineseness"? Do those who profess to be bilingual-educated and who move beyond the old paradigmatic labels of "Chinese-educated" and "English-educated" indicate a totally new conception of "Chineseness" that will include the criteria of bilingualism and, by extension, biculturalism? Will the older generation of *Huaxiaosheng* teachers, who view the younger generation teachers as less competent in their command of Mandarin, consider the younger generation as less "Chinese" or even afflicted with the condition of "ethnicity drift" or "cultural erosion" (Tong and Chan, 1994: 3)? The cultural dynamics of "Chineseness" across generations await further exploration.

The assumption that "English-knowing bilingualism" is one of the major reasons for Singapore's economic success and, therefore, survival is widely acknowledged. Yet, the association of English language knowledge with economic growth raises the more pertinent question of the human costs involved in effecting such a phenomenally swift transformation in post-independence Singapore. The question of human cost in terms of setting back an entire generation's life chances aside, the personal sufferings and indignity registered in the painful biographies of the older teachers, especially "converted" teachers, seem to be less understood by the mainstream. The scars of suffering have been laid bare with the emergence of *Shanghen Wenxue*, or the Literature of the Wounded.[12] It is a new genre that has emerged after the post-independence era of societal and educational change, and records the inner lives and emotional turmoil of the social category of *Huaxiaosheng*. One of the themes reflected in the Literature of the Wounded is the plight of converted teachers. In one of Zhang Hui's micro-short stories, "The Classified Secret in the 45.45 Meeting" (Zhang, 1990b: 2–4), the nameless school principal blames converted teachers for the problem of falling percentage rates in English:

> These figures illustrate that among the Mathematics and Science teachers, 45.45% are converted teachers. Although they're teaching in English, they use and speak it incorrectly. This is a fact. It's not that I despise them. Under their tutelage, the English of our students will definitely be polluted . . . Finally, I've located the root cause of the problem.

The narrative of the agonizing humiliation and injustice endured by these teachers is just one of the many literary works highlighting the plight of Chinese language teachers, especially converted teachers.

The problem of the *Huaxiaosheng* identity has contemporary resonance in Singapore politics. The recent Tang Liang Hong incident in the 1997 general election, in which the 61-year-old Chinese-educated lawyer was accused by the PAP government of being a "dangerous Chinese chauvinist"[13] (*The Straits Times*, 29 December 1996) once again highlights the labelling of the Chinese-educated as a political category. As a collective, it was not to be placated as was

[12] The term "Literature of the Wounded" first appeared in the Chinese literature of mainland China. It is a new genre "dating back to the Tiananmen poems of 1976", and "contains the accounts, sometimes fictionalized, often real, of people's experiences during the Cultural Revolution" (Thurston, 1988: 36). The Chinese-educated intellectuals in Singapore have appropriated this term. As noted by Liu, "After the Cultural Revolution in China, there emerged a large body of 'Literature of the Wounded'. Some people once said that Singapore also has its body of 'Literature of the Wounded' with a different content" (Liu, 1994).

[13] Tang was accused of playing to the popular gallery of a largely "Chinese-educated" ground by commenting on the over-representation of the English-educated and Christians in Parliament (*The Straits Times*, 29 December 1996).

the case in the 1991 general election when the governing PAP attributed its electoral reverses largely to the so-called Chinese-educated "silent majority" residing in the HDB heartlands (Gopinathan, 1994: 89). Instead, as a collective, it is to be disciplined by the label of "Chinese chauvinism" that will endanger the ideal of multiracialism inherent in nation-building and endorsed by the PAP government. The Tang incident indicates the problematization of the older Chinese-educated generation in communal terms and highlights the state's essentialist treatment of ethnic issues. The Singapore state endorses the CMIO (Chinese—Malay—Indian—Others) model of ethnicity. Such a model comprises respective racial groups, each marked by common descent and skin colour. Based on this multiracial model, each ethnic group is assumed to possess a distinctive common cultural and linguistic domain. Thus, as a Chinese-educated rooted within "Chinese culture" and speaking Mandarin, one is "naturally" a Chinese by descent first and foremost. Essentializing ethnicity in terms of blood and descent, being a Chinese-educated necessarily becomes a question *not* of cultural identification *per se*, but is rooted in and complicated by communal ties and sentiments.

Finally, I want to comment on the question of the class identity of the Chinese-educated. The mass media in Singapore sometimes represents the social category of *Huaxiaosheng* as "working-class people fluent only in their mother tongues", "Chinese-educated lower-income Singaporeans" (George, 1996). At other times, the "silent majority" refers to "the CDAC-type of target audience", comprising the "Chinese-speaking but not necessarily Chinese-educated" (Chua, 1997). The language and politics of class appear to be masked by the issues of language and culture. There is a need, therefore, to refer to the Chinese-educated as, strictly, a specific social category of people educated in a particular language and subjected to a process of socialization in Chinese-medium schools from the secondary school level upwards. This category of Chinese-educated includes intellectuals such as teachers, journalists and artists. Inadequate delineation of this term results in confusing the Chinese-educated with the lower-income strata and the less educated. The class identity of the Chinese-educated and that of the Chinese-speaking or even dialect-speaking need to be differentiated.

REFERENCES

Ahmat, S. (1973) "University Education in Singapore: The Dilemma of the Malay-Medium Educated", in Y. H. Yip, ed., *Development of Higher Education in Southeast Asia: Problems and Issues*. Singapore: Regional Institute of Higher Education and Development, pp. 161–84.

Ang Beng Choo (1994) "The Teaching of Chinese Language in Singapore", in S. Gopinathan et al., eds., *Language, Society and Education: Issue and Trends*. Singapore: Times Academic Press, pp. 313–29.

Ang, Ien (1973) "To Be or Not to Be Chinese: Diaspora Culture and Post-modern 1993 Ethnicity", *Southeast Asian Journal of Social Science*, 21(1): 1–17.

Borthwick, Sally (1988) "Chinese Education and Identity in Singapore", in Jennifer Cushman and Wang Gungwu, eds., *Changing Identities of the Southeast Asian Chinese since World War II*. Hong Kong: Hong Kong University Press, pp. 35–59.

Chew, Shirley (1976) "The Language of Survival", in Riaz Hassan, ed., *Singapore: Society in Transition*. Kuala Lumpur: Oxford University Press, pp. 148–54.

Chua Mui Hong (1997) "How the PAP Govt Manages the Divisions in the Chinese Ground", *The Straits Times*, 11 January 1997.

Cui Gui Qiang (1994) *Xinjiapo Huaren: Cong Kaibu Dao Jianguo* [The Chinese in Singapore: Past and Present]. Singapore: EPB Publishers.

De Vos, G. and Romanucci-Ross, L. (1982) *Ethnic Identity, Cultural Continuities and Change*. Chicago: The University of Chicago Press.

Doraisamy, T. R. (1969) *150 Years of Education in Singapore*. Singapore: TTC Publications.

Franke, W. (1965) Problems of Chinese Education in Singapore and Malaya", *Malaysian Journal of Education* 2(2): 182–93.

George, Cherian (1994) "Tang Affair and PAP effort to Manage Chinese Ground", *The Straits Times*, 30 December 1996.

———. (1997) "Tang Liang Hong Affair: A View from the Shelters", *The Straits Times*, 10 January 1997.

Goh Keng Swee et al. (1979) *The Report on the Ministry of Education 1978*. Singapore: Ministry of Education.

Gopinathan, S. (1973) *Towards a National System of Education 1945–1973*. Singapore: Oxford University Press.

———. (1994) "Language Policy Changes 1979–1992: Politics and Pedagogy", in S. Gopinathan et al., eds., *Language, Society and Education in Singapore: Issues and Trends*. Singapore: Times Academic Press, pp. 65–91.

Guo Pei Xian (1965) "Xianshou Muyujiaoyu de Zhongyao Liyou" [Significant Reasons for Receiving an Education in the Mother Tongue First]. *Nanyang Wenzhai* 6(9): 31–32.

Hill, Michael and Lian Kwen Fee (1994) *The Politics of Nation-Building*. London: Routledge.

Khoo Swee Hoon, Jean (1988) "Once a Chinese, Always a Chinese: Education and Ethnic Identity among the Chinese in Singapore". Academic Exercise. Department of Sociology, National University of Singapore.

Kwok Kian Woon (1994) "Social Transformation and the Problem of Social Coherence: Chinese Singaporeans at Century's End", *Asiatische Studien/Etudes Asiatiques* XLLX (1): 217–41. Bern: Peter Lang.

Lau Wai Har (1992) "Huawen Zhishifenzi—tamen de Yijian he Xintai" [Chinese-educated Intellectuals—Their Opinions and Mentality], in *Biezuo Dulexian de Fengzheng* [Don't be a Stray Kite]. Singapore: Shanjing Chubanshe, pp. 20–27.

———. (1994) "Suoduan Huajiaozhe Yu Yingjiaozhe de Juli" [Narrow the Gap between the Chinese-educated and the English-educated], *Lianhe Zaobao*, 11 October 1994.

Li Yuan Jin (1994) "Xinjiapo Huawenjiaoyu Bianqian (1959–1987) xia, Zhishifenzi de Baogen Xintai" [Changes in Chinese Education in Singapore and the Attitude of Intellectuals towards the Preservation of Roots], in *Traditional Culture and Social Change*. Singapore: Tung Ann District Guild, pp. 47–97.
Lian Kwen Fee (1982) "Identity in Minority Group Relations", *Ethnic and Racial Studies* 5(1): 42–52.
Liu Pei Fang (1994) "Lishi Changhezhong de yiduan Jiyi" [A Section of Memory in the Long River of History], *Lianhe Zaobao*, 25 September 1994.
Mannheim, Karl (1952) "The Sociological Problem of Generation", in Paul Kecskemeti, ed., *Essays on the Sociology of Knowledge*. London: Routledge & Kegan Paul, pp. 276–321.
Murray, D. P. (1971) "Multilanguage Education and Bilingualism: The Formation of Social Brokers in Singapore". Unpublished Ph.D. dissertation. Stanford University, USA.
Pakir Anne (1992) "English-knowing Bilingualism in Singapore", in Ban K. C. et al., eds., *Imagining Singapore*. Singapore: Times Academic Press, pp. 234–262.
———. (1993) "Two Tongue-Tied: Bilingualism in Singapore", *Journal of Multilingual and Multicultural Development* 14(1 & 2): 73–90.
Sai Siew Yee (1995) "Between Two Worlds: Post-Independence Educational Change and Chinese Language Teachers in Singapore". Unpublished Academic Exercise. Department of Sociology, National University of Singapore.
Thurston, Anne F. (1988) *Enemies of the People: The Ordeal of the Intellectuals in China's Great Cultural Revolution*. Cambridge, Massachusetts: Harvard University Press.
Tong Chee Kiong and Chan Kwok Bun (1993) "One Face, Many Masks: The Singularity and Plurality of Chinese Identity". Unpublished paper.
Wang Xiu Nan (1970) *Xinma Jiaoyu Fanlun* [Education in Malaysia and Singapore]. Hong Kong: Southeast Asia Research Institute.
Yen Ching-hwang (1993) *Community and Politics: The Chinese in Colonial Singapore and Malaysia*. Singapore: Times Academic Press.
Yeo, K. W. (1973) *Political Development in Singapore: 1945–55*. Singapore: Singapore University Press.
Zhang Hui (1990a) *Ma de Laodao* [Complaints of a Horse]. Singapore: Xinjiapo Zuojia Xiehui, Xinya Chubanshe.
———. (1990b) *45.45 Huiyi Jimi* [The Classified Secret in the 45.45 Meeting]. Singapore: Xinjiapo Zuojia Xiehui.
———. (1992) *Shimenglu* [Record of Ten Dreams]. Singapore: Xinjiapo Zuojia Xiehui.

NEWSPAPERS

Nanyang Wenzhai (1963) "Xinjiapo Huaxiao Xuesheng Ruijian Wenti" [The Problem of Declining Enrolment in Chinese Schools], 4(11): 17–18.
———. (1965) "Huazu Zinu ying Xianshou Huayu Jiaoyu Gongkaixin" [The Open Letter Expounding that Children of Ethnic Chinese Should Receive a Chinese-medium Education First], 6(10): 27.
The Straits Times, 29 December 1996.

RACE AND RACIALIZATION IN MALAYSIA AND SINGAPORE

Lian Kwen Fee

When the British decided to extend colonial rule and established a permanent presence throughout the Malay peninsula in 1874, it marked the beginning of the construction of a plural society, by bringing into contact subsequently significant numbers of people from different historical and cultural origins. This is collectively referred to in the local social sciences as indigenous (Malay) and migrant (Chinese and Indian) communities. These two communities, particularly the Malays and the Chinese, are regarded as the major protagonists that have dominated the political stage of Malaysia since decolonization began with the ill-fated Malayan Union proposal in 1946. In the language of racialization, the protagonists have been variously described as *ketuanan Melayu* (Malay supremacy) and *bumiputera* (prince of the soil) with reference to indigenes and *kaum pendatang* (migrant community or newcomers). The terms *bumiputera* and *kaum pendatang* have been coined by the Malays, as the political majority, to ascribe and exclude the Chinese (and by default Indians) from a society they perceived to be increasingly appropriated by the latter in the late 1960s and early 1970s. These words have been quickly embedded in the language of racialization, in both public and private discourses, as the protagonists sought to assert themselves in the post-independence era. It comes as no surprise to even the most casual of observers of these two societies that race and ethnicity have been and continue to influence how Malaysians and Singaporeans conduct themselves at all levels—from the public and political discourse of racial politicking, decision-making and policy formation to the private and everyday discourse of where to eat, how to educate their children, where to worship, and how to relate to different peoples socially and professionally.

Yet until recently, scholars who have written about inter-group relations in the two societies have only been too willing to assume that race and ethnicity, and their related processes are unproblematic. In many instances, these writers have been guilty of conflating the two terms. My intention is to examine the significance of race and racialization in Malaysia and Singapore and their implications in relation to the contributions in this volume.

Racialization and Its Origins

Any course or textbook on race and ethnic relations invariably, until recently, refers to the dubiousness of any claim to the scientific status of "race". Notwithstanding, "race" has been accepted as a social science concept for most of the last century, as having a real influence on relations among groups and with which such relations can be analysed. This accumulated view has been directly challenged by Robert Miles (1989: 72–3), who argues that social scientists have perversely prolonged the life of an idea by uncritically employing the common-sense notion of race and thus reified it. This objection has been refuted by writers such as Omi and Winant (2000: 202) who, in rejecting the view that race is an ideological construct, believe that American society in everyday life is so thoroughly racialized that to be without racial identity is close to not having an identity.

Racialization refers "to a political and ideological process by which particular populations are identified by direct or indirect reference to their real or imagined phenotypical characteristics in such a way as to suggest that the population can only be understood as a supposedly biological unity" (Cashmore, 1988: 246). To Cashmore's description, I would add genotypical characteristics. People do not distinguish and exclude others on the basis of their knowledge of biology or genetics (Goldberg, 1992: 556). They do so because they assume that such differences are natural. They naturalize such differences and relations among such groups, in very much the same way as people assume gender distinctions are natural. If this is the common-sense understanding of race, then social scientists are required to address how race comes to be socially constructed and used in everyday life. As Miles (1989: 73) puts it, researchers have the responsibility of inquiring into "the reasons and conditions for the social process whereby the discourse of race is employed in an attempt to label, constitute and exclude social collectivities".

Racialization and the rendering of identity in racial terms are possible only in conditions associated with the emergence of modern society, and within economic, political, legal, and cultural relations that have no equivalent in pre-modern society (Goldberg, 1992: 556). Guillaumin (1995: 73–77) specifically identifies bourgeois or industrial society, which made possible the appropriation of labour, as critical to the social and ideological construction of race. She argues that it was only under conditions of capitalist production that a person's labour could be annexed, as opposed to the annexation of his or her whole physical body, as in slavery. The enslavement of population groups in pre-modern societies, however, was never a racial phenomenon. Enslavement was first and foremost a political phenomenon, even if it had its economic benefits. It was an expression of power relations significant to the status of the powerful, whether a ruler or chief. Anyone on the wrong side of the relationship could be enslaved, irrespective of whether they shared a similar phenotype. Enslavement was localized, unlike the appropriation of labour in modern society. The demand for labour power under capitalist production was so insatiable that the search for labour supply inevitably extended to other societies through colonization. "The more the methods of appropriating people's bodies or labour came to be rationalized and systematized," Guillaumin (1995: 75–76) asserts, "the more, at the same time, the ideologists sought for a natural explanation of social groups. And the ideological explanation tended to be transformed into scientific and legal categories". If mass labour could only be appropriated under conditions of domination, as in colonial society, its justification was readily sought in naturalizing differences among population groups. Hence, the dominated became the object of naturalization, racialization and racism. What is also implicit in racialization is that it is the dominated groups that are most often referred to in racial terms (Guillaumin, 1995: 76).

The roots of racialization in Malaysia and Singapore may be traced to the British colonial presence in the late nineteenth century. I identify three points that are worth highlighting. First, the British conception of race was informed by Social Darwinism, particularly by the turn of the twentieth century when scholar-administrators like Hugh Clifford, Frank Swettenham and Richard Winstedt were influential figures in determining policy on local development. Social Darwinism combined the idea of a fixed hierarchy with that of progress (Malik, 1996: 91)—those at the top of the hierarchy arrived there on merit, because of their natural superiority in the struggle for existence. For this group of scholar-administrators, it was doubtful that the Malay "race" could fully attain the benefits of civilization

(Maier, 1988: 51–7). Second, because the British colonists saw the potential for appropriating the natural resources of Malaya and the need to import labour to realize this potential, Darwinism was applied to rationalize how such labour could be exploited and best utilized: docile Tamil labour was ideal for the plantations, the self-reliant Chinese would be effective in commercial activities, and the indolent Malay peasant was best left alone in the *padi* fields. Capability, as far as the British colonists were concerned, was determined by the contribution that non-White labour could make to the colonial economy. Differential abilities could easily be explained by racializing the local population in Social Darwinist terms. The British practice of the racial division of labour, despite its diminution over the post-independence years, has left a lasting ideological impression on Malaysians and Singaporeans, and has influenced race and ethnic relations in the two societies. Even today, the Chinese in both societies refer to the Malays as lazy, backward and uncompetitive. Contemporary discourse on race and racialization in Malaysia and Singapore has its origins in colonial society. Third, the British administrative practice of ascribing the local population with racial identities—official classification in census and identity cards—has been maintained by the post-independence governments of Malaysia and Singapore.

Racialization in Colonial and Post-Colonial Malaysia

Racialization in colonial society, however, is not the same as racialization in post-colonial society. Dr. Mahathir, from long before he became Prime Minister of Malaysia in 1981, has been an unwavering advocate for improving the economic position of the Malays within a modern industrial society. In response to the deteriorating position of the Malays relative to the Chinese and Indians since independence in 1957, he wrote *The Malay Dilemma* in 1970. In this, he sought to explain why the Malays were unable to compete with the other communities. As a medical doctor himself, his views are interesting. In naturalizing differences among population groups, he is partial towards explanations related to genetic determinism. He argues that Malay economic weakness may be attributed to two causes, environment and heredity (Mahathir, 1970: 20–25). As the physical environment of the Malay peninsular was well-endowed with food resources, the early Malays, even the weakest and less diligent, were able to live in comparative comfort with little exertion. At the same time, the debilitating climate of the tropics did not encourage rigorous work or mental activity. As far as heredity was concerned, the Malay practice of in-breeding through first cousin marriages has had the cumulative effect of producing a race that was uncompetitive. In Dr. Mahathir's words, "the absence of inter-racial marriages in the rural areas resulted in purebred Malays" (Mahathir, 1970: 29). In contrast, the Chinese immigrants in the country were the products of a harsh environment in China where natural disasters were common. In addition, the Chinese custom of not marrying within the clan and cross-breeding had produced a hardy "race".

In comparing British racialization in the colonial period with Dr. Mahathir's racialization in the post-colonial period, both share a common premise in Social Darwinism. In the former, the *object* of colonial racialization was all the non-White population—regarded as racially inferior—for the expressed purpose of legitimizing British rule and economic exploitation. In these circumstances, colonial racialization is no less than racism. In Dr. Mahathir's arguments, the Malays are the *subject* of racialization. His explanation provided the intellectual justification—the Malays through no fault of their own were lagging behind the other communities—for affirmative action instituted through the New Economic Policy in 1971, which privileged the indigenous population as *bumiputra* and provided them access to advantages denied to non-indigenous communities.

There is another sense in which post-colonial racialization is different from colonial racialization. When Malays engage in racialization, they racialize themselves as subjects but the Chinese and others as objects. Similarly, the Chinese racialize themselves as subjects but the Malays as objects. Post-colonial discourse in racializing is, therefore, dialectical: the Chinese claim to a racial identity is seen as a counter to a Malay racial identity and vice-versa. The reason is that neither group can claim to be in a position of complete dominance; the Malays are politically dominant whereas the Chinese are economically dominant. In naturalizing differences between each other, they do so as both subject and object. Yet, because the Malays have historically been regarded by the British as a weaker "race", a view that has been passed down and shared by both Malays and Chinese today, it may be argued that the Chinese racialization of Malays is likely to be racist. It is unlikely that the Malay racialization of Chinese is racist. By contrast the Tamils, who constitute 80 percent of the

Indian population and are one of the most marginalized communities in Malaysia, have neither political nor economic influence relative to the Malays and the Chinese. They are, therefore, likely to be the objects of racialization in Malaysian society; together with their phenotypical distinction, they are vulnerable to racism.

Racialization, Miles (1989: 75) is also a dialectical process of signification: "ascribing a real or alleged biological characteristic with meaning to define the Other necessarily entails defining the Self by the same criterion". So, when a Chinese disparagingly refers to Malays as lacking drive and motivation, he or she does so as if to reaffirm the work ethic of the Chinese as a racial trait. Similarly, when a Malay describes the Chinese as being *kasar* (lacking refinement), it is to underline the significance of *adat* (custom) for Malayness.

While I have been arguing that the significance of race and racialization in understanding inter-group relations in Malaysia is yet to be fully realized, this is not to suggest that ethnicity has become redundant. Here, I draw on Goldberg's conception (1992: 553) of "ethnorace" to indicate that race and ethnicity need not be mutually exclusive in practice. A population group may be referred to as a race and ethnic group simultaneously, by insiders and outsiders. For example, the Chinese in Malaysia and Singapore may regard themselves as sharing a common language (Mandarin) and a common biological origin because of perceived phenotypical similarities; they do not necessarily make the distinction between cultural and physical origins, and distinguish themselves as either an ethnic group or race. In response to a question on how he defines being a Chinese, a male Chinese-educated shopkeeper in Singapore replied (Tong and Chan, 2001: 369):

> Chinese are Chinese because of their colour. The older generation used to feel that skin colour mattered a lot . . . . the "blacks" were the Malays and Indians . . . . "white-skinned" people were the "whites" and yellow were the Chinese. So my father used to say that we Chinese are from China. . . . First, our skin colour is yellow, our language is different . . . . those were the most important distinguishing factors . . . . then our habits, likes and dislikes, are all completely different.

The claims that a group makes in distinguishing itself may refer to a rhetoric of cultural content (ethnicity) or a rhetoric of descent (race) (Goldberg, 1992: 555).

Chinese identity in Malaysia and Singapore has always been racialized. I suggest that this is because the Chinese who came to Malaya in the late eighteenth and first half of the twentieth century, the period in which Chinese immigration to the region was at its peak, were influenced by ideas of race extant in China. Reformist writings at that time presented the impression of a dichotomous world in which the Chinese were engaged in a battle for supremacy against the white race, at a time of increasing Western encroachment. The reformers perceived race as a biological extension of the lineage, which encompassed all the population that lived on the soil of the Yellow Emperor; hence, the expression "the yellow race" (Dikotter, 1990: 426). In contrast, the Malays had no notion of race, even well into British colonization. The Malay equivalent of *bangsa* is explained by Nagata (1981: 98):

> The term *bangsa* conveys the double ideas of a people sharing both a common origin and a common culture. Etymologically, it is derived from the Sankskrit *vamsa*, 'line of descent'. Emically, it has a primordial quality, for it implies that the cultural traits are inalienably and inextricably associated with a particular people, that is, carried by a community whose ulitimate unity derives from a single origin.

Bangsa is equivalent to the French description of *ethnie*, which Schnapper (1998: 16) describes as "groups of men who live as heirs of an historical and cultural community (often expressed in terms of common descent) and who share the desire to maintain it". While *bangsa*—as expression of the political identity of the Malays—has been the subject of contestation in the political development of the community, the Malay language has been a potent basis of the Malay *ethnie* during the years of decolonization (1940s to 1950s), independence (1960s) and post-colonization (1970s to 1980s).

It is timely here to caution against any simplistic reading of how racialization occurs and what its consequences are. It is a far more complex and contextual process than we can imagine. By way of illustration, I draw on Benjamin's (2002) discussion of the relations between what the so-called "Malay" peasant population and the aboriginal inhabitants or the Orang Asli of Peninsular Malaysia, who anthropologists identify as being tribal. For most people, the Orang Asli are regarded as racially distinguishable from the Malays. Benjamin (2002: 9) suggests that even in pre-Islamic times, the aboriginal population had assimilated into Malay peasant society so that the Malays can trace their origins to the Orang Asli; the proportion is higher in some regions than in others. Indeed, so close is the linguistic and cultural characteristics between the two that he uses the descriptions

"Malay proper" and "tribal Malay" to distinguish between the two (Benjamin, 2002: 37–38). Sharing a common background with many of the aboriginal communities in the region from time immemorial, there is evidence that Malays in colonial society had expressed fears of their tribal origins being discovered or being reassimilated into tribality—a threatening prospect in a political culture that has a premium on pride in exogenous descent and cultural advancement. As the Malay population was increasingly seen as backward in colonial society, Hirschman (1986: 339) argues, the belief of an even more backward people in the remote interior may be compensatory in Malay culture.

It is, therefore, unsurprising to find that the Orang Asli are vulnerable to racialization in post-colonial society. Benjamin (2002: 19) reports picking up a textbook used in Malaysian school that describes the Senoi as being cleverer and more capable than the *Negritos*, and the proto-Malays in turn being cleverer than the *Senoi*. Contemporary applications of racial hierarchy have undoubtedly Darwinist and colonial origins. In so far as Malay racialization of the Orang Asli involves claims to racial superiority, it constitutes racism. Racism, it may be argued, not only exists in colonial but also in post-colonial society.

Sumit Mandal's (2003: 55) discussion of the significance of racism and racialization with regard to Malaysia is instructive. Racism, Mandal comments, is both structural and ideological in South Africa under apartheid and is a particular manifestation of racialization, but it is certainly not reflective of state and society in Malaysia. Although racist discourses have appeared from time to time, they have neither been consistently supported by the state nor have they been widely socialized. Hence, it is preferable to speak of racialization because it is a function of politics in Malaysia and not the consequence of racist beliefs and politics. For example, one of the major consequences of the New Economic Policy in the early 1970s Malaysia is the institutionalization of race by the state construction of the preferential status of *bumiputera*, bestowed exclusively until recently on the Malays on account of their indigenous status. In effect, this is positive discrimination but the formalization of *bumiputera* status, that is, the practice of exclusionary citizenship, has proved to be most divisive for Malaysians and has dominated local political discourse over the past three decades. This is a clear illustration of what Goldberg (1992: 561) refers to as racial formation, namely, it "involves the structural composition and determination of groups into racialized form, the imparting of racial significance and connotation at given socio-structural sites to relationships previously lacking them". Hence, racial formation is structurally determined.

Mandal's reading of racism, however, is narrow as he regards racism to be confined to institutional and formal activity. As I have referred to earlier, it is likely for the Chinese to be racist towards the Malays; the Malays towards the Orang Asli; and the Malays and Chinese towards the Tamil population. Indeed, racism is always one step away from racialization.

The consequences of racialization, Mandal (2003: 55) cautions, are complex, uneven and contested. Furthermore, Mandal (2003: 59) asserts, the racial division of labour in colonial Malaya did not lead to a deep but a provisional socialization of race as a marker of identity, which was subsequently modified after independence. Mandal draws attention to the potential significance of racialization in examining Malaysian society, and I want to extend the conceptualization of this process in order to appreciate its utility. Racialization refers to the "process of delineation of group boundaries and of allocation of persons within those boundaries by primary reference to . . . . inherent and/or biological (usually phenotypical) characteristics" (Miles, 1982: 157). The effect of racialization is to subordinate a group to a materially and politically disadvantaged position, but it also elicits a political and ideological response from this group (Miles, 1982: 185). "The response", Miles asserts, "is ideological in so far as those who are the object must construct a way of conceptualizing themselves and their circumstances. The response is political in so far as those who are the object negotiate a strategy by which to actively challenge their subordination".

I have argued earlier how Tamils in Malaysia have come to be racialized by the colonial and racist division of labour, and by participation in the politics of power-sharing in an independent and consociational state. The colonial labour policy in the early decades of the twentieth century had created a predominantly Tamil labour force captive in the estates. With the declaration of Emergency in 1948, which led to the banning of the Communist Party of Malaya and the collapse of the urban-based and Chinese-led trade unions, the British authorities seized the opportunity to nurture an Indian labour movement managed by pro-British and moderate Indian leaders. The National Union of Plantation Workers (NUPW) at its height claimed a membership of one-third of the total labour force in the estates and was the largest organization representing Indian labour. The NUPW was so well racialized that its leadership eschewed any political role, destroying any potential it had as a class movement. The major political party representing Indians, the Malaysian Indian Congress, was first led by non-Tamil middle class leaders but was Tamilized by the 1950s with popular support from Tamil estate workers. With the inauguration of a consociational government on independence in 1957, power-sharing by the three founding races—the Malays, Chinese and Indians—was instituted in a coalition party that took power, the Alliance. As power-sharing within such an arrangement was based on the principle of proportionality, the MIC was the weakest partner, and it exerted neither significant political nor economic influence. At the mercy of the dominant partner, UMNO, for its position in government, the MIC leadership could only maintain its legitimacy through maintaining a working-class Tamil identity. The racialization of the Tamil population was exacerbated in the 1970s by the appearance of overt caste politics in the community. Hence, the racialization of Tamil society in post-colonial Malaysia is a consequence of a consociational polity that is, in turn, driven by it.

Racialization is real and widespread in Malaysian society but poorly documented. It has its origins in colonial society and the practice of the colonial state. Within a consociational state and a semi-democracy, where elections are moderately competitive but the government is dominated by a single dominant party (Case, 2004: 29), racialization is no less significant. It is, however, as Mandal asserts, complex, uneven and contested. The discussion on relations among Malays, Chinese, Orang Asli, and Tamils clearly illustrates this. In contrast, racialization appears to be less variegated in Singapore, where the state is a dominant influence in people's lives.

The Corporatist State and Racialization in Singapore

The concept of the corporatist state is particularly useful in understanding racialization and its consequences in Singapore society. The corporatist state is one dominated by bureaucrats and technocrats and is depicted as an autonomous agency seeking the stability, unity and development of society through efficient management (Brown, 1994: 70). Such a state is not subject to challenge from popular or particularistic demands; instead, it co-opts various groups in society whose co-operation is necessary for the realization of state goals. The legitimacy of the corporatist state is maintained through a nationalist ideology that portrays the nation as a consensual and organic community. For this reason, the PAP government has assiduously sought to depoliticize ethnicity but ironically, racializes society through the ideology of multiracialism.

The corporatist state, Brown continues, manages and structures the politics of ethnicity in three ways. In its political manifestation, race and ethnicity is regarded by the state elite as dangerous to social stability and subversive of national loyalty. Hence, the public and political articulation of racial/ethnic issues may be construed as endangering national cohesion, a ploy that the PAP is ready to use to alienate public support for and discredit opposition candidates in parliamentary elections. Furthermore, there is legislation such as the Maintenance of Religious Harmony Act 1990, which can be used against individuals who promote religion for political ends. In its cultural expression, race and ethnicity is perceived as fundamental to the national ideology of multiracialism. Being a Singaporean is necessarily a hyphenated identity; hence, one is Singapore Chinese or Singapore Malay. Finally, the expression of racial and ethnic interests is only legitimate if they are aired in forums and channels acceptable to the state. One example of this are the state-sponsored ethnic self-help associations designed to manage the problem of the underclass in the respective ethnic communities. Another is the introduction of several Group Representative Constituencies that require political parties to field minority candidates so that their views are represented in Parliament.

Multiracialism, used interchangeably with multiculturalism in the discourse of nation-building, has been articulated by the first generation PAP government as the founding ideology of Singapore, even prior to independence in 1965. The adoption of racial/ethnic group as the official classification of the Singapore population and the basis of multiracialism was rationalized by its leaders that the four groups (Chinese, Malays. Indians, and the all-inclusive "Others", or the acronym CMIO) enjoyed the status of founding communities (Hill & Lian, 1995: 103). As I referred to earlier, the official concept of multiculturalism assumed that each of these groups was a race with a distinctive and identifiable culture, language, and to an extent possessed a common religious affiliation; hence, the ease with which multiculturalism is officially and simultaneously regarded as multiracialism. The commitment of the PAP government to the ideology, policy and practice of multiracialism is so consistent and comprehensive that many Singaporeans have come to accept the CMIO model, which is essentially racial, as a reference point in their relations with the state if not in their everyday lives in relation to other ethnic groups.

For instance, the PAP commitment to bilingualism in education even before it became the government requires every Singapore student to learn a second language, his or her so-called mother tongue, in addition to English. The justification for bilingualism in the early years of PAP rule was that the mother tongue was synonymous to the culture of the child. The promotion of Mandarin as the mother tongue of all Chinese children and Confucianism as the basis of Chinese culture in the late 1970s had the effect of homogenizing a heterogeneous Chinese population that was previously organized along dialect groups. A similar policy was applied to the Malay and Indian minorities, with Malay and Tamil designated as their respective mother tongues.

Maintaining the ethnic balance of the population (approximately 78 percent Chinese, 14 percent Malay, and seven percent Indian), though not always explicitly stated, is implicitly acknowledged by the state as a desirable policy. This is, however, seen by some members of minority groups as maintaining the numerical and political dominance of the Chinese (Lai, 1995: 168). Maintaining an ethnic balance is also reflected in the allocation of public housing, which accommodates more than 80 percent of the island's population. Until the late 1980s, public housing and resettlement was based on a first-come-first-served basis thar, while not eliminating racial enclaves, had the effect of dispersing them (Chua, 1991: 347–48). By the late 1980s, however, the government alleged that resale of HDB flats had resulted in excessive concentrations of Malays in certain estates, and it introduced a policy of restricting Malay occupation to a quota of 20 percent. Finally, the educational performance of students in subjects in public examinations is published yearly in the major newspapers, and prominence is given to the racial affiliation of these students. The Ministry of Education assiduously maintains a database on the educational achievements of students based on their racial groups. The ethnic self-help associations were set up to address underachievers in schools on the basis of their racial affiliation. In summary, the policies and practices of the state—the ascription of racial-ethnic identity, political participation, education, housing, and population planning—is very much based on a discourse that racializes Singaporeans and maintains how they should organize their lives.

Racialization, Ethnicization and the State

Many of the contributions in this volume are relevant to the issues raised in this chapter, one of which I have discussed earlier. Alexius Pereira (Chapter One) argues that significant numbers of Eurasians migrated from Singapore in the 1970s mainly because they were uncertain of their future in a society managed by a Chinese-dominated PAP government that no longer privileged a community—well-treated by the colonial administration in the past—as embodied in the policies of multiracialism and meritocracy. The Eurasians who stayed back felt they were being marginalized as a consequence of state racialization. During the 1990s, they made representations that they should no longer be considered as "other" but as a race in their own right. The state's tacit recognition of their contribution, despite their numerical insignificance, to Singapore society encouraged Eurasians to rediscover their origins. They readily found this in their Portuguese-Malaccan descent, drawing on food, language and dance to engage in the rhetoric of cultural content. The Eurasians, who were ambivalent about their mixed European-Asian ancestry in colonial society and racialized in an independent state, were now ethnicized. This does not mean they have become an ethnic group; rather they are an ethnorace, a term I referred to earlier to indicate a situation in which race and ethnicity are not mutually exclusive.

Alice Nah's discussion of how the aboriginal population of Malaysia came to be named Orang Asli underlines the ascriptive power of the state. Early attempts at racial classification of the aboriginal groups were undertaken by ethnographers, missionaries and anthropologists through philology and anthropometric measurements. These inevitably led to a veritable minefield that was impossible to sort out, as culture, language and genetic typology became hopelessly entangled. As a consequence of the Communist insurrection in the 1950s, the government issued identity cards to the local population—which it regarded as potential sympathizers of the Communist cause—to keep track of its movements. The aborigines, particularly mobile within the remote interior, were regarded as vulnerable and were given personal names to facilitate identification; a practice that was out of step with cultural reality. In 1966, well after the end of the insurgency, the Malaysian government renamed the aborigines Orang Asli as a means of overcoming the perjorative connotations of the various descriptions used in the past. Citing Carey, Alice Nah comments that *asli* is derived from the Arabic *asali*, which means original. The introduction of the NEP in 1971 and the conferment of *bumiputra* status on the Malays in recognition of their privileged status as the indigenous people, raised questions among Malay leaders about the description of the aborigines as original inhabitants. Unilateral attempts by these politicians to replace the term "Orang Asli" resulted in the formation of an association, *Persatuan Orang Asli Semanajung Malaysia*, that supported the retention of the name (Nicholas, 2002: 121). The racialization and collectivization of the aboriginal population inadvertently led to their self-identification as a racial/ethnic group.

With regard to the Chinese in Malaysia, Tong Chee Kiong argues that other than blood and descent, there is little agreement on what constitutes Chinese culture or identity. His Chinese informants referred consistently to phenotype and the notion of "pure blood" in describing their identity. As the Chinese generally regard preserving their lineage as a priority, it is understandable why they place a premium on birth, blood, and descent in referring to their identity. Once this condition—which Tong describes as primary or core—is satisfied, then everything else is negotiable, instrumental and situational. Where it really matters, the Chinese have a racialized conception of themselves, and this may explain why they are so ready to racialize others. Tong also makes the useful distinction between understanding race and ethnic relations in Malaysia at the micro and macro levels. In public and political discourse, relations between Chinese and Malays are very much racialized. In personal and everyday discourse, the Chinese, he suggests, are more inclined to adopt a more individualistic style. Racializing discourses in everyday life at least, it seems, are not as widespread in Malaysian society than scholars and political commentators have led us to believe.

REFERENCES

Benjamin, Geoffrey (2002) "On Being Tribal In The Malay World", in G. Benjamin and C. Chou, eds., *Tribal Communities in the Malay World*. The Netherlands: IIAS & Singapore: ISEAS, pp. 7–76.

Brown, David (1994) *The State and Ethnic Politics in Southeast Asia.* London: Routledge.
Case, William (2004) "Testing Malaysia's Pseudo-Democracy", in E. Gomez, ed. *The State of Malaysia.* London: RoutledgeCurzon, pp. 29–48.
Cashmore, Ellis (1988) *Dictionary of Race and Ethnic Relations.* Second edition. London: Routledge & Kegan Paul.
Chua, Beng Huat (1991) "Race Relations and Public Housing Policy in Singapore", *Journal of Architectural Planning Research* 8(4): 343–54.
Dikotter, Frank (1990) "Group Definition and the Idea of Race in Modern China", *Ethnic and Racial Studies* 13(3): 420–31.
Goldberg, David (1992) "The Semantics of Race", *Ethnic and Racial Studies* 15(4): 544–69.
Guillaumin, Colette (1995) *Racism, Sexism, Power and Ideology.* London: Routledge.
Hill, Michael and Lian, Kwen Fee (1995) *The Politics of Nation Building and Citizenship in Singapore.* London: Routledge.
Hirschman, Charles (1986) "The Making of Race in Colonial Malaya: Political Economy and Racial Ideology", *Sociological Forum* 1(2): 330–61.
Lai Ah Eng (1995) *Meanings of Multiethnicity: A Case Study of Ethnicity and Ethnic Relations.* Kuala Lumpur: Oxford University Press.
Mahathir Mohamad (1970) *The Malay Dilemma.* Singapore: Donald Moore.
Maier, Hendrik (1988) *In the Center of Authority.* Ithaca: Cornell University, Southeast Asia Program.
Malik, Kenan (1996) *The Meaning of Race.* London: Macmillan.
Mandal, Sumit (2003) "Transethnic Solidarities in a Racialised Context", *Journal of Contemporary Asia* 30(1): 50–68.
Miles, Robert (1989) *Racism.* London: Routledge.
———. (1982) *Racism and Migrant Labour.* London: Routledge & Kegan Paul.
Nagata, Judith (1981) "In Defense of Ethnic Boundaries: The Changing Myths and Charters Of Malay Identity", in C. Keyes, ed.), *Ethnic Change.* Seattle: University of Washington Press, pp. 88–115.
Nicholas, Colin (2002) "Organizing Orang Asli Identity", in G. Benjamin and C. Chou, eds., *Tribal Communities in the Malay World.* The Netherlands: IIAS & Singapore ISEAS, pp. 119–36.
Omi, Michael and Howard Winant (2002) "On the Theoretical Status of the Concept of Race", in J. Wu and S. Min, eds., *Asian American Studies: A Reader.* New Brunswick: Rutgers University Press, pp. 199–208.
Schnapper, Dominique (1998) *Community of Citizens.* New Brunswick: Transaction Publishers.
Tong Chee Kiong and Chan Kwok Bun (2001) "One Face, Many Masks: The Singularity and Plurality of Chinese Identity", *Diaspora* 10(3): 361–89.

INDEX